CAMBRIDGE
UNIVERSITY PRESS

Click Start

INTERNATIONAL EDITION

Learner's Book 8

University Printing House, Cambridge CB2 8BS, United Kingdom

One Liberty Plaza, 20th Floor, New York, NY 10006, USA

477 Williamstown Road, Port Melbourne, VIC 3207, Australia

314–321, 3rd Floor, Plot 3, Splendor Forum, Jasola District Centre, New Delhi – 110025, India

79 Anson Road, #06–04/06, Singapore 079906

Cambridge University Press is part of the University of Cambridge.

It furthers the University's mission by disseminating knowledge in the pursuit of
education, learning and research at the highest international levels of excellence.

www.cambridge.org
Information on this title: www.cambridge.org/9781108951944

First published 2021

20 19 18 17 16 15 14 13 12 11 10 9 8 7 6 5 4 3 2 1

Printed in Malaysia by Vivar Printing

ISBN 9781108951944 Paperback

Cambridge University Press has no responsibility for the persistence or accuracy
of URLs for external or third-party internet websites referred to in this publication,
and does not guarantee that any content on such websites is, or will remain,
accurate or appropriate. Information regarding prices, travel timetables, and other
factual information given in this work is correct at the time of first printing but
Cambridge University Press does not guarantee the accuracy of such information
thereafter.

....

....

Every effort has been made to trace the owners of copyright material included in this
book. The publishers would be grateful for any omissions brought to their notice for
acknowledgement in future editions of the book.

Introduction

The international edition of *Click Start: Computing for Schools* is designed around the latest developments in the field of computer science, information and communication technology. Based on Windows 7 and MS Office 2010, with extensive updates on Windows 10 and MS Office 2016, the series aids the understanding of the essentials of computer science including computer basics, office applications, creative software, programming concepts and programming languages.

Each level of the series has been designed keeping in mind the learning ability of the learners as well as their interests. Efforts have been made to use examples from day-to-day life, which will help the learners to bridge the gap between their knowledge of the subject and the real world. The books are designed to offer a holistic approach and help in the overall development of the learners.

KEY FEATURES

- **Snap Recap:** Probing questions to begin a chapter and assess pre-knowledge
- **Learning Objectives:** A list of the learning outcomes of the chapter
- **Activity:** Interactive exercise after every major topic to reinforce analytical skills and application-based learning
- **Exercise:** A variety of questions to test understanding
- **Fact File:** Interesting snippets to improve concept knowledge
- **Quick Key** and **Try This:** Shortcuts and useful tips on options available for different operations
- **Glossary:** Chapter-end list of important terms along with their definitions
- **You Are Here:** Quick recap
- **Lab Work:** Practical exercises to enable application of concepts through learning-by-doing
- **Project Work:** Situational tasks to test practical application of the concepts learnt
- **Who Am I?:** Biographies to inspire young learners
- **Sample Paper:** Practice and preparation for exams

The books make learning fun and help the learners achieve expertise in this fast-changing world of computer science.

Overview

Snap Recap
Probing questions to begin a chapter and assess pre-knowledge

SNAP RECAP

1. What do you understand by the term open source software?
2. Which software program(s) do you generally use for editing a document or creating a presentation?

Learning Objectives
A list of the learning outcomes of the chapter

LEARNING OBJECTIVES

You will learn about:

- various OpenOffice applications
- introduction to OpenOffice Writer
- main components of the OpenOffice Writer window
- File, Edit and Format menus in OpenOffice Writer
- introduction to OpenOffice Impress
- creating, modifying and running a presentation in OpenOffice Impress.

Activity
Interactive exercises after every major topic to reinforce analytical skills and application-based learning

ACTIVITY

A slide master is a slide that controls all information about the Theme, Layout, Background, Color, Fonts and Positioning of all slides. The settings that we select in the Slide Master will be applicable to all the slides created in a presentation. Go to **View ⟹ Master ⟹ Slide Master**. Make the following changes in the Slide Master:

- Change the Title of the slides to font size = 50, bold, Comic San MS, Color = Purple.
- Change the font settings of the content to different bullets, colors, sizes and types.

FACT FILE

The JavaScript files have an extension of .js, and are identified by an icon. These files contain just the code, and no <SCRIPT> tag is required.

Exercise
A variety of questions to test understanding

EXERCISE

A. Fill in the blanks.

1. Cut and Paste are present in the .... menu.
2. To create and edit a document we use OpenOffice ....
3. The .... view shows miniature form of all slides in a presentation.
4. The .... option in File menu will save the file for the first time.
5. The .... is used to give animation to the objects on the slides.

B. State true or false.

1. The file extension of OpenOffice Impress presentation is .ods.
2. Slides can be easily rearranged and deleted in the Slide Sorter View.
3. F6 is used to run a presentation.

Fact File
Interesting concept-related snippets to improve knowledge

Quick Key and **Try This**
Shortcuts and useful tips on options available for different operations

TRY THIS

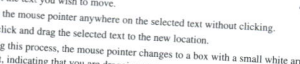

Dragging and dropping a selected text is equivalent to cut and paste in the same or another document.

- Select the text you wish to move.
- Place the mouse pointer anywhere on the selected text without clicking.
- Left click and drag the selected text to the new location.
- During this process, the mouse pointer changes to a box with a small white arrow over it, indicating that you are dragging text.
- When you reach the new location, release the mouse button to drop the text.

Glossary
Chapter-end list of important terms along with their definitions

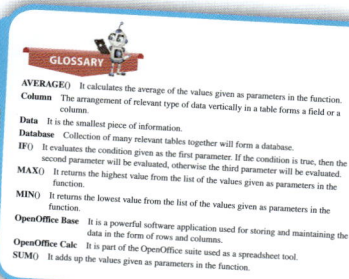

You Are Here
Summary for a quick recap

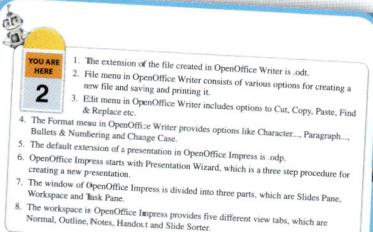

Lab Work
Practical exercises to enable application of concepts through learning-by-doing

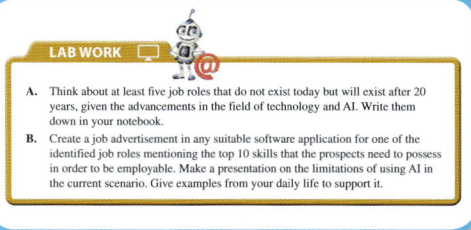

Project Work
Situational tasks to test practical application of the concepts learnt

Sample Paper
Helps to test learners' understanding at the end of the course

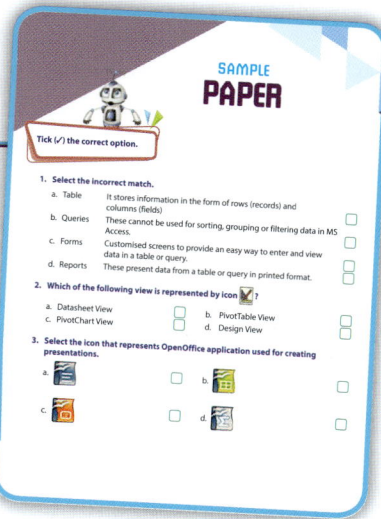

Who Am I?
Biographies to inspire young learners

Cntents

MS Access 2010

1

SNAP RECAP

1. Why do you need to store data in tables? Give an example.
2. Name some applications you can use to store tabular data.

LEARNING OBJECTIVES

You will learn about:

- important terms related to databases
- functions of DBMS and database objects
- starting MS Access 2010
- creating a new database in MS Access 2010
- components of the MS Access 2010 window
- data types and the primary key
- changing the view
- creating and modifying tables in MS Access 2010
- saving a database in MS Access 2010
- opening an existing database
- queries, forms and reports in MS Access 2010.

Introduction

A database refers to the arrangement and storage of data in a way that allows it to be retrieved easily. Microsoft Access is a database program that is used for storing all kinds of information in the form of tables, queries, forms, reports, etc. It has many built-in features to assist you in constructing and viewing the information stored in the database. Once the information is stored in the Microsoft Access database, it is easy to find, analyse and print. This chapter uses MS Access 2010. For MS Access 2016 updates, go to the end of the chapter.

Important database terms

Database: A database is an integrated collection of logically related records in the form of tables. It offers an organised mechanism for storing, managing and retrieving information related to a particular subject or purpose. For example, a database can be created for schools, libraries, banks, etc.

Database Management System (DBMS): A DBMS is a set of computer programs that controls the creation, maintenance and use of the computerised database by the user. Some examples of popular DBMS software are MS Access, FoxPro and FoxBASE.

Table: A table is a collection of related information in the form of rows and columns. For example, the diagram below shows the structure of a School database where the tables Student, Library and Staff store different pieces of information related to students, the books in the library and the school staff.

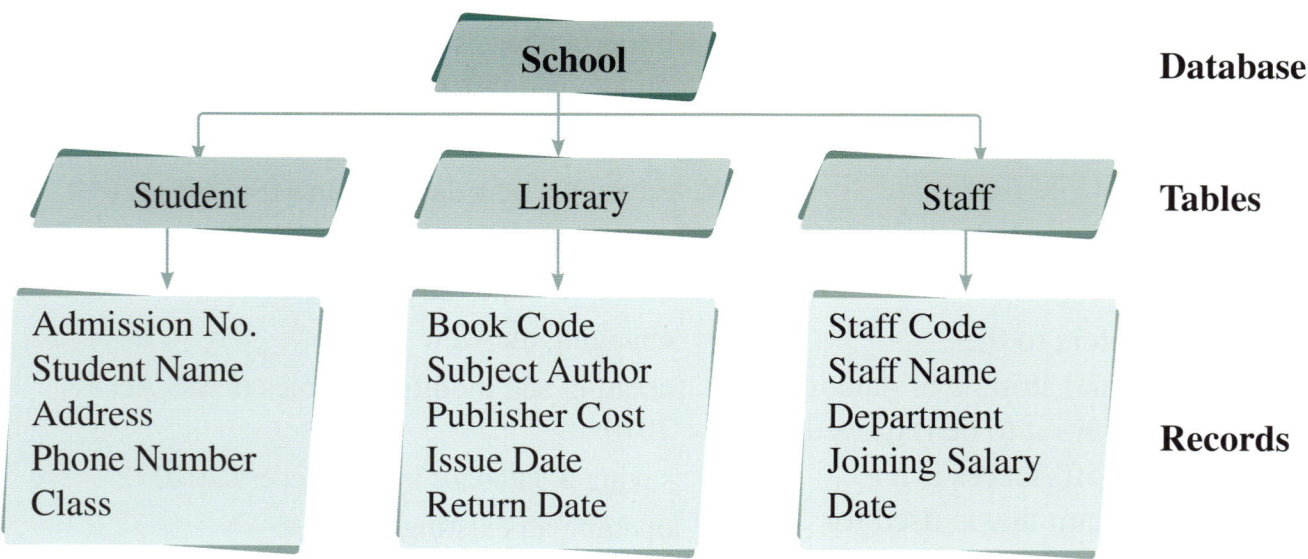

Structure of a database

Record: A record is one row of a table. It includes complete information arranged horizontally. For example, the Student table may contain the complete information for a student, such as Admission No., Student Name, Address, Phone Number and Class.

Field: A vertical column in a table that stores information of the same type. For example, Admission No. is a field that stores only admission numbers, and Student Name stores only the names of the students.

Functions of DBMS

A DBMS performs the following important functions to ensure the integrity and consistency of data in the database:

- **Reduces data redundancy**: Data redundancy means duplication of data. A DBMS helps to remove duplicate data. For example, in a library, the name of a book may occur under the author's name and the ISBN number.

- **Facilitates sharing of data**: Different users can access and use the same database. For example, the Admissions department can use the School database for storing and retrieving Admission No. of the students, while the teachers can use the same database for retrieving the Student Name.

- **Controls data inconsistency**: A change in any one file is automatically updated in all the related files. For example, in a library, if there are two records for a single book, one under the author's name and another under new stock, the details might be changed under one record. This may lead to inconsistency as both the records for the same book would contain different information. A DBMS stops this from happening.

- **Enforces standards**: In a DBMS, certain standards can be applied in data representation, such as the naming, structure and format of data. For example, if Name of Student is a field in a table, it should be consistent everywhere.

- **Ensures data security**: The access to any record can be protected in a DBMS. The files can be accessed only by those who are authorised to do so.

- **Maintains integrity**: A DBMS maintains integrity by keeping some constraints when the data is entered. These constraints are rules designed to keep data consistent and correct. They act like a check on the incoming data.

FACT FILE

A relational database management system (RDBMS) was proposed by E.F. Codd in 1970. It is a type of database where data is organised as related tables. These databases are more powerful as relevant data can be extracted and tables extended and modified without having to reorganise the existing tables.

Database objects

The following table identifies the database objects you can use while creating a Microsoft Access 2010 database:

Object	Description
Table	Stores information in the form of rows (records) and columns (fields). For example, one table could store a list of friends along with their details, while another table could store their exam marks.
Queries	These are used for sorting, grouping or filtering data in the database. For example, a query might only display a list of students in Class 7 out of all the school students.
Forms	Customised screens to provide an easy way to enter and view data in a table or query. For example, when you apply for admission in a school, you fill out an online form. The data that you enter in the admission form is stored inside the school's database.
Reports	These present the data from a table or query in a printed format. For example, teachers can create a report of all the students opting for Fine Arts as a subject.

ACTIVITY

A. Create a presentation on the topic 'Databases and their concepts'. The slides should include:

   1. Key features   2. History   3. Real-life usage

B. List the various types of database programs available along with their latest versions.

C. Think of a Hospital database. What do you think the table names might be in this database? Suggest the different fields of information in the tables. Draw the structure of this database using a software program of your choice.

Starting MS Access 2010

Follow these steps to open the MS Access 2010 application.

1. Click on **Start** button ⟹ **All Programs** ⟹ **Microsoft Office** ⟹ **Microsoft Office Access 2010**.
2. MS Access 2010 window appears.

Creating a database

In MS Access 2010, a database can be created in two ways:

1. Using a blank database.
2. Using sample templates.

Using a blank database

To create a blank database, you need to follow the steps given below:

1. In the default MS Access window, a blank database is already selected. Also, the **Blank database** pane appears on the right.
2. Type a name for your database in the **File Name** box. The location of your database appears below this box.

> You can change the location of the database by clicking on the 📂 **Browse** icon in the right pane.

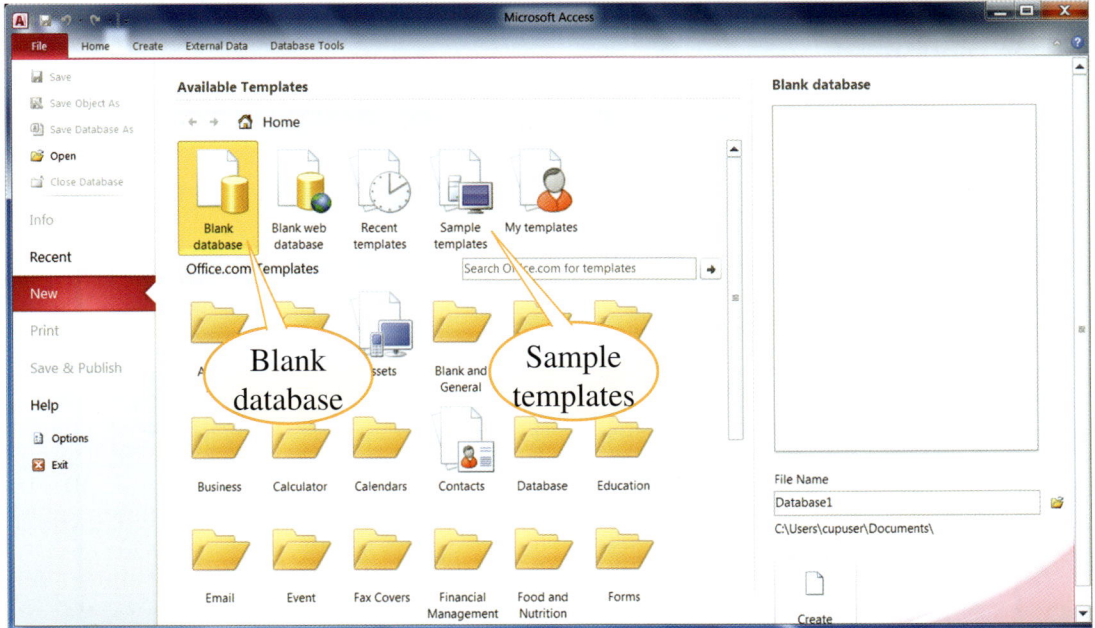

MS Access 2010 window

3. Click on the **Create** button. A new database titled **Table1** will be created, as seen in the **Datasheet View** (see below). The table has a field labelled as **ID**. The header fields can be changed or added by double-clicking on it.

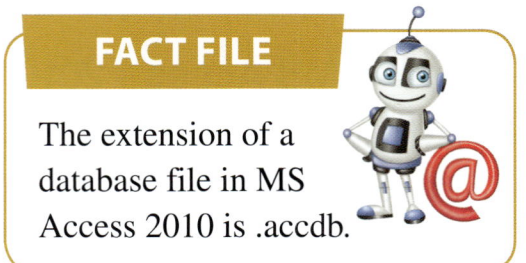

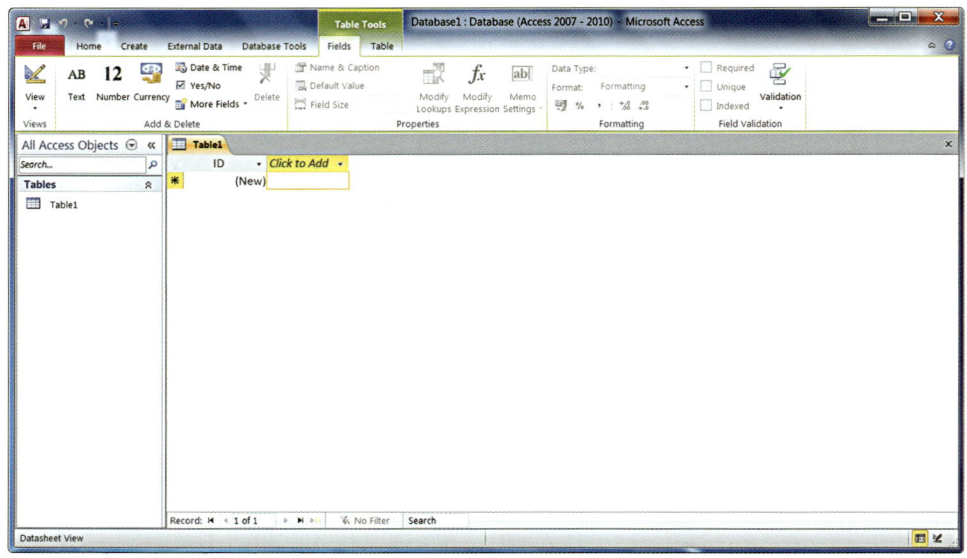

A new database using a blank database

Using sample templates

1. Click on the **Sample Templates** in the pane of the MS Access 2010 window.
2. Select the template of your choice, say Faculty, from the Available Templates section.

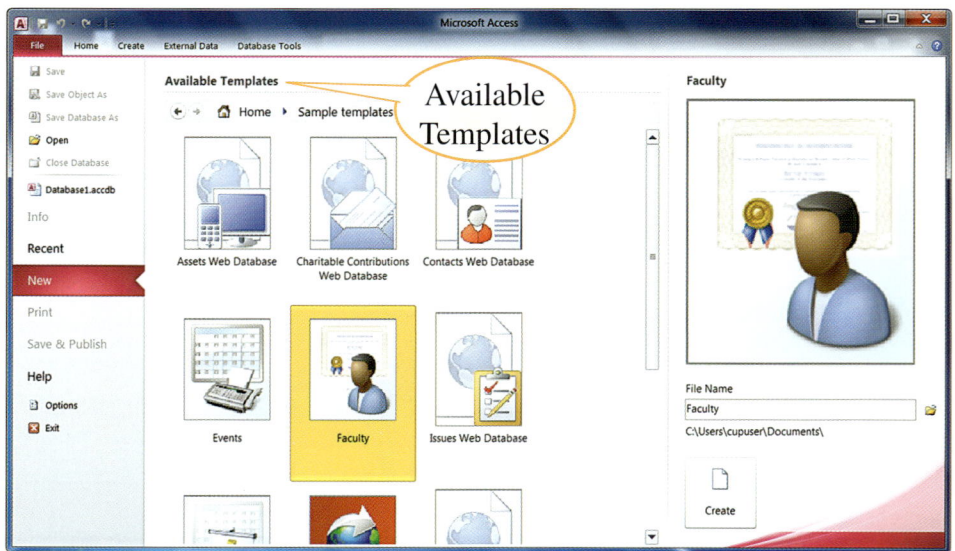

Available Templates in the MS Access 2010 window

3. A pane appears on the right as shown on the previous page. Change the name of the file in the **File Name** box and change the location of the database using the Browse button. After clicking on the **Create** button in the right pane of the MS Access 2010 window, you will get the sample database Faculty List.

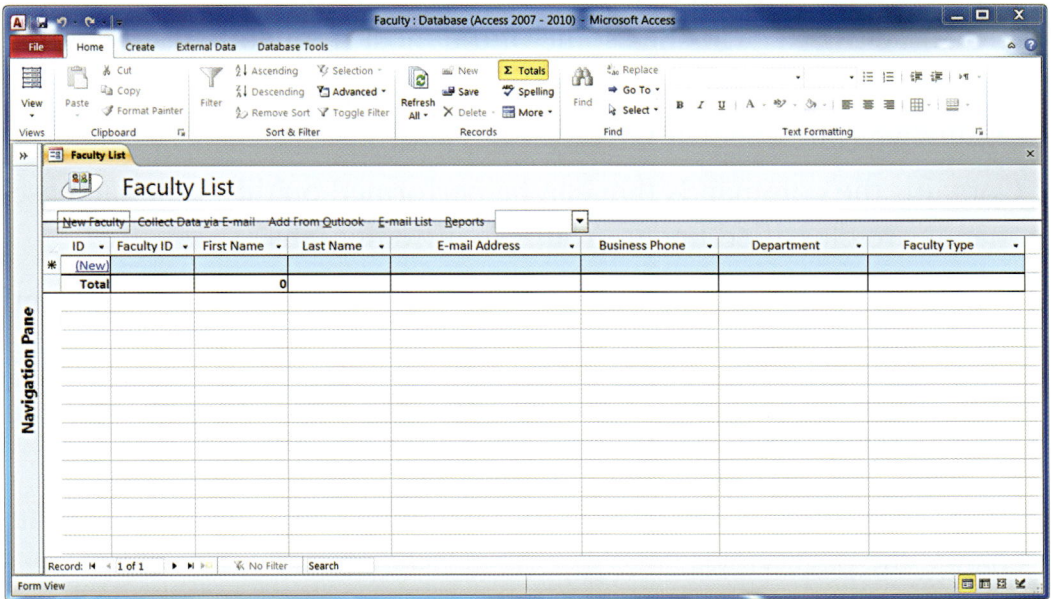

Creating a database using a template

Components of the MS Access 2010 window

The Database window has the components (parts) shown below.

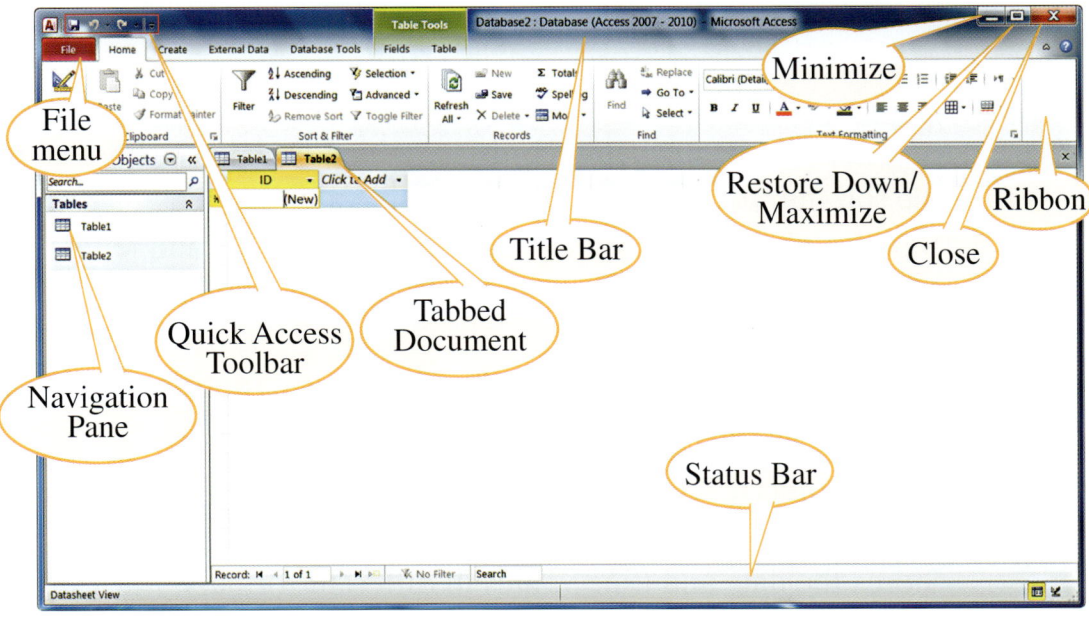

Components of a Database window

Title Bar: Shows the name of the database created. The **Minimize, Maximize/Restore Down** and **Close** buttons are also found in this area.

File Menu: The button on the left of the Title Bar. It contains commands like New, Open, Save and Print.

Quick Access Toolbar: This has some of the most frequently used commands in MS Access like Save, Undo and Redo. The toolbar can be shifted below the Ribbon, and more commands can be added to it.

Ribbon: Contains the commands that can be performed on different database objects. These commands are classified under groups in different tabs.

Navigation Pane: The left pane of the window. Database objects in currently open or new databases are displayed.

Tabbed Document: The database objects appear in tabs, unlike the overlapping windows in the earlier versions.

Status Bar: This is found at the bottom of the window and displays the status and buttons to change the page views.

Data Types

The Data Type for every Field Name describes the form in which the data is accepted. Descriptions of some of the commonly used Data Type values that appear in the drop-down list are shown in the table below.

Data Type	Description
AutoNumber	An integer that automatically generates an increasing or decreasing order of numbers when records are added or deleted. For example, the roll number of a student can be an AutoNumber.
Text	Stores alphanumeric values that is, both numbers and letters. Maximum 255 characters can be stored. For example, a product ID or an address.
Memo	Used for lengthy text and numbers such as definitions or descriptive notes. A maximum of 65,536 characters are allowed.
Number	Holds numeric data that is used for calculations. Both decimals and non-decimal digits are allowed.
Date/Time	Stores the date and time values in different formats.
Currency	Specifies different currencies and displays them in different formats.

Yes/No	This can have only one of the two values True/False, Yes/No or On/Off.
Hyperlink	A link to an internet resource.

Commonly used Data Types in MS Access 2010

Setting Data Type

To set a data type for each field, follow the steps given below:

1. Select the chosen field you want to set the Data Type for.

2. Click on the **Fields** tab ⟹ **Formatting** group ⟹ **Data Type** drop-down list (see below). Select the chosen data type from the list. By default, AutoNumber is selected.

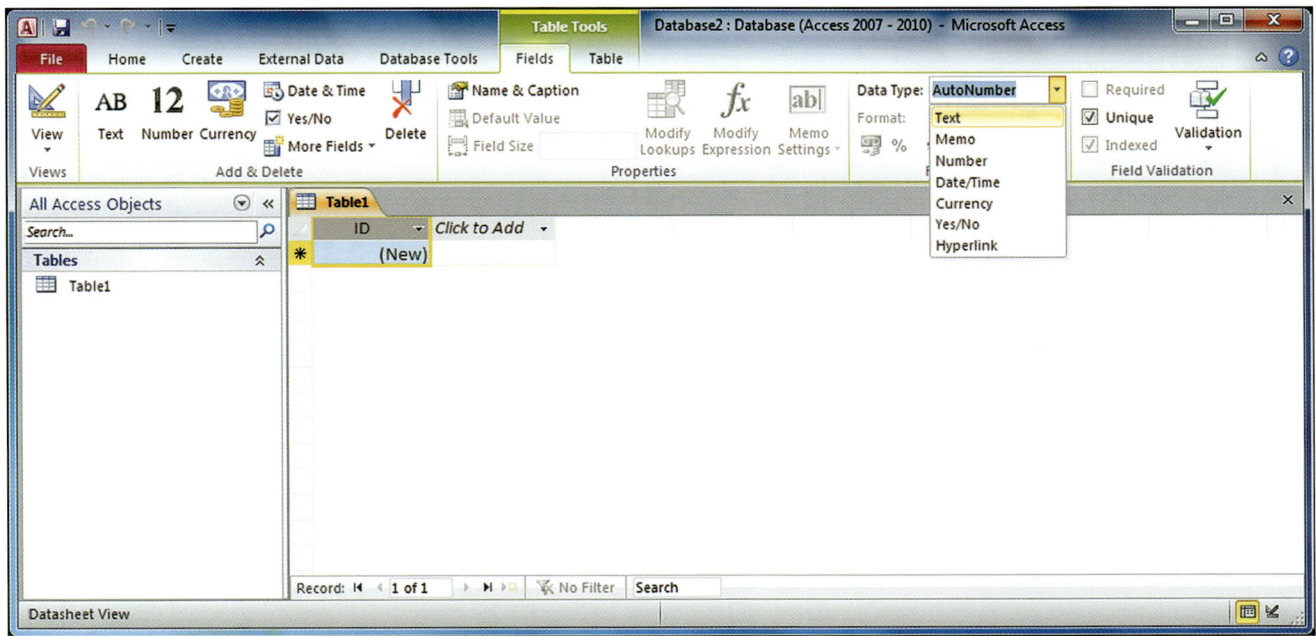

Setting Data Type

Primary Key

Every table in the database must have at least one field that uniquely identifies each record in the table. This field is known as the **Primary Key**. This key should always have a value that is not repeated for any other record.

For example, in a table of students, it is possible that there are two students with the same name. Here, you can assign Admission No. as the primary key to identify each student.

If the primary key is not assigned, it is automatically added as an ID at the time of creating the table.

FACT FILE

You can have multiple primary keys for a table. However, these should be unique values. To do this you must hold down the Ctrl key and then select the row selector for each field.

Assigning a Primary Key

To access the **Design** tab, right-click on Table1 in the left pane, then select the **Design View** option.

To assign a primary key to the table fields, select the required field. For example, select the field and then click on the **Design** tab ⟹ **Tools** group ⟹ **Primary Key** option (see below).

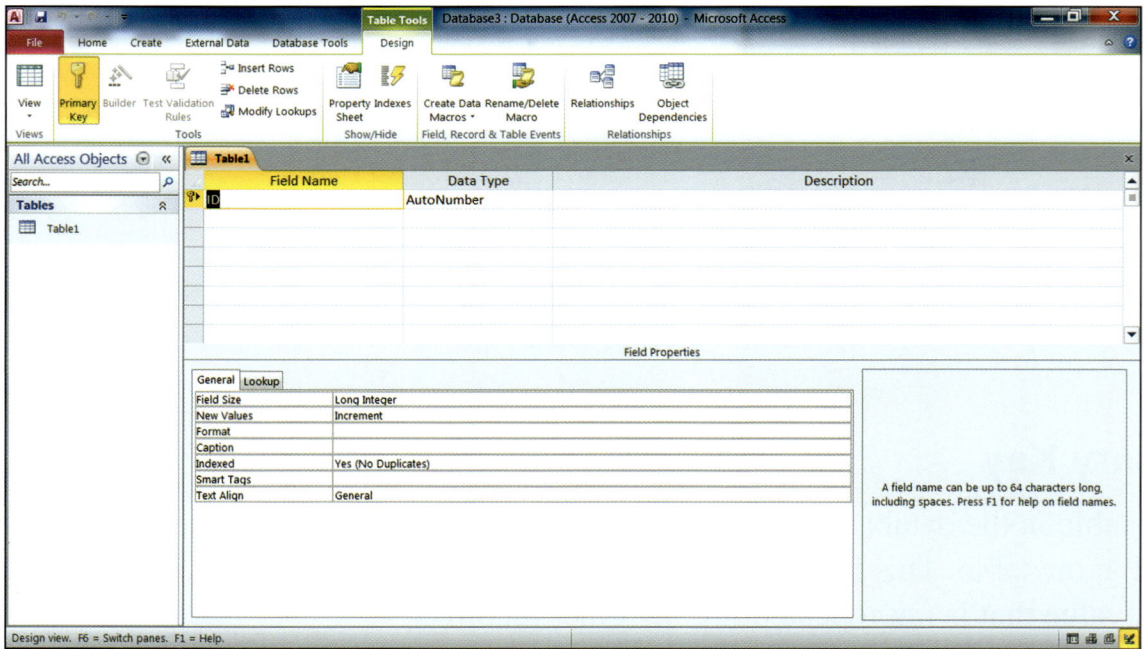

Assigning a primary key

Select the required field and right-click on it. A shortcut menu opens. Select the **Primary Key** option (see below).

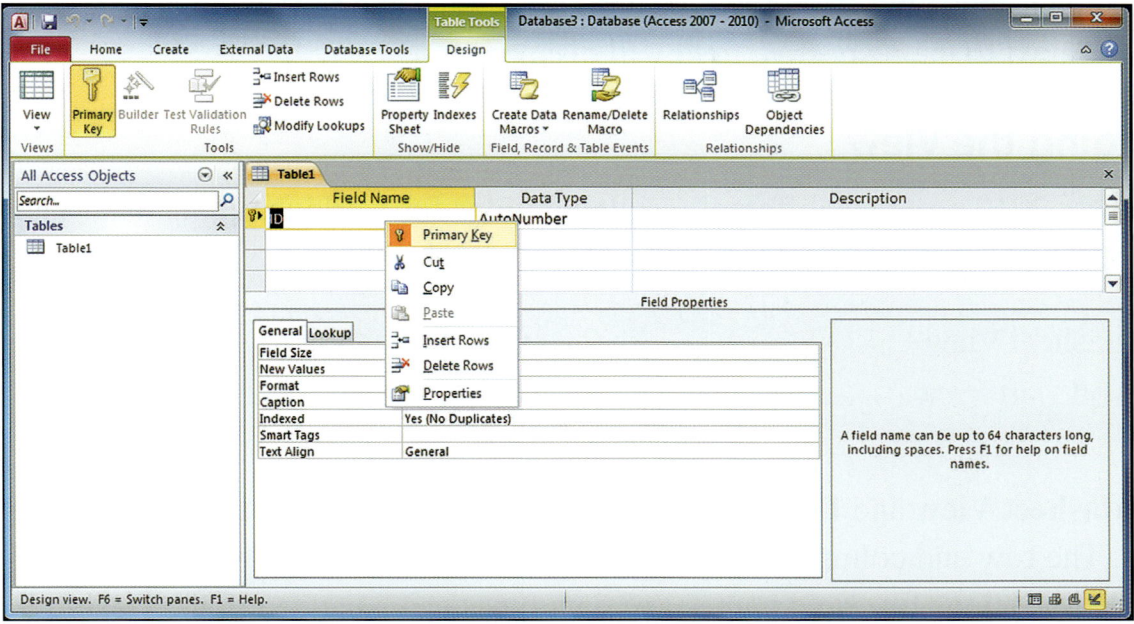

Assigning a primary key using the shortcut menu

A key will be displayed in front of the column name to show that the column is now working as a primary key in the table (see below).

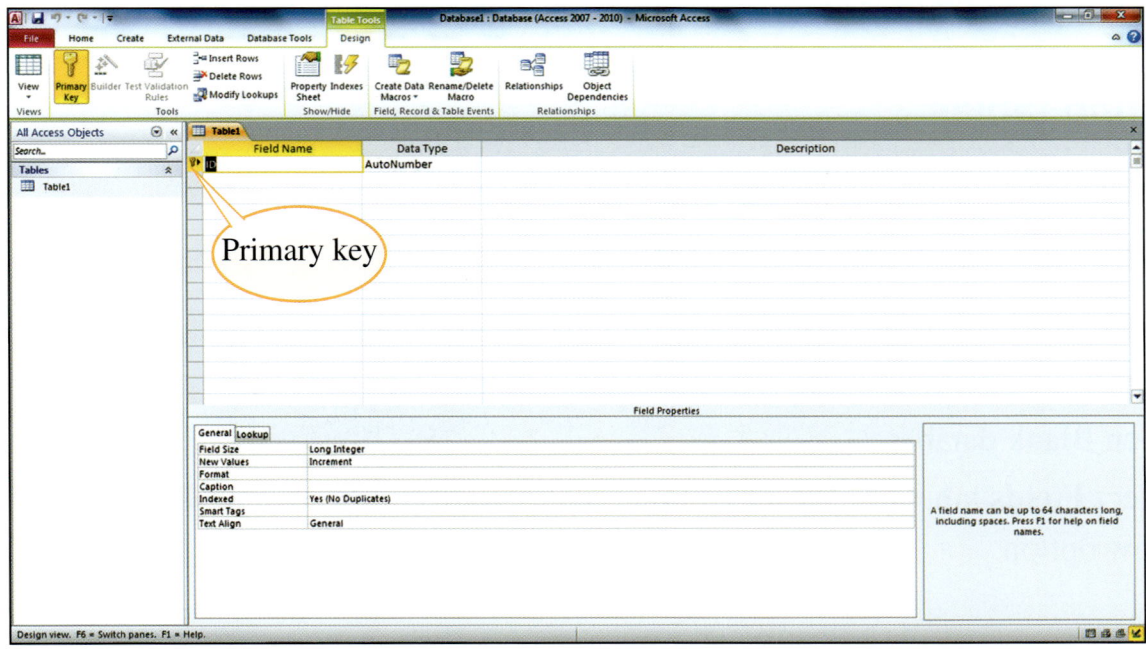

A column working as the primary key

Removing a Primary Key

To remove a primary key, select the required field and select the **Primary Key** option in the **Tools** group of the **Design** tab. Alternatively, you can select the field, right-click on it and then select the **Primary Key** option from the shortcut menu. The key symbol appearing next to the respective field will disappear.

Changing the View

MS Access 2010 provides different viewing options for working on the data. The **Views** group of the **Home** tab provides four options in which users can view their data.

1. Datasheet View
2. PivotTable View
3. PivotChart View
4. Design View

The **Datasheet View** and **Design View** are the two most commonly used views in MS Access. The row and column format is seen in the **Datasheet View** where data can be added. Descriptions like field names and data types can be added in the **Design View**.

It is possible to switch from one view to another using the **View** drop-down list in the **Views** group of the:

- **Datasheet** tab, while switching from Datasheet View to Design View.
- **Design** tab, while switching from the Design View to Datasheet View.

Creating tables

There are two ways to create a table in MS Access 2010:

Creating a table in Datasheet View

This will give you a blank datasheet with unlabelled columns that looks like an Excel worksheet. Follow these steps to create a table in the Datasheet View.

1. Open Blank database.
2. Select **Fields** tab ⟹ **Views** group ⟹ **View** drop-down list ⟹ **Datasheet View** option.

3. Click on **Table** in the **Tables** group in the **Create** tab.

4. A new tabbed document will be formed. **Click to Add** field header will be seen next to the ID field.

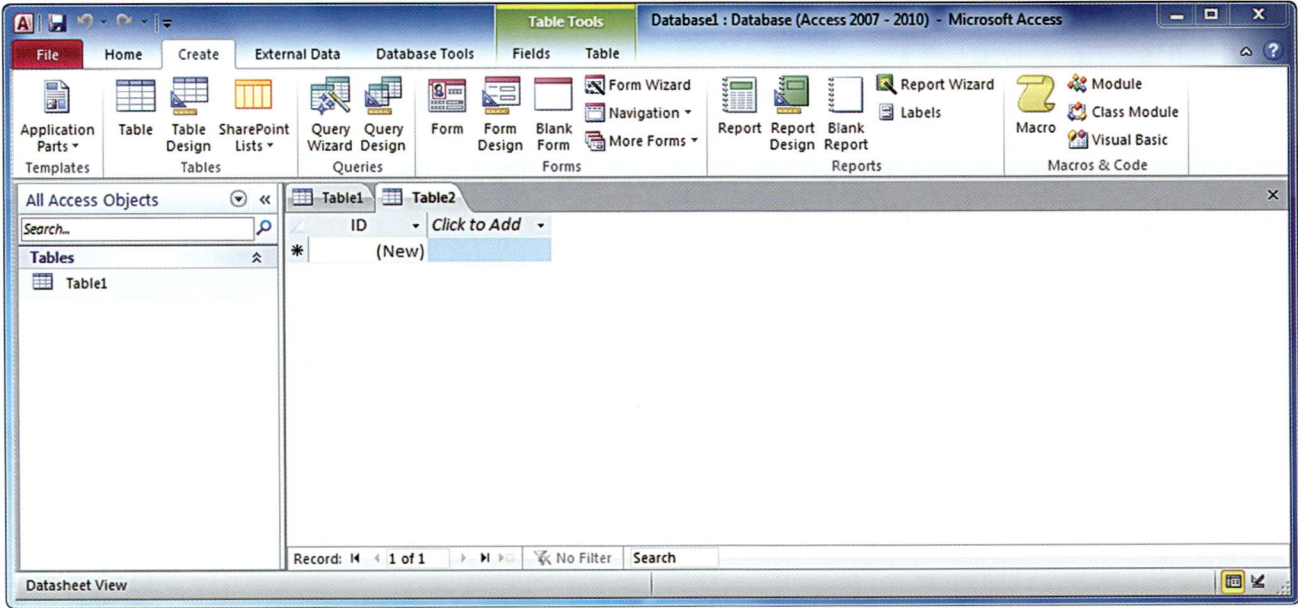

Datasheet View option

5. Click on the field header and select the data type. Add the data to the fields.

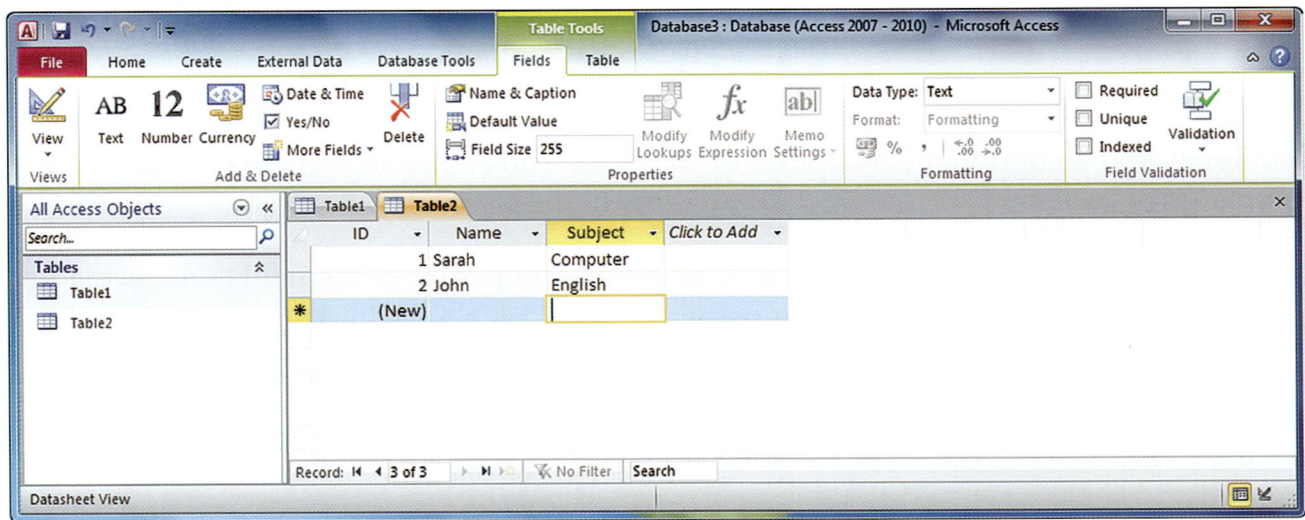

Creating a table in Datasheet View

Create a table in Design View

With this option you define the structure of the table by specifying the field name, data types and properties for each column. This is the most common way of creating a table. Follow these steps to create a table in the Design View.

1. Open Blank database.
2. Select **Fields** tab ⟹ **Views** group ⟹ **View** drop-down list ⟹ **Design View** option.
3. The Design View window is divided into two parts: **Field Grid** pane and **Field Properties** pane. These are discussed below.

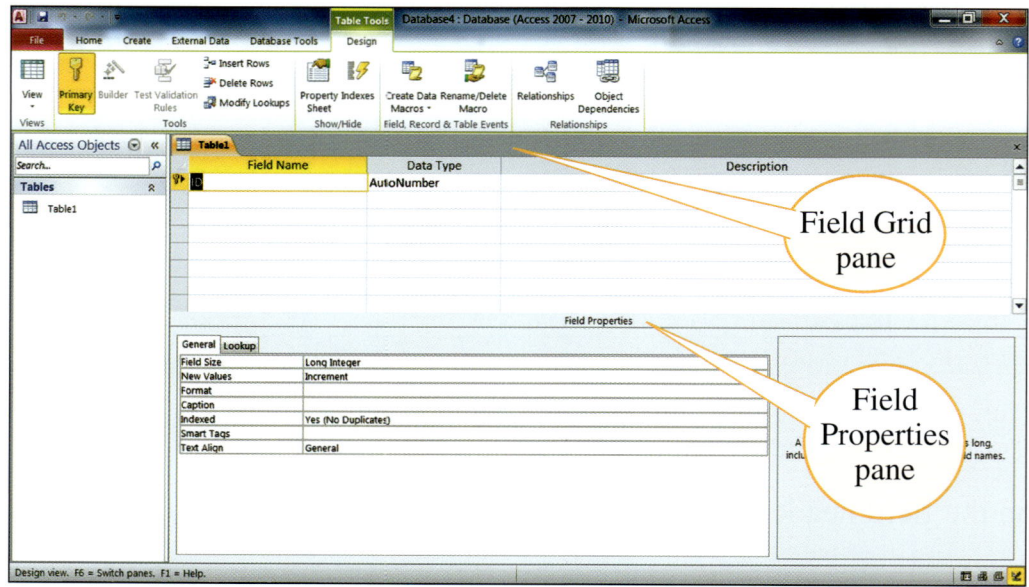

Creating a table in Design View

Field Grid pane: This pane is used to define the fields in the table along with their data types and an optional description of the field. You can change the data type of the field in this view.

Field Properties pane: You can give additional properties to the field name using this pane. It is used to specify the field properties in detail such as field size and validation.

Some of the commonly used options that can be filled in the **Field Properties** pane are explained in the table below.

Property	Description
Field Size	Used to set the maximum size for data stored in the field set to the Text or Number data type.
New Values	Used to set the order of numbers in the fields either in an incremental or random order.

14

Format	Allows you to display data in a format which is different from the way it is stored. For example, you can choose a predefined format or other symbols for creating a custom format to define a currency.
Caption	Used to display an alternative name for the field to make it more explanatory.
Indexed	This speeds up sorting but may slow down the database.
Smart Tags	Adds tags like date, telephone number, financial symbol or person name to the field. Each tag is associated with an action or a list of actions.
Text Align	Used for the alignment of the text entered in the field.

Some of the Field Properties in MS Access 2010

4. Enter the required information in the **Field Grid** and **Field Properties** panes in the **Design View** window (see below). Use the Tab or the Enter key to move through the different fields.

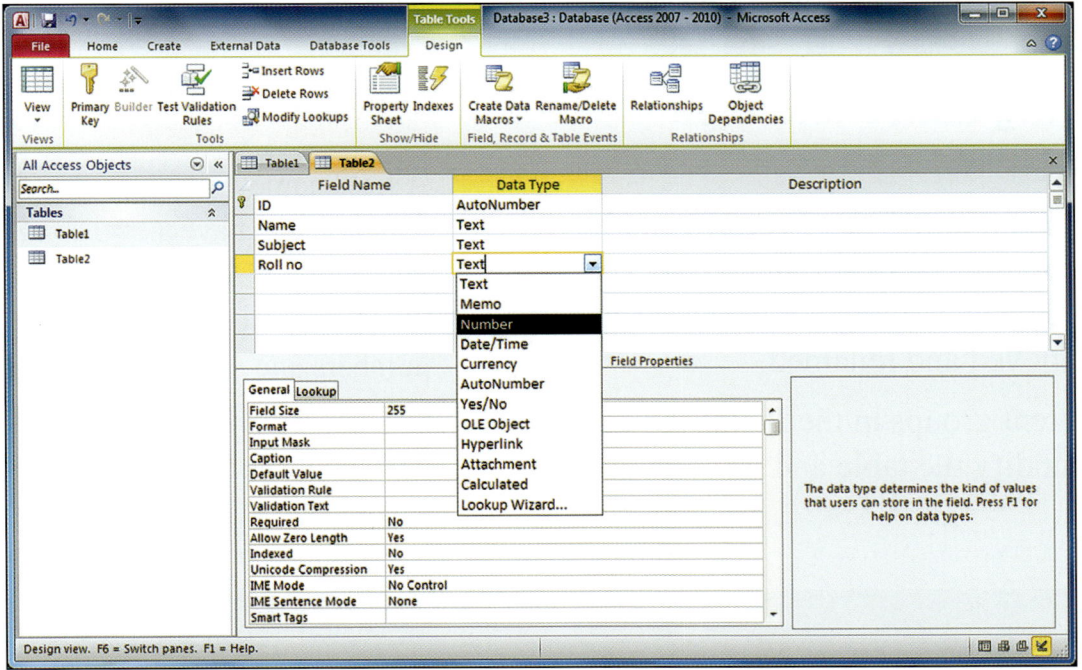

Filling the field information

5. Assign one of the fields in the **Field Grid** pane as the primary key. A key will be displayed in front of the column name to show that the column is now working as a primary key in the table (see the figure on the next page).

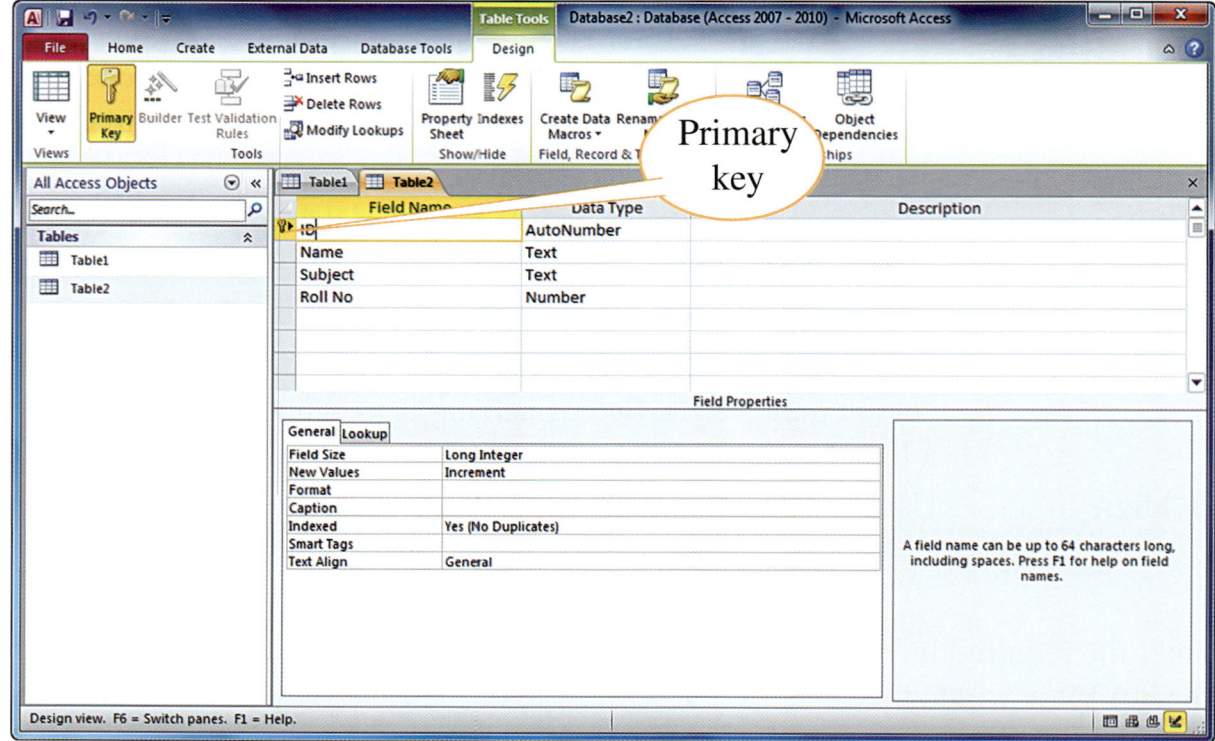

A column working as a primary key

Modifying tables and their content

Tables created in MS Access 2010 can be modified in the Datasheet view. Data types can be changed and columns/fields can be added, deleted, moved and renamed.

The different groups in the Fields tab can be used to modify the table and its contents.

FACT FILE

A field name in the database can have a maximum of 64 characters in upper, lower or mixed case; letters, numbers and some special characters can also be used. However, it cannot have brackets or a full stop and it cannot start with a blank space.

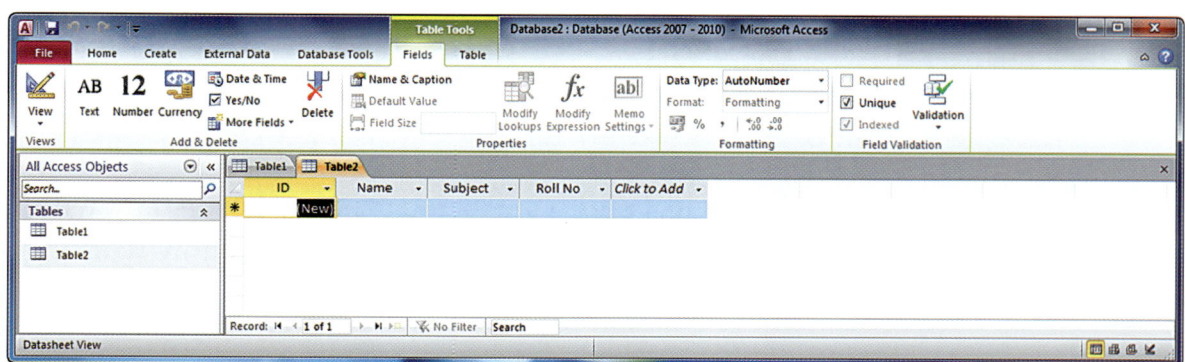

Fields tab

Changing Data Types

1. Select the chosen column header.
2. Click on the drop-down list next to the **Data Type** option in the **Formatting** group and select the chosen option.

Inserting a new field

1. Select the column header where you wish to insert a field.
2. Click on the chosen field option in the **Add & Delete** group of the **Fields** tab.

Deleting a field

1. Select the column header of the field you wish to delete.
2. Click on the **Delete** option in the **Add & Delete** group of the **Fields** tab.
3. Click on **Yes** in the **Microsoft Office Access** dialog box.

Moving a field

1. Select the field to be moved. A thick blue line appears along the left edge of the field.
2. Hold the left mouse button till the cursor changes to 🖑.
3. Drag and drop the field in the desired location.

FACT FILE

Deleting records is permanent. It cannot be reversed through an Undo operation.

Rows in a table can also be moved using the above steps.

Renaming a field

1. Select the column header whose heading you want to change.
2. Right-click on the column and click on the **Rename Field** option.

TRY THIS

Select a column/field. Click on the drop-down arrow next to the column header. Sort the data in the column as required.

Design a database for a shop, with three tables named Item, Order and Customer. Add two columns in each table as shown below. Enter at least eight records in each table.

Item	Data Type	Order	Data Type	Customer	Data Type
Quantity in Stock	Number	Item Ordered	Number	Order No.	Number
Rate per Item	Currency	Customer No.	Text	Amount	Currency

Saving a database

1. Click on the **File** menu.
2. Select the **Save Database As** option from the drop-down list.

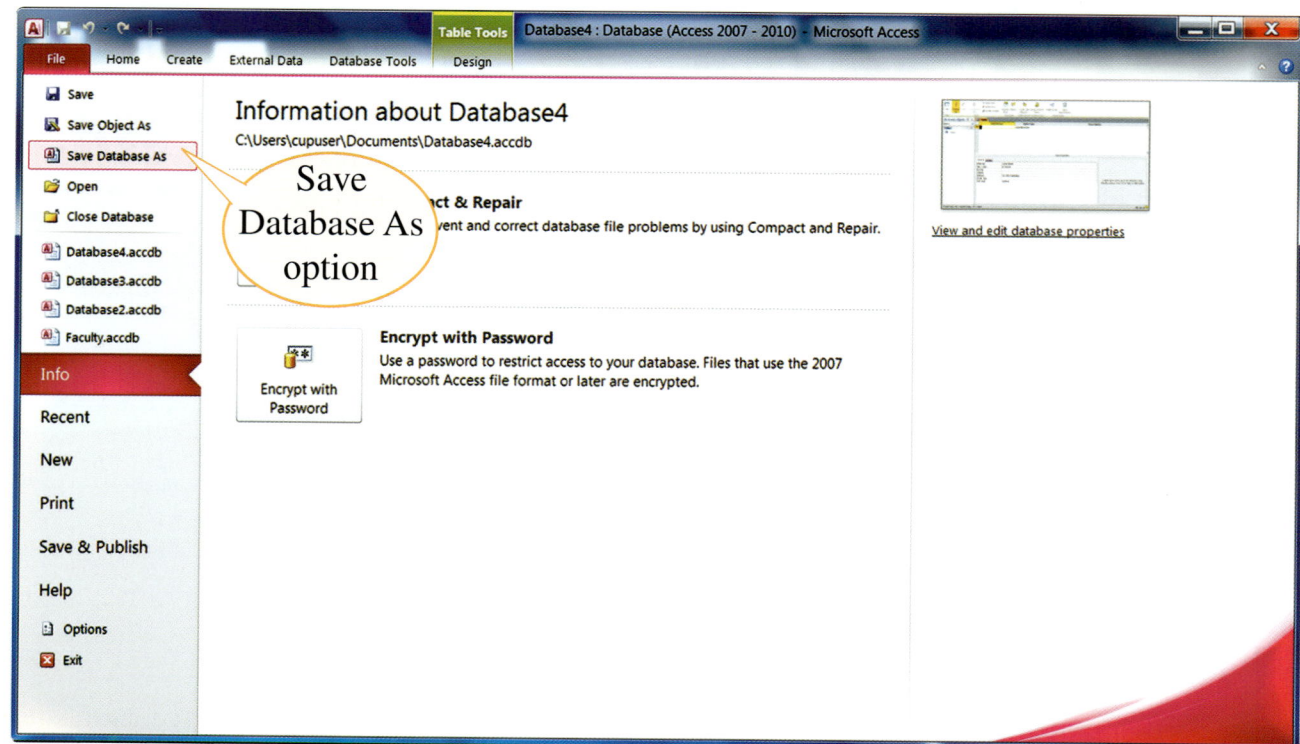

Selecting the Save Database As option

3. The **Microsoft Access** dialog box appears. It seeks permission to save all the opened objects before saving the file. Click on **Yes**.

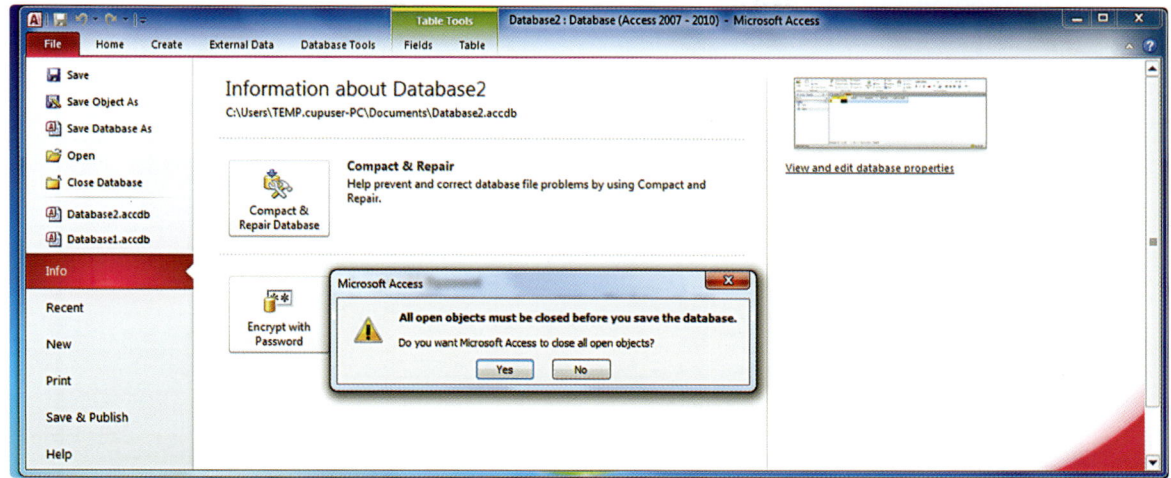

Microsoft Access dialog box

4. The **Save As** dialog box appears. Select the chosen location for saving the file and enter the file name in the **File name** box. Click on the **Save** button.

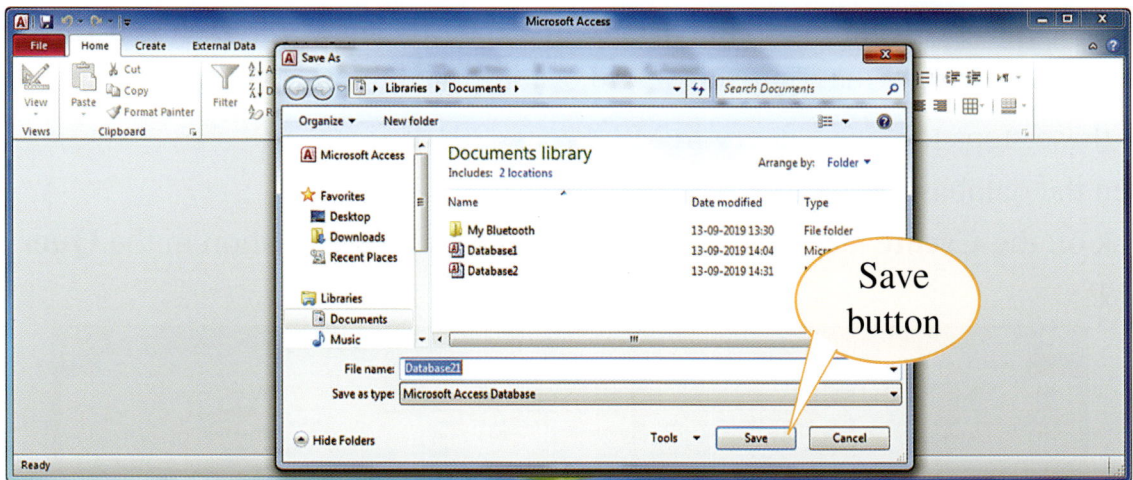

Save As dialog box

Opening an existing database

A database saved in MS Access 2010 can be opened by following these steps:

1. Open the MS Access 2010 window.
2. Click on the **File** menu and select **Open** from the drop-down list.
3. The **Open** dialog box appears. Select the location of the database in the left pane

and enter the name of the file in the **File name** box. Select the file extension from the drop-down list, if required. Then click on the **Open** button.

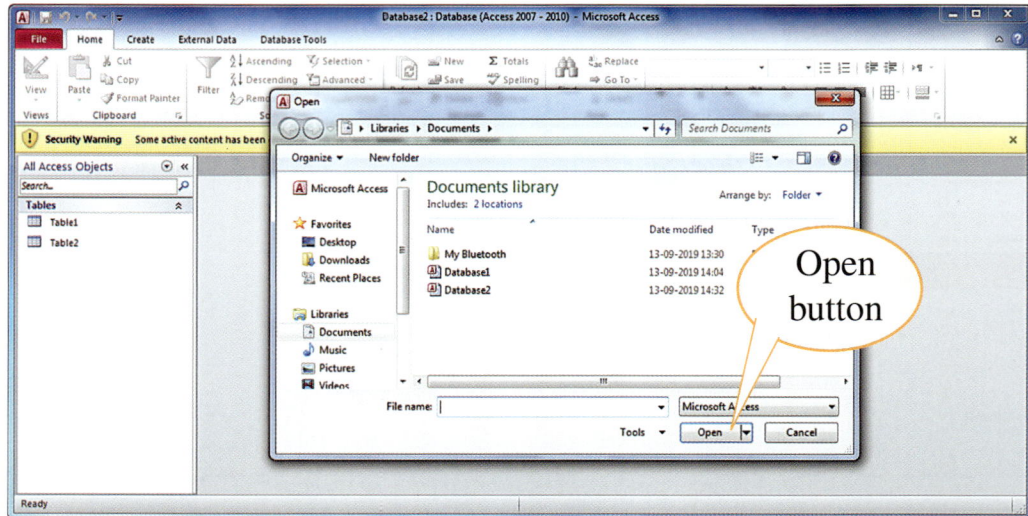

Open dialog box

Queries

A query is a question relating to the data with a specific answer to it. It is a way of retrieving specific information from single or multiple tables of the database.

Follow these steps to raise a query in MS Access 2010:

1. Open the database.
2. Click on the **Create** tab and then select the **Query Design** option in the **Queries** group.

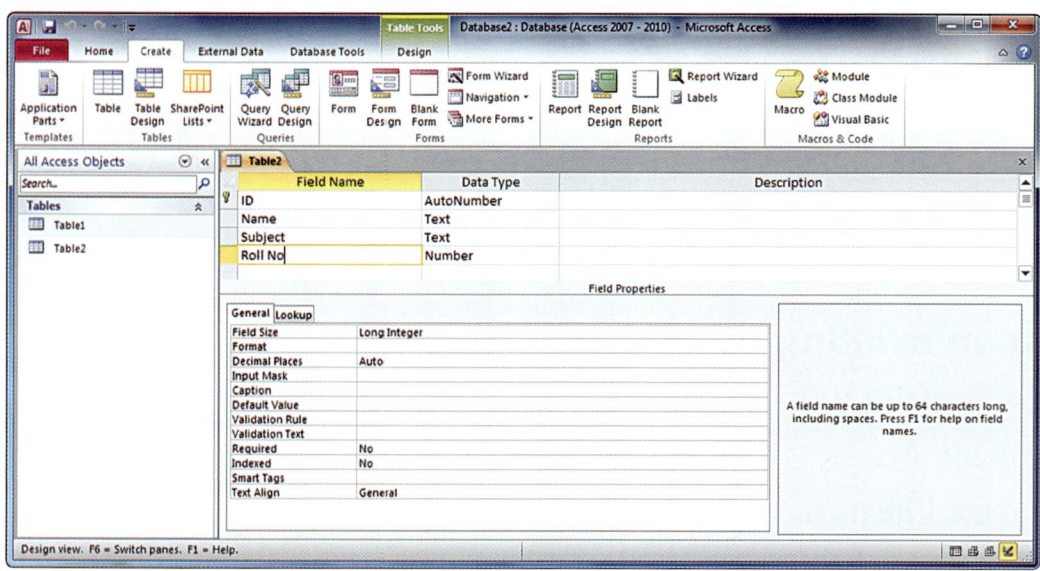

Queries group in the Create tab

3. The **Show Table** dialog box appears. In the **Tables** tab, select the table from the list of tables created and click on **Add**.

4. Repeat the same step to add more tables. Click on **Close** after the required tables have been added.

5. The **Query** tab opens. The upper pane displays the tables selected. The lower pane represents the **Design Grid**.

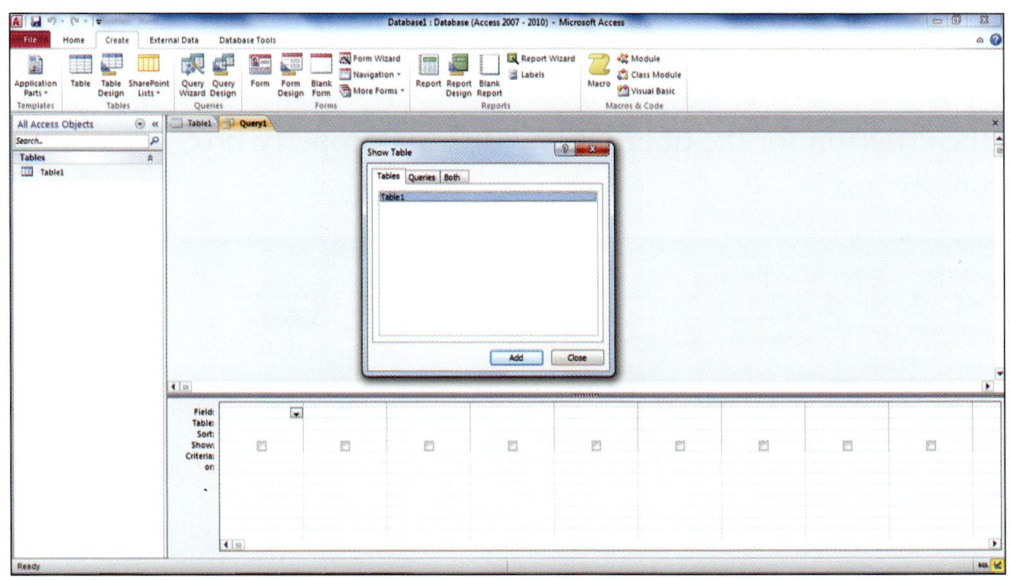

Show Table dialog box and Design Grid pane

Design Grid pane: The portion of the Query tab where fields and criteria for the query are added.

Some of the commonly used options that can be filled in this pane are explained in the table below.

Property	Description
Field	Shows the fields in the selected table to be included in the query.
Table	Displays the name of the table from which the field has been added.
Sort	Determines the sorting order of the data in the datasheet produced by the query.
Show	A checkbox that shows or hides the fields.
Criteria	Specifies the condition on which the query will have to be answered.
or	For specifying alternative criteria on which the query will be resolved.

Design Grid properties

6. Click on the down arrow in the Field property boxes and add the fields in the chosen order. The corresponding name of the table will appear in the Table property.

> Click on the table name with the asterisk (*) symbol in the drop-down list, to add all the fields of the table to the query. You can also double-click on a field name in the upper pane or drag it to the chosen box to add it to the Field property in the Design grid.

7. Sort the data in the selected field based on your preference using the Sort property.
8. Specify the criterion for the query in the Criteria property box. Add multiple criteria in the property box.

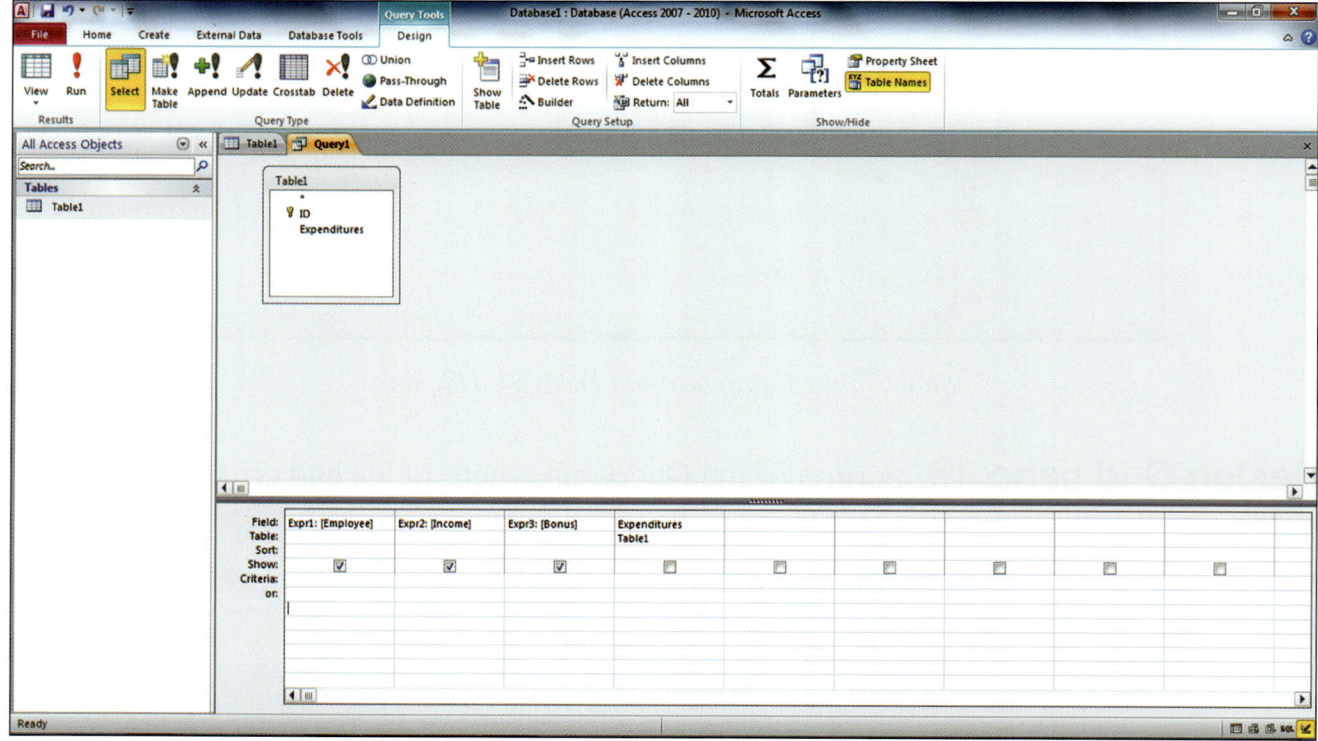

Design grid filled for the query

If required, click on the **Save As** option from **File** menu to save the query.

To run a query

Follow these steps to run a query:

Click on the **Design** tab ⟹ **Results** group ⟹ **Run** option.

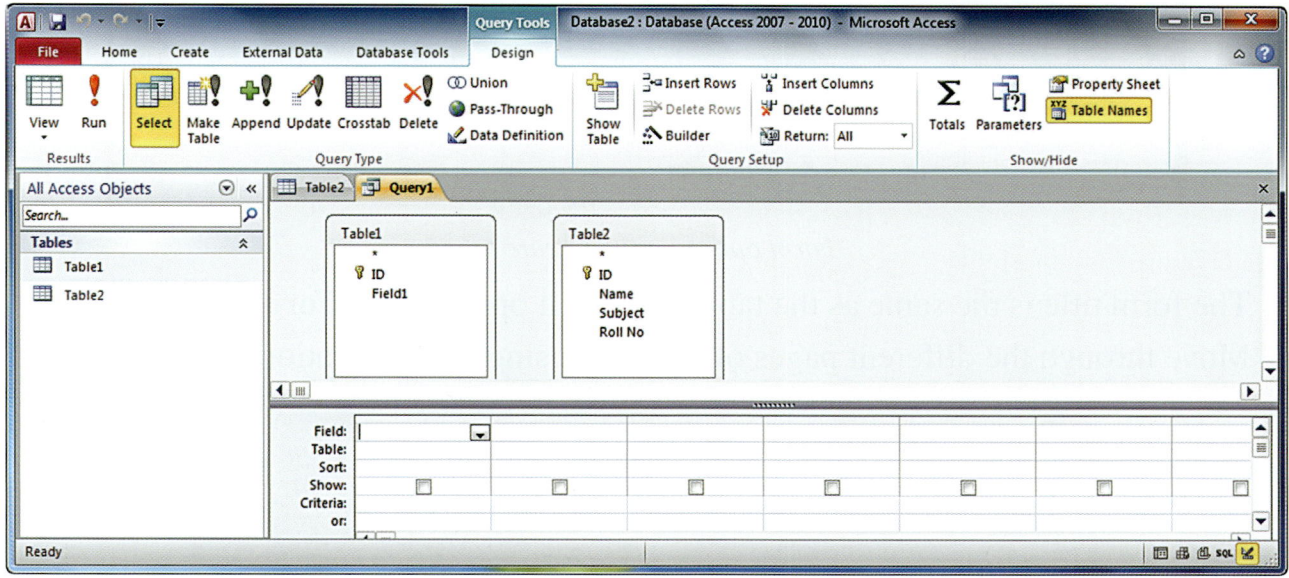

Run option

The result for the query appears in the **Query** window in the Datasheet view.

Forms

Forms are customised screens for viewing, entering, modifying and deleting data in a table or a query. You can create a form in MS Access 2010 using the following steps:

1. Open a database.

2. Click on the **Create** tab ⟹ **Forms** group ⟹ **Form** option.

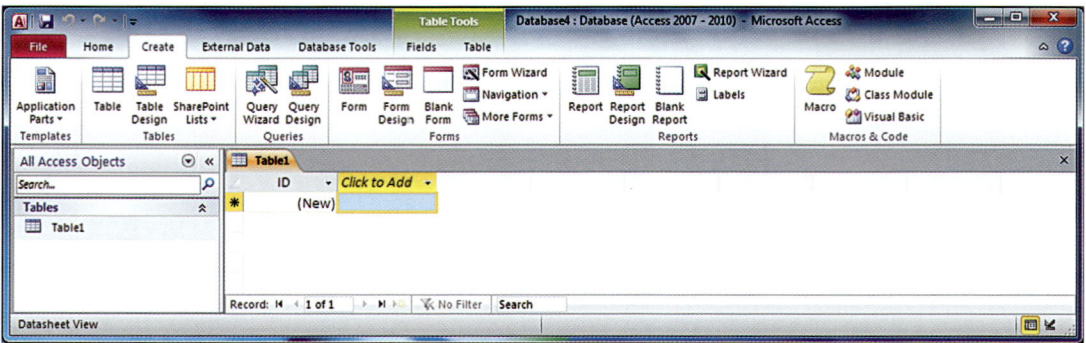

Form option in the Create tab

3. The form title is the same as the table chosen. It opens in the **Form View**.
4. Move through the different pages of the form using the Navigation bar.

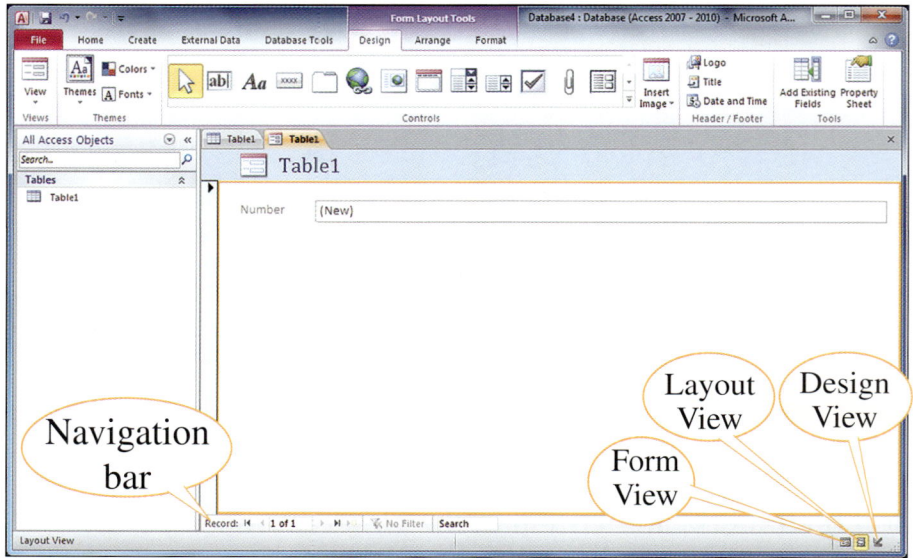

Creating a form

5. Save the form using the **Save As** option in the **File** menu drop-down list.

6. You can change the view of your form using the icons given in the Status bar. The **Layout View** can be used to change the layout. A style can be selected from the **Auto Format** group of the **Format** tab. The **Design View** can help in changing the design.

24

Reports

Reports are the representation of data in a printed format. The size, appearance and layout of the print can be customised based on the requirements.

Follow these steps to create a report in MS Access 2010.

1. Open the database. Select the table or the query for which a report has to be created.

2. Click on the **Create** tab ⟹ **Reports** group ⟹ **Report** option.

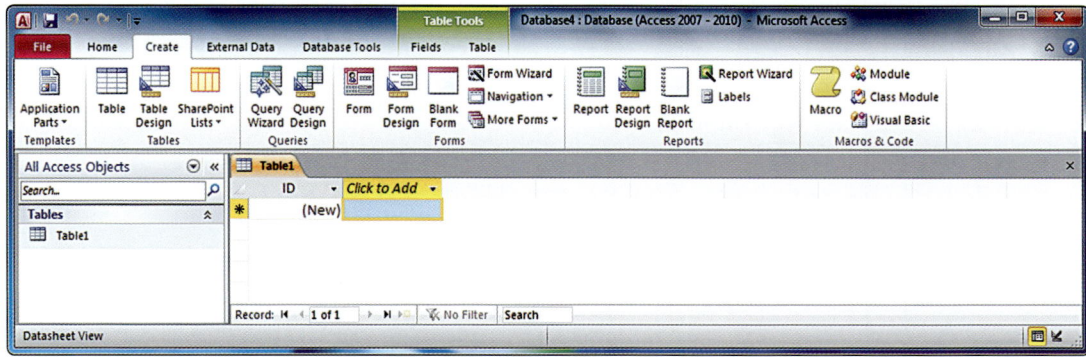

Report option in the Create tab

3. A report is created by Access and it will appear on the screen.

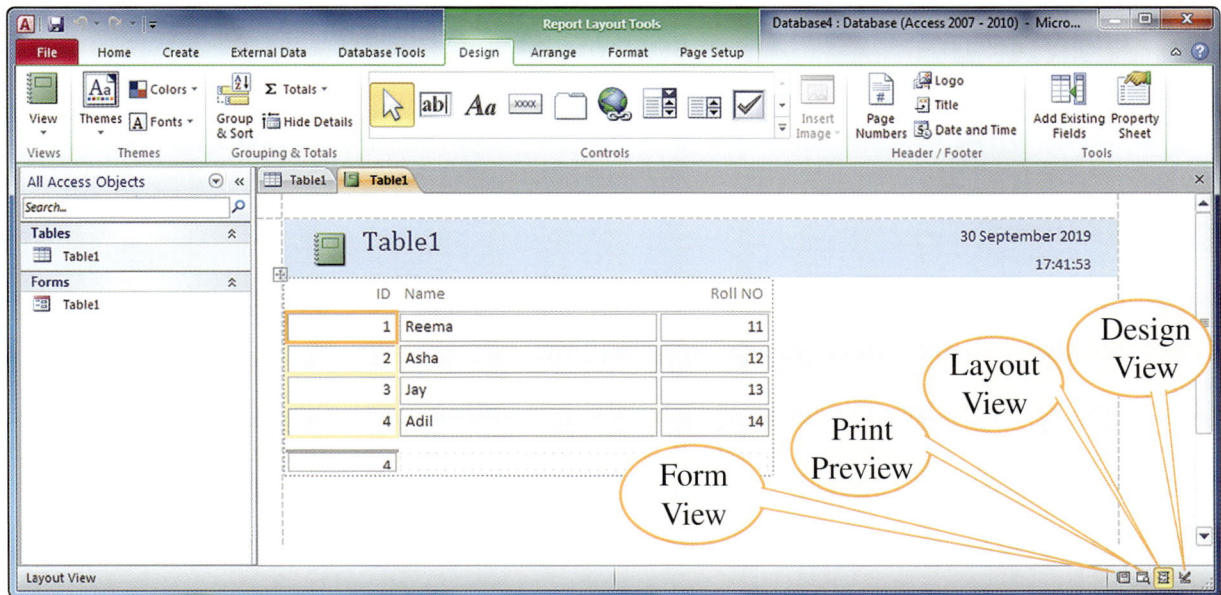

Report created for the selected table

4. Use the **Layout View** in the Status bar to format the report.

5. Use the **Print Preview** to see how the report will look on paper when printed (see below).

6. Print the report using the **Print** option in the **File** menu drop-down list.

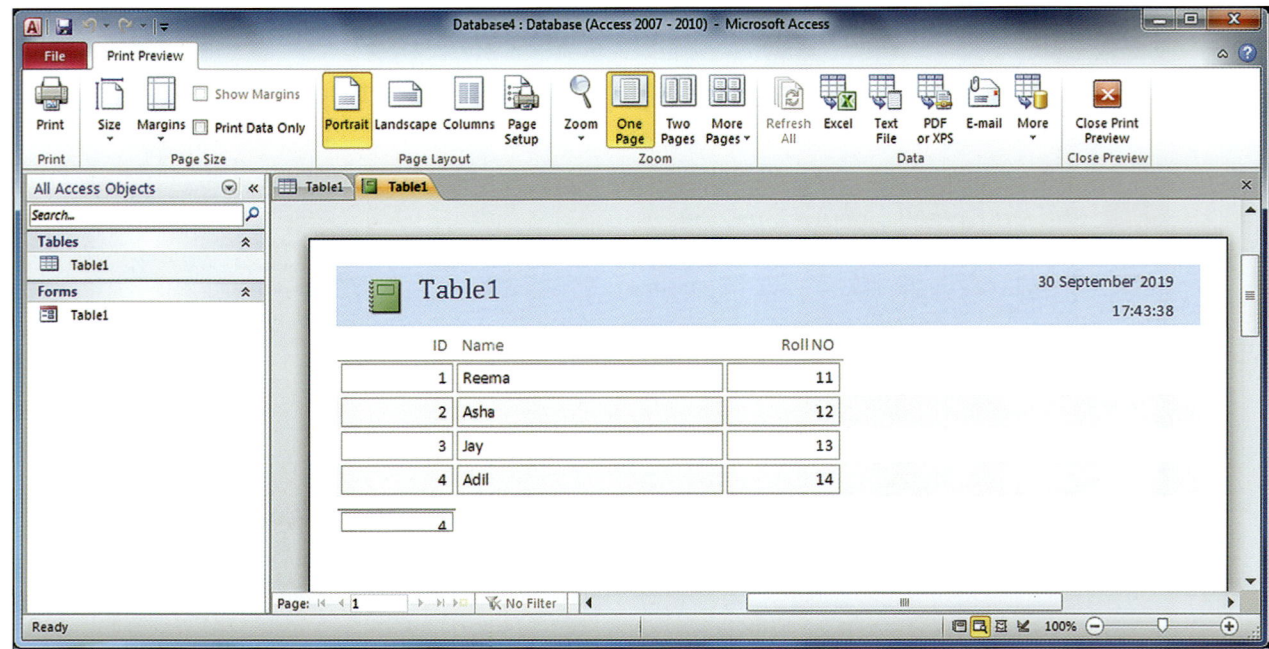

Print Preview of the Report

ACTIVITY

A. A query has been generated for a group of related tables in a database. Is it possible to get a hardcopy of the query? If yes, suggest how.

B. Create a table with the records of sports lovers in your class using MS Access 2010. Use different descriptive fields such as Student Numbers, Student Names and Favourite Sports with appropriate data types. Set a unique primary key for the table. After the table is created:

   1. Enter at least 10 records in the table.

   2. Change the address of record 3 and favourite sport of record 6 in the table.

   3. Delete the last record from the table.

4. Create a query based on the favourite sport. For example, create a query to display only football lovers.

5. Generate a report for the table.

6. Create a form and enter a new record into the table.

7. Save all changes made to the table.

8. Close the table and the database.

GLOSSARY

Data type   The format in which the data is accepted.

Database   An integrated collection of logically-related records in the form of tables.

Database objects   Components (parts) of MS Access.

DBMS   A set of computer programs that control the creation, maintenance and the use of databases in the computer.

Field   A column arranged vertically in a table that stores information of the same type.

Form   A customised screen for viewing, entering, changing and deleting data in a table or a query.

Primary key   A unique value that identifies each record in the table.

Query   A question about the data with a specific answer to it.

Record   Includes complete information about a particular record arranged horizontally in a table.

Report   The representation of data in a printed format.

Table   A collection of related information in the form of rows and columns.

YOU ARE HERE

1

1. Microsoft Access 2010 is a database program used for storing information in the form of tables, queries, forms, reports, etc.

2. A DBMS reduces data redundancy, makes file sharing easier, controls data inconsistency and enforces standards.

3. A new database can be created either using a Blank database or Sample templates.

4. Tables can be created either in Datasheet View or Design View.

5. The Design View consists of two panes: Field Grid pane and Field Properties pane.

6. Queries are raised to get specific information from a table or tables.

7. Forms provide different views for adding, deleting, formatting and designing the data.

8. Queries, forms and reports created for a table can be saved in a database.

EXERCISE

A. True or false?

1. Customised screens that provide an easy way to enter and view data in a table or query are called reports.

2. A new database can only be created using a blank database.

3. Queries are raised to get specific information from a table.

4. One or more of database objects are found when a database is created.

5. The primary key should always have a value that is not repeated for any other record.

B. Match the following.

1. Status bar		a.	Information arranged horizontally in a table
2. Hyperlink		b.	Information arranged vertically in a table
3. Field		c.	Data from a table or query in printed format
4. Report		d.	Displays buttons to change the page views
5. Record		e.	A link to an internet resource

C. State the difference between:

1. Record and Field

2. Table and Queries

3. Forms and Reports

4. Field Grid pane and Field Properties pane

5. Datasheet View and Design View

D. Answer the following questions.

1. What is a DBMS? Discuss its functions.

2. Suggest two ways to create a database.

3. Discuss two ways of creating tables in MS Access 2010.

4. What are Data Types? Name some commonly used Data Types in MS Access 2010.

5. What is the importance of the Primary Key?

LAB WORK

A. Create a database to maintain the library records of your school. Design a form for new students joining the library.

B. Prepare a table listing the names and taste of your ten favourite food items. Delete the rows in which the names of junk food items have been listed. Insert new rows and complete the list with healthy foods.

C. Create the following tables in MS Access 2010.

US States

S_Code	S_Name	S_Capital
GA	Georgia	Atlanta
MA	Massachusetts	Boston
ME	Maine	Augusta
RI	Rhode Island	Providence
WI	Wisconsin	Madison

US Cities

C_Code	C_Name	S_Code
9	Augusta	ME
10	Atlanta	GA
11	Boston	MA
12	Cambridge	MA
13	Madison	WI
14	Milwaukee	WI
15	Providence	RI

- Assign Primary Keys to both the tables.
- Add five records in both the tables.
- Generate a report.

PROJECT WORK

Create tables to store the details of the students going to visit a monument. The number of tables and their contents should be discussed in the class. Create a form and enter one more record into your table(s). Create a report to generate a printed version of the database.

WHO AM I?

I was born on 16 July 1951 in Philadelphia, Pennsylvania, USA.
I co-created the software program VisiCalc, the first electronic spreadsheet.
I am also known as 'the father of the spreadsheet'.
I received the Grace Murray Hopper Award in 1981 for VisiCalc.
I am ……………..……

MS Office 2016 Updates

MS Access 2016 has the same layout as MS Access 2010. There are a few minor differences listed below.

- The default window of MS Access 2016 is given below. It gives you multiple templates to select from.

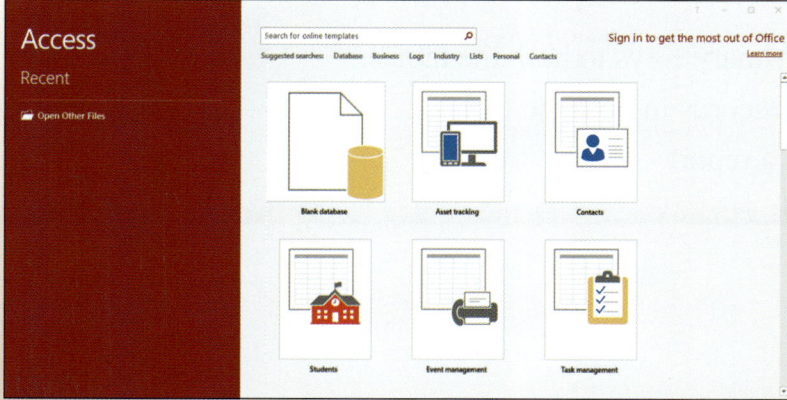

- In Access 2016, the top menu has a background color so that it can be easily differentiated from the rest of the screen. In MS Access 2010, there was no difference between the color of this menu and the rest of the screen.

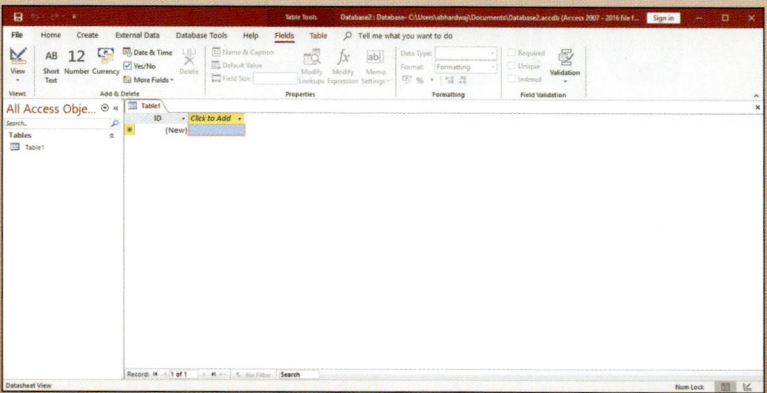

- In Access 2016, there are two Microsoft Office themes that can be used: 'Colorful' and 'White'.

- There is a user-friendly 'Tell Me' option to help you with any problems while working on MS Access 2016.

Introduction to OpenOffice I

SNAP RECAP

1. What do you understand by the term open source software?
2. Which software program(s) do you generally use for editing a document or creating a presentation?

LEARNING OBJECTIVES

You will learn about:

- various OpenOffice applications
- introduction to OpenOffice Writer
- main components of the OpenOffice Writer window
- File, Edit and Format menus in OpenOffice Writer
- introduction to OpenOffice Impress
- creating, modifying and running a presentation in OpenOffice Impress.

Introduction

OpenOffice is a collection of application software just like Microsoft Office. It is compatible with many operating systems like Windows, Linux and MacOS. **Sun Microsystems** released the first version of OpenOffice 1.0 but it was taken over by **Apache Foundation** in 2011. The software was renamed as **Apache OpenOffice**.

OpenOffice is an open source software application, and its source code is available and can be freely downloaded from openoffice.org. It consists of six applications as shown in the table.

OpenOffice Application	Used for	Logo
Writer	Processing text documents	
Calc	Creating spreadsheets	
Impress	Making presentations	
Math	Editing maths formulae	
Draw	Drawing diagrams	
Base	Creating tables and databases	

OpenOffice applications

OpenOffice Writer

OpenOffice Writer is a word processor used to create, edit, format and print a document. It is just like MS Word with similar features but with a different layout. The extension of the file created in OpenOffice Writer is .odt.

It can be used to create and edit:

- documents with text, images and charts
- brochures and invitations
- newsletters with multiple columns.

Main components of OpenOffice Writer window

To open OpenOffice Writer, after downloading it, click on **Start** button ⟹ **OpenOffice** ⟹ **OpenOffice Writer**. The main components of OpenOffice Writer window are shown below.

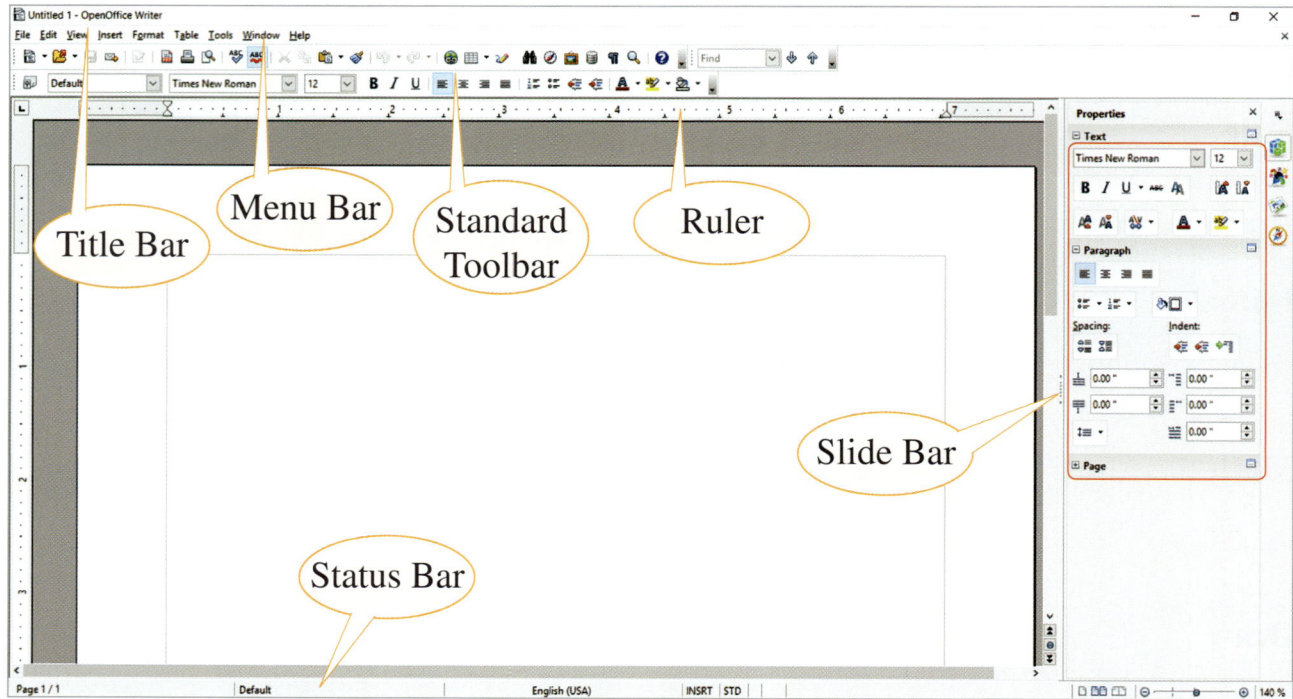

OpenOffice Writer window

Title bar

This is the bar on the top of the application window with the document name Untitled 1 and the program name OpenOffice Writer.

Menu bar

This is made up of several drop-down menu tabs: File, Edit, View, Insert, Format, Table, Tools, Window and Help.

Standard toolbar

This includes tools for frequent tasks such as open, save, copy, cut, paste, etc.

Ruler

Both vertical and horizontal rulers are available to show dimensions, tabs, columns, margins of the page, etc.

Slide bar

This contains frequently used tools grouped in a deck.

Status bar

This bar displays information about the current page, current template, zoom percentage, insert or overwrite mode, selection mode, unsaved changes and digital signature.

Menus in OpenOffice Writer

The Menu bar in OpenOffice Writer consists of various drop-down menu tabs like File, Edit, View, Insert, Format, Table, Tools, Window and Help. Let us discuss some of these menus in detail.

File menu

The File menu in OpenOffice Writer is shown below, with a list of the various options available.

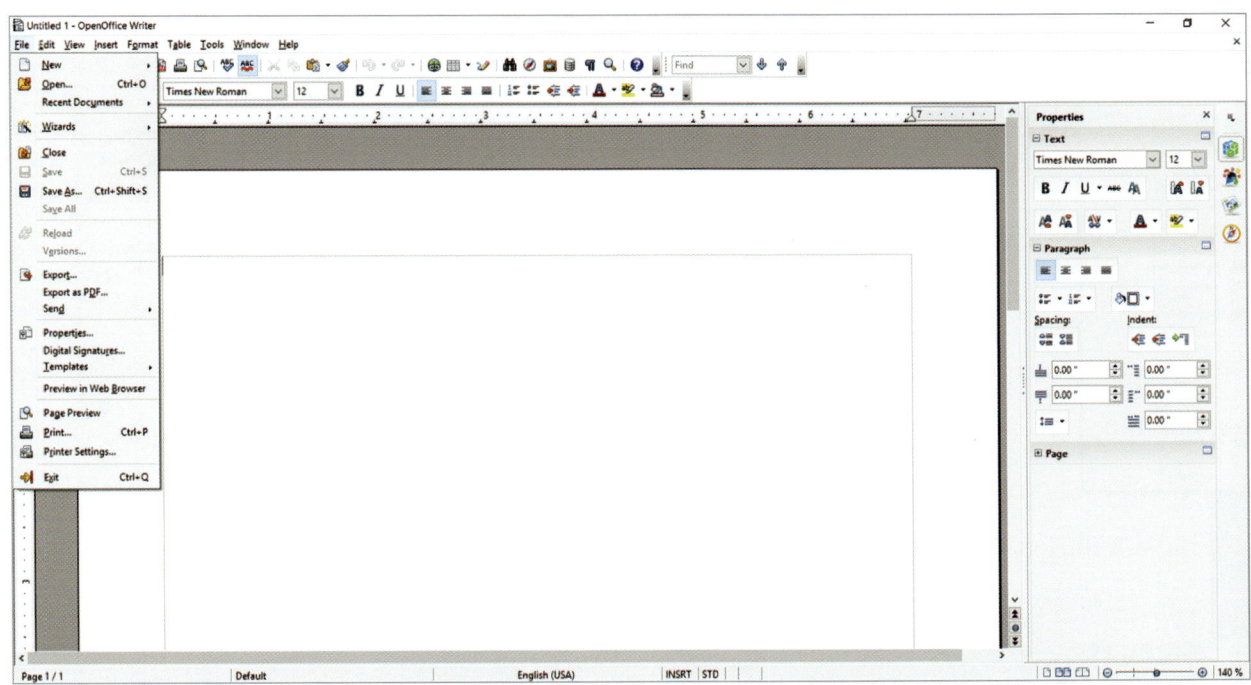

File menu in OpenOffice Writer

New: Creates a new file.

Open...: Opens an already created file.

Close: Closes a file.

Save: Saves the changes in an already created file.

Save As...: Saves a new file for the first time or saves an existing file with a different name.

Save All: Saves all open files.

Page Preview: Previews the document before taking a printout.

Print...: Prints a document.

Printer Settings...: Changes the printer settings for a document to be printed. When clicked, it opens the printer setup dialog box which shows you the name of the printer and its details, such as Status, Type and Location. You can also change printer properties from here.

Exit: Exits OpenOffice Writer.

Edit menu

The Edit menu in OpenOffice Writer is shown below, with a list of the various options available.

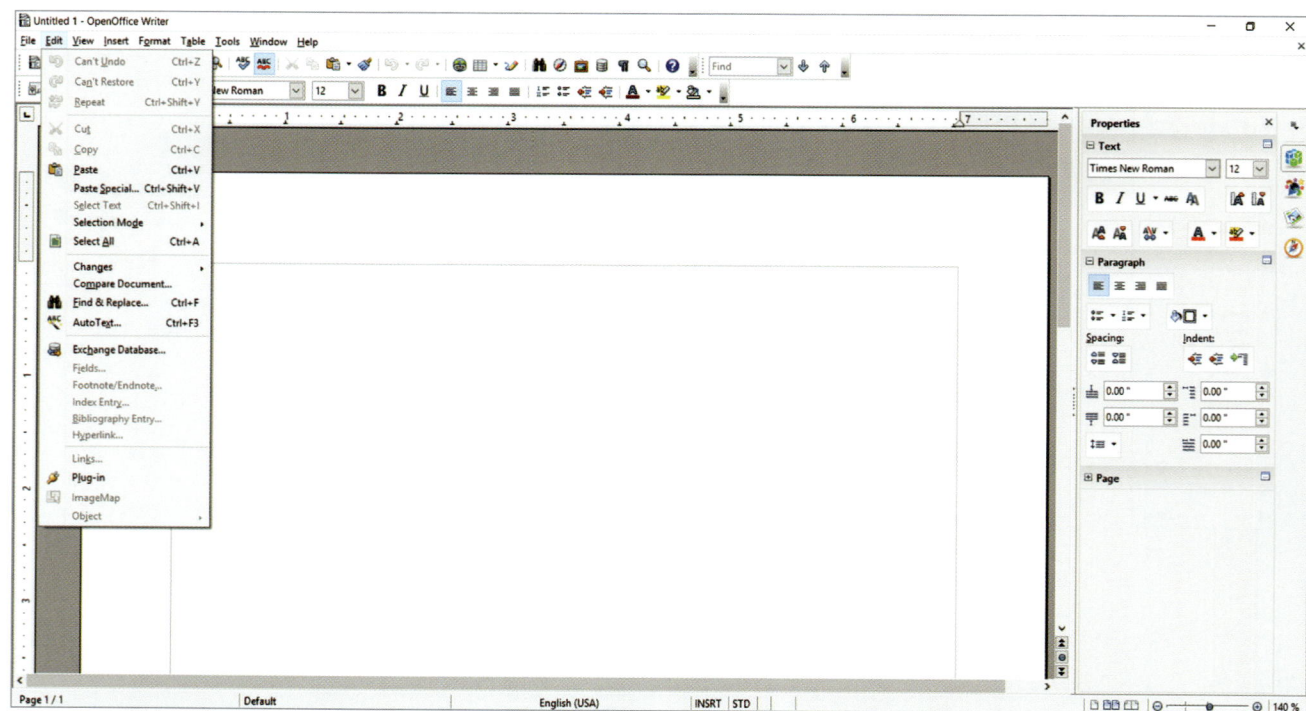

Edit menu in OpenOffice Writer

Undo: Used to undo the last action in a document. This can also be done by using the undo tool from the standard toolbar.

Restore: Used to redo the last action in a document. This can also be done by using the redo tool from the standard toolbar.

Cut: Cuts the selected text and places it in the clipboard.

Copy: Copies the selected text in the clipboard.

Paste: Pastes the cut/copied text from the clipboard into the document.

Paste Special...: Pastes the formatted or unformatted text in a document.

Select All: Selects the complete document.

Find & Replace...: Searches for a selected word and replaces the searched word with a new word.

Format menu

The Format menu in OpenOffice Writer is shown on the right, with a list of the various options available.

Character...: The formatting related to the character like Font, Font Effects, Position,

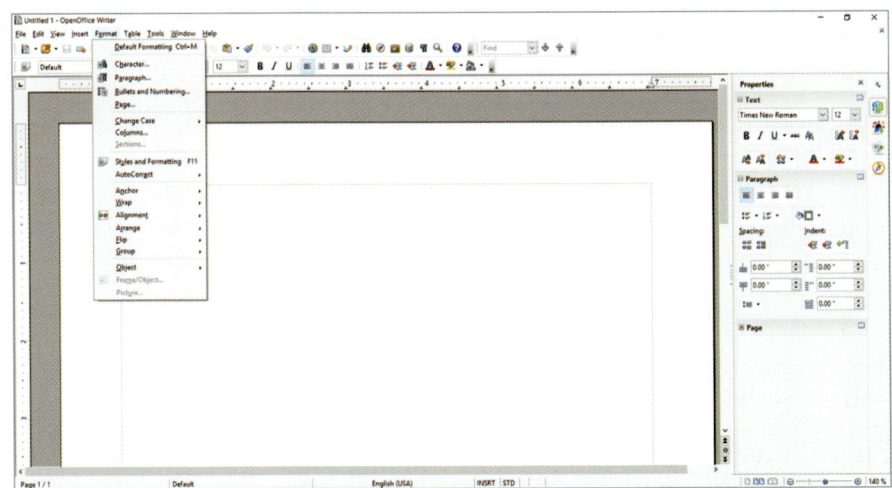

Format menu in OpenOffice Writer

Hyperlink and Background. The Character dialog box is shown below.

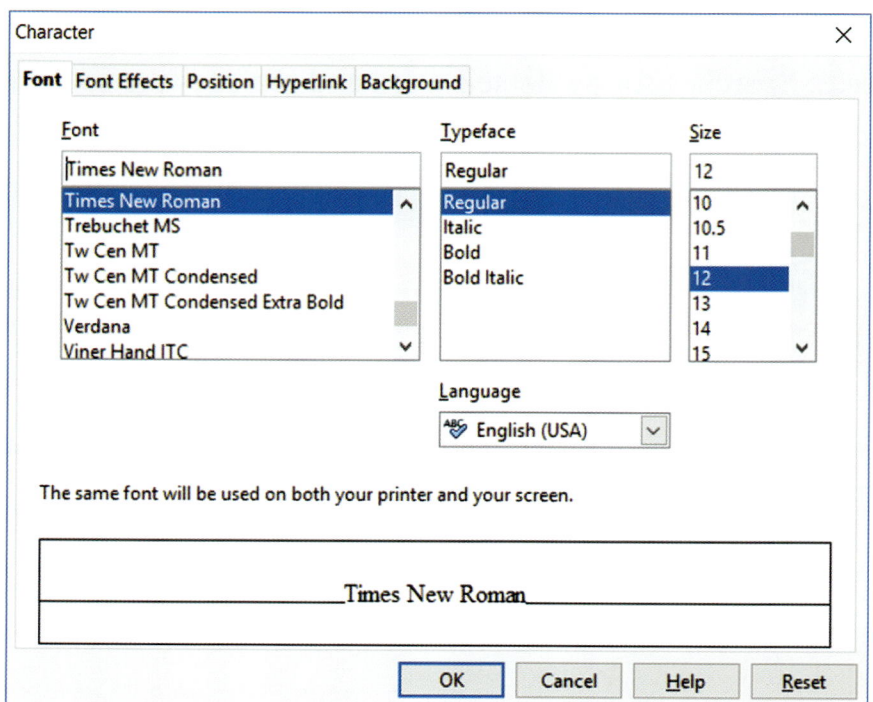

Character dialog box in the Format menu

Paragraph...: The formatting related to paragraph Indents & Spacing, Alignment, Text Flow, Outline & Numbering, Tabs, Drop Caps and Borders can be done using the paragraph dialog box.

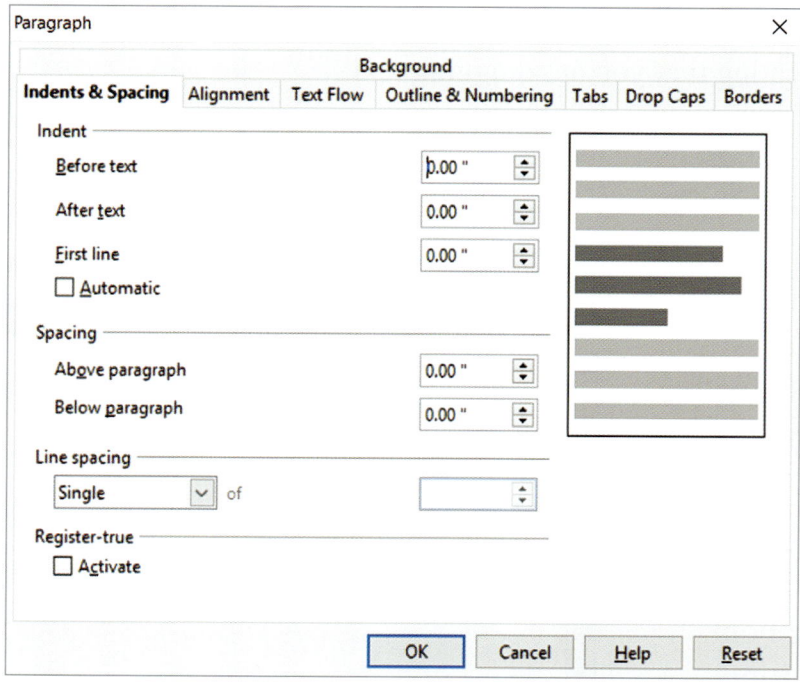

Paragraph dialog box in the Format menu

Bullets and Numbering...: An ordered or unordered list can be created by using bullets and numbering. OpenOffice Writer has different ways of representing bullets and numbers as shown below.

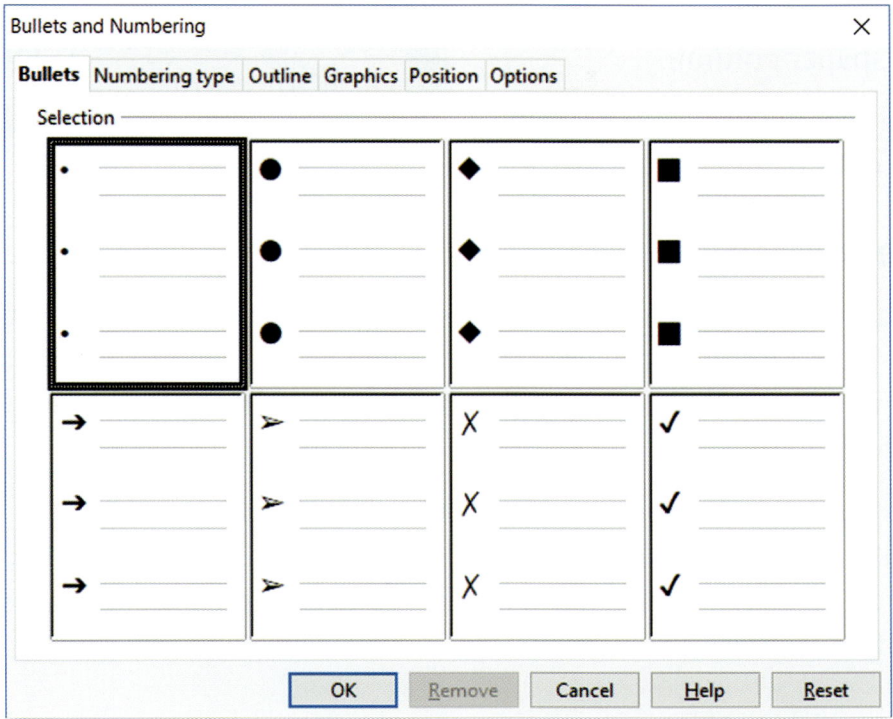

Bullets and Numbering in the Format menu

Page...: Changing the page borders and background, margins, applying columns and adding headers and footers, etc. can be done using the Page Style dialog box.

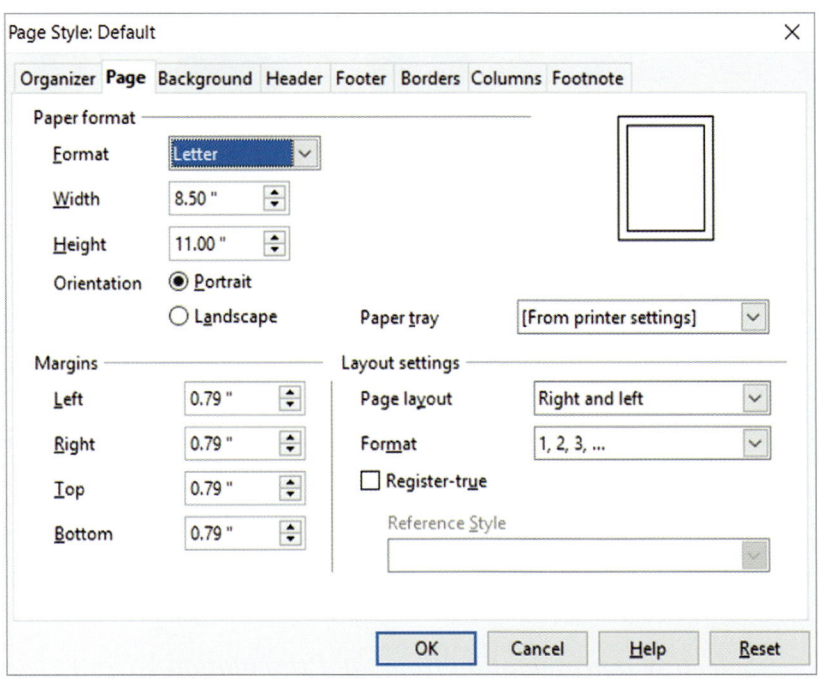

Page Style dialog box

Change Case: Converts the text into uppercase, lowercase, toggle case, title case or sentence case.

Columns...: Creates multiple columns on a page. It is used to create articles just like a newspaper column.

Alignment: Aligns the text as left, right, center or justified.

OpenOffice Impress

OpenOffice Impress is a presentation tool used to create multimedia presentations. It is a part of the OpenOffice suite. Presentations can be used by professionals in offices or by students in schools and colleges. It is an easy way to present a topic with lots of multimedia effects.

A presentation consists of one or more slides with different elements like text, bulleted or numbered lists, tables, charts, clipart and a wide range of graphic objects. The default extension of a presentation in OpenOffice Impress is .odp. Let us now learn how to use OpenOffice Impress.

Creating a presentation

To create a presentation, click on **Start** ⟹ **Openoffice.org** ⟹ **OpenOffice Impress**. It opens by showing the wizard as below, which gives three options.

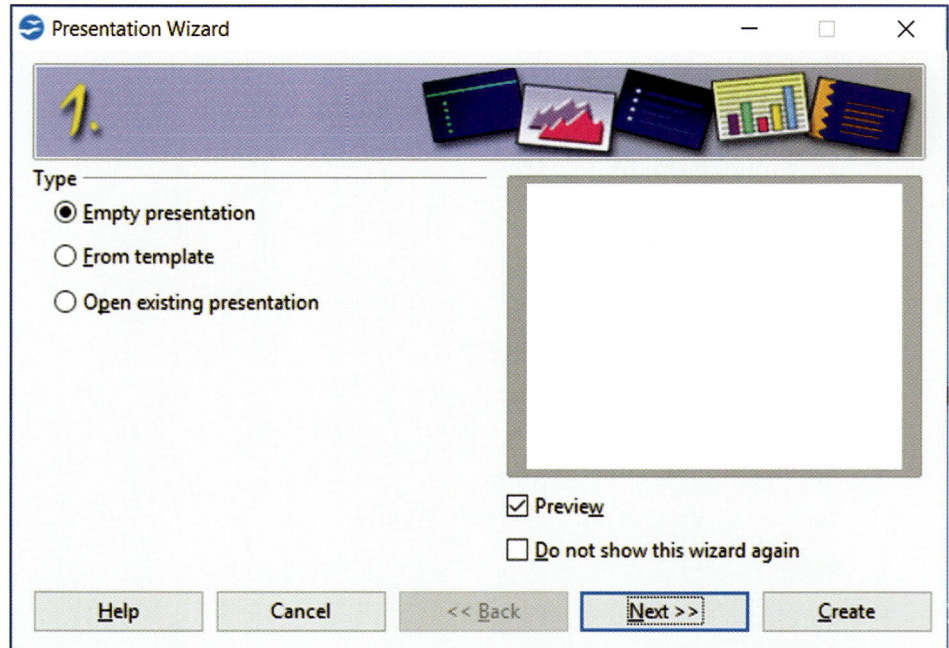

Selecting a presentation from the Presentation Wizard

These options are:

- **Empty presentation**: Creates a blank presentation.
- **From template**: Provides some predefined templates to choose from.
- **Open existing presentation**: Opens presentations which were created earlier.

1. Select **Empty presentation** and then click on **Next>>**.
2. **Select a slide design** according to the suitability of your presentation. Click on **Next>>**.

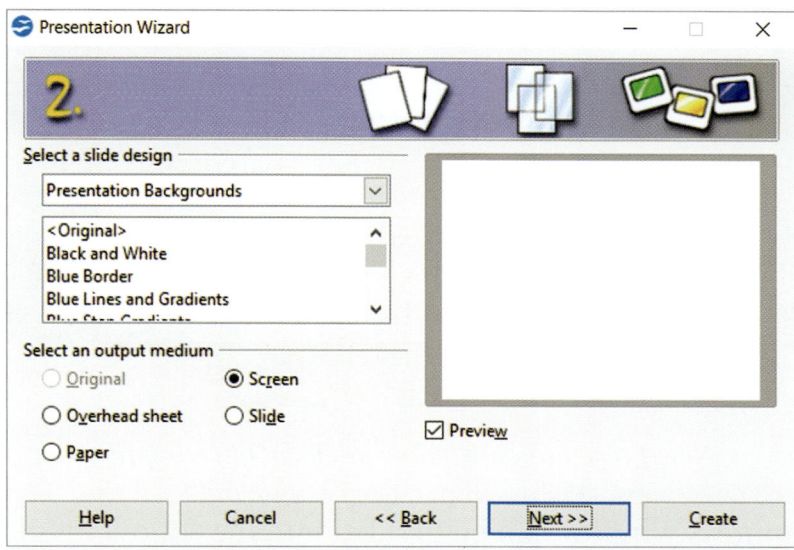

Selecting a slide design from Presentation Wizard

3. First, **Select a slide transition** and then **Select the presentation type**. Click on **Create** to create a presentation with the settings done using this three-step presentation wizard.

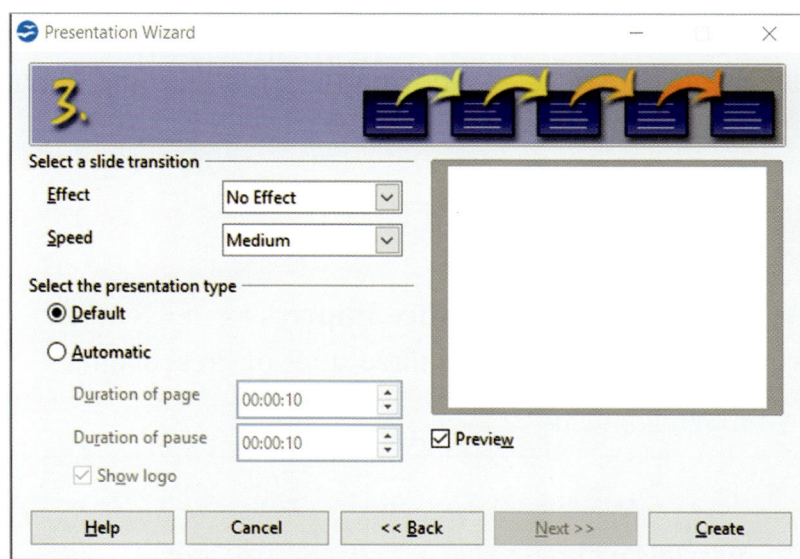

Creating a slide using Presentation Wizard

4. After you click on **Create** you will get the OpenOffice Impress window as shown below.

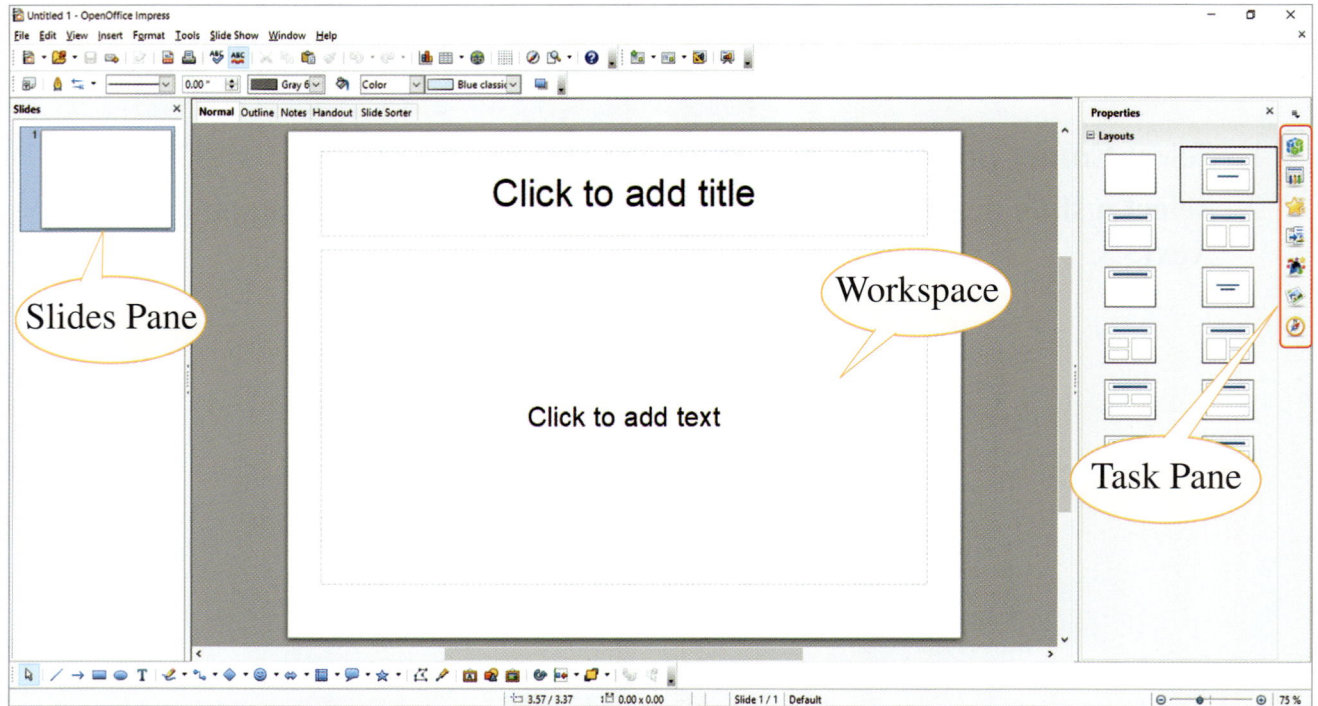

New Presentation window in OpenOffice Impress

The OpenOffice Impress window can be divided into the following three components:

- **Slides pane**: This is on the left side of the window. It shows a thumbnail of all the slides in the presentation. The slides are in the order of creation. You can drag and change the order of the slides.

- **Workspace**: This is the main area where you can design your slides.

- **Task pane**: This displays different tasks like Properties, Slide Transition, Custom Animation, Master Pages, Styles and Formatting, Gallery and Navigator which can be used to design slides.

Presentation views

The workspace window in OpenOffice Impress provides five different view tabs, as described below:

Normal: A slide can be created, edited and viewed. It displays the complete slide with text and graphics.

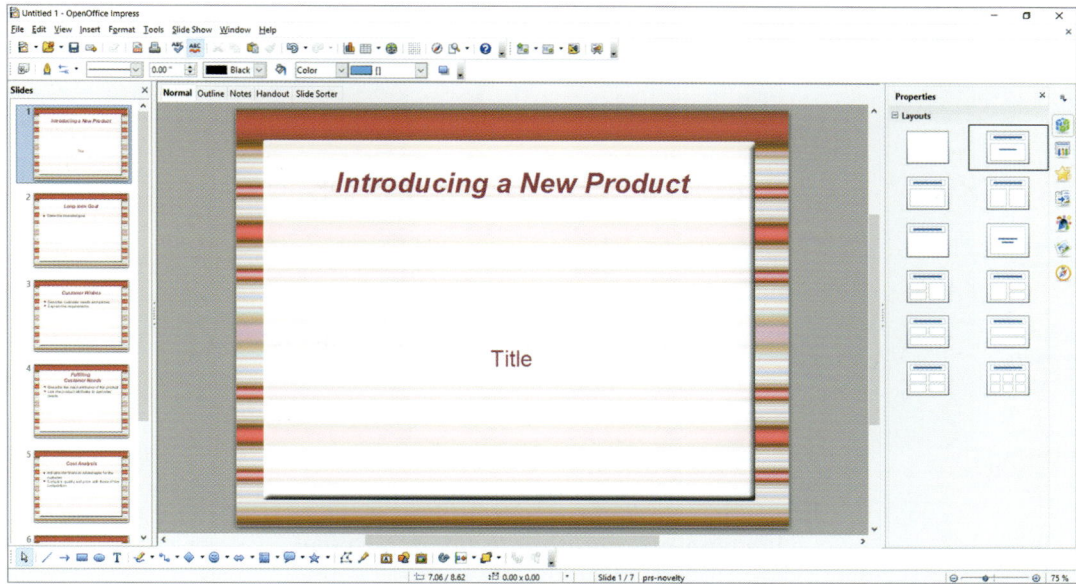

Viewing presentation in the normal view

Outline: This view can display only the text of the slides. It can be used to plan the text and rearrange the content on a slide.

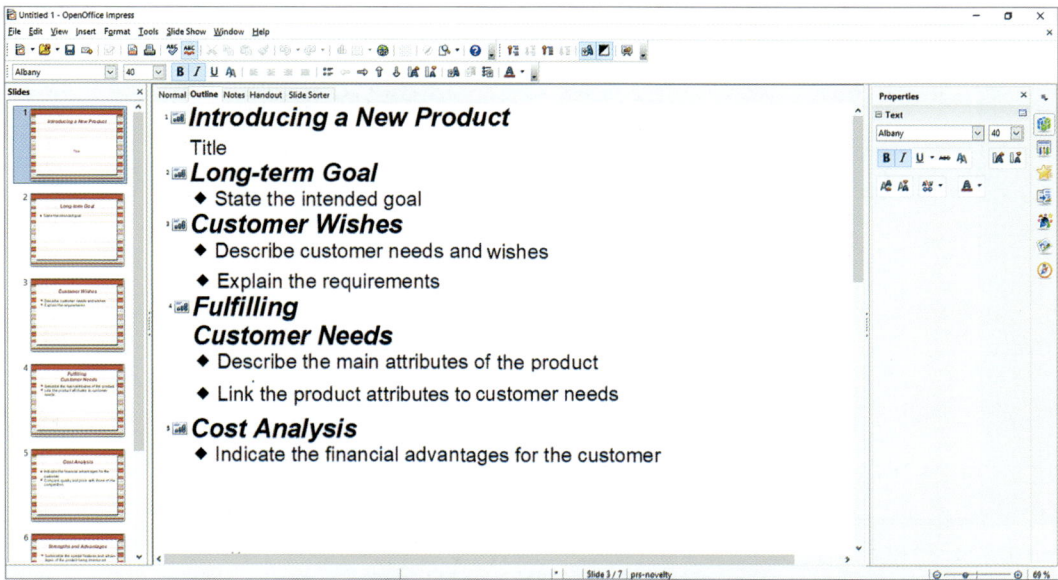

Viewing presentation in the outline view

Notes: This view is used to add extra notes to the slide. It acts as reference for the presenter during the slide show.

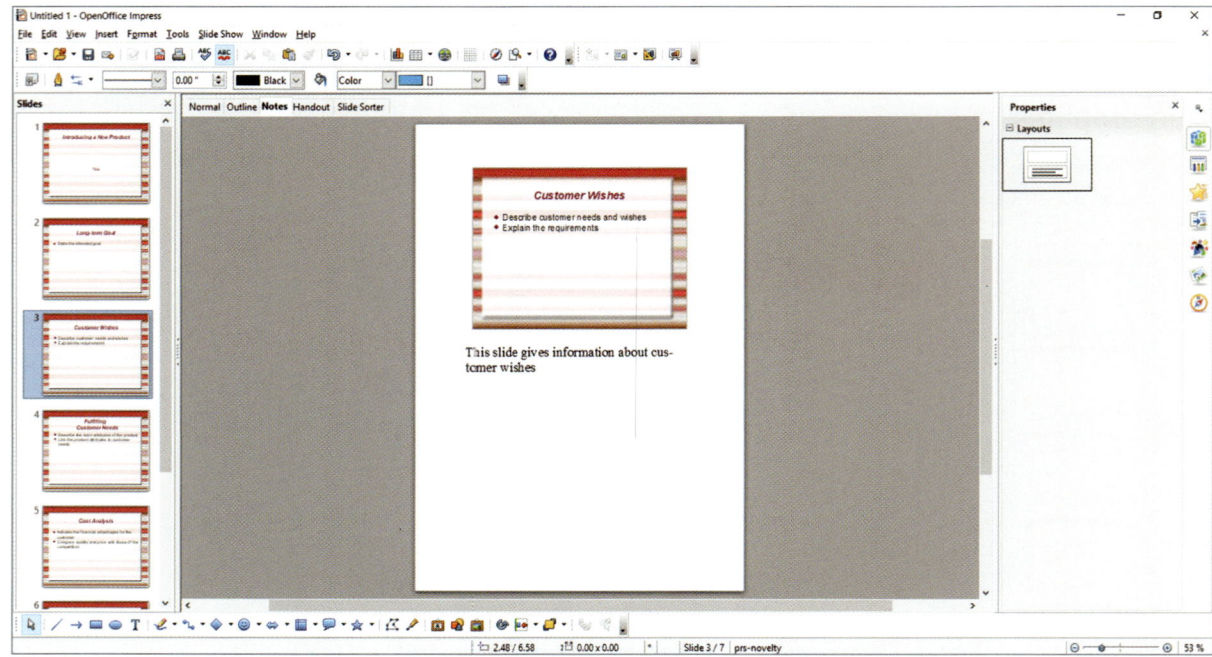

Viewing presentation in the notes view

Handout: This view creates a handout with more slides on one page. It displays the layout with single, two, three, four, six or nine slides per page.

Viewing presentation in the handout view

44

Slide sorter: Displays all the slides of the presentation in a miniature form. We can rearrange the slides in this view.

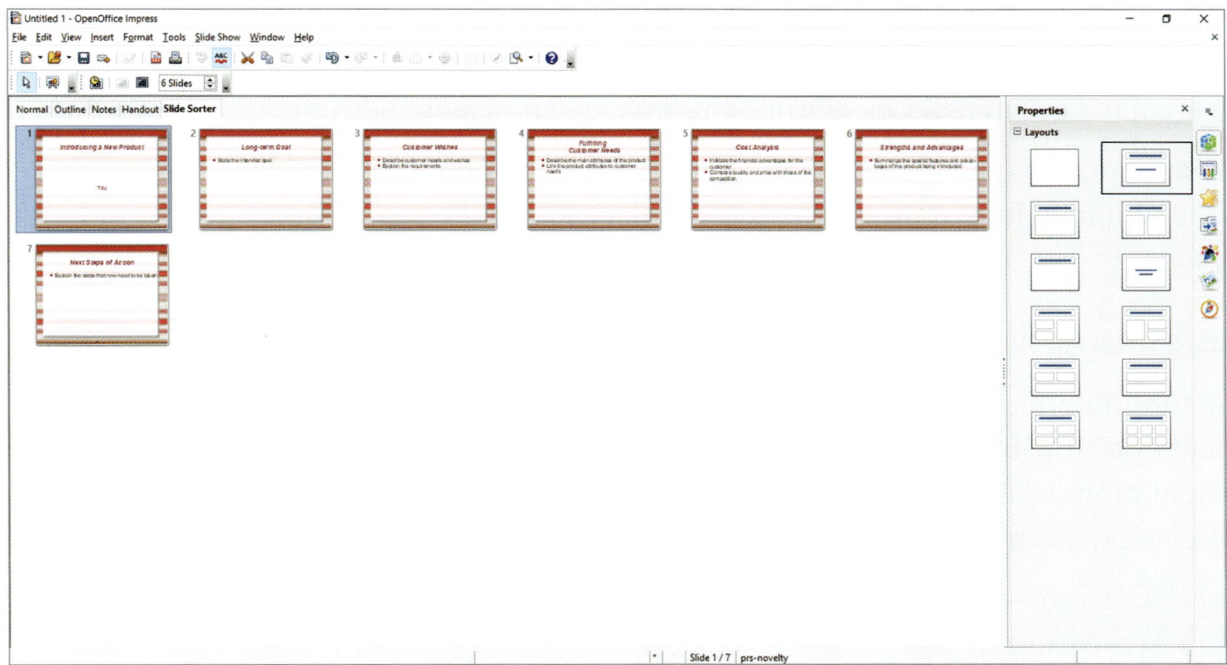

Viewing presentation in the slide sorter view

ACTIVITY

A slide master is a slide that controls all information about the Theme, Layout, Background, Color, Fonts and Positioning of all slides. The settings that we select in the Slide Master will be applicable to all the slides created in a presentation. Go to **View** ⟹ **Master** ⟹ **Slide Master**. Make the following changes in the Slide Master:

- Change the Title of the slides to font size = 50, bold, Comic San MS, Color = Purple.

- Change the font settings of the content to different bullets, colors, sizes and types.

TRY THIS

Go to **Edit** ⟹ **Navigator** in OpenOffice Impress to display all the objects contained in a presentation. It provides a convenient way view all slides and its objects. You can also use the navigator button on the standard toolbar.

Slide layouts

The basic elements of the slides are Title, Content, Footer, Header, Slide Number, Graphics and Images, Charts, Table and Movie. All these elements can be arranged on a slide in different layouts. Some of the layouts available in OpenOffice Impress are shown on the right.

These Slide Layouts are available in the Task Pane on the right side of the window. In case it is not visible, select **Format** ⟹ **Slide Layout**.

Slide transition

The motion effect of the slides during the slide show is the Slide Transition. It is how one slide changes to the next during the presentation during the slide show. We can add transitions in the Slide Sorter view or in the Normal view.

Slide Transition can be applied by Selecting **Slide Show** menu ⟹ **Slide Transition...**

Select **Slide Transition** from the Task Pane on the right side of the OpenOffice Impress window.

From the Slide Transition window (on the right), you can select transition, speed, sound, etc.

Custom Animation

This is a set of animated effects that can be applied on objects like titles, content and graphics. Animations can make a presentation more lively and memorable. Animation effects are applied from Normal View so you can select individual objects on a single slide.

Custom Animation can be applied by selecting **Slide Show** menu ⟹ **Custom Animation...**

Select **Custom Animation** from the Task Pane available on the right side of the OpenOffice Impress window.

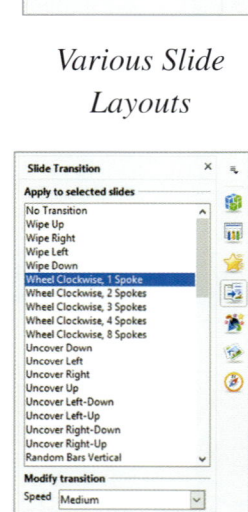

Various Slide Layouts

Selecting Slide Transitions

Steps to apply Custom Animation

1. Select the element to which an animation is to be applied, then click on the **Custom Animation** tab.

2. Click on the **Add** button to add animation effects (on the left below). It opens another window with the list of effects as shown on the right below.

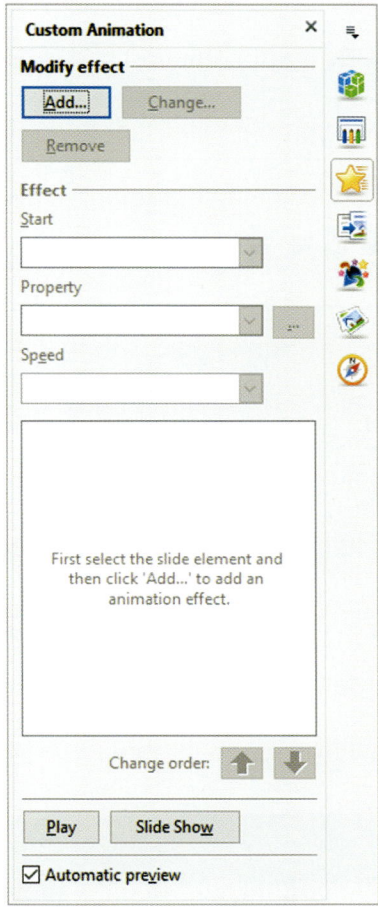

*Custom
animation window*

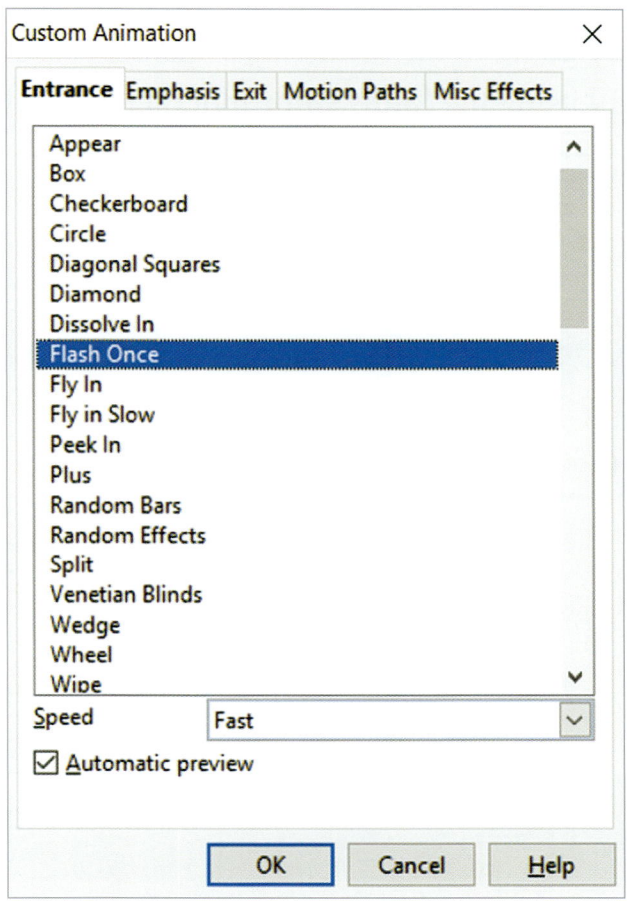

Selecting custom animation

3. Select an effect, for example, **Flash Once**. Select the **speed** of the effect as Very fast, Fast, Very slow, Slow and Medium. Click on OK.

4. This will bring you back to the Custom Animation window. Now you can select options for **Start**, such as **On click**, **With previous** or **After previous** depending upon whether you wish to start the animation by clicking the object, or with the previous effect, or after the previous effect has stopped playing.

5. Click on the **Play** button to see the animation effect applied.

Running a presentation

While running a presentation, the slides appear one by one on the screen showing the transition of the slides with the animated text and graphics. This is called a **Slide Show** of the presentation.

You can run a slide show in three different ways:

- By pressing the **F5** function key.
- By going to the **Slide Show** menu ⟹ **Slide Show** option.
- By using the **Slide Show** tool on the Toolbar.

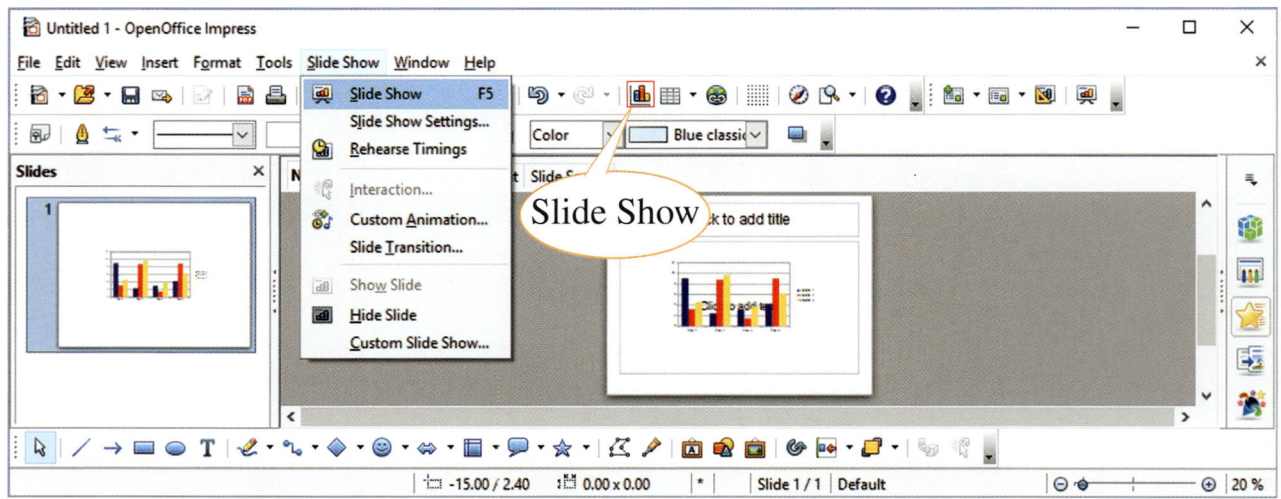

Running a slide show

QUICK KEY

To run a Slide Show in OpenOffice Impress	**F5**

GLOSSARY

OpenOffice   An open source software application which can be used on any operating system like Windows, Linux and MacOS.

OpenOffice Impress   A presentation tool used to create multimedia presentations.

OpenOffice Writer   A word processor used to create, edit, format and print a document.

YOU ARE HERE

2

1. The extension of files created in OpenOffice Writer is .odt.
2. The File menu in OpenOffice Writer consists of various options for creating a new file, saving and printing it.
3. The Edit menu in OpenOffice Writer includes options to Cut, Copy, Paste, Find & Replace, etc.
4. The Format menu in OpenOffice Writer provides options like Character, Paragraph, Bullets & Numbering and Change Case.
5. The default extension of a presentation in OpenOffice Impress is .odp.
6. OpenOffice Impress starts with Presentation Wizard, which is a three-step procedure for creating a new presentation.
7. The window of OpenOffice Impress is divided into three parts: Slides Pane, Workspace and Task Pane.
8. The workspace in OpenOffice Impress provides five different view tabs: Normal, Outline, Notes, Handout and Slide Sorter.

EXERCISE

A. Fill in the blanks.

1. Cut and Paste are found in the .... menu.

2. To create and edit a document we use OpenOffice ....

3. The .... view shows all slides in a presentation in a miniature form.

4. The .... option in the File menu will save the file for the first time.

5. The .... is used to give animation to the objects on the slides.

B. True or false?

1. The file extension of OpenOffice Impress presentation is .ods.

2. Slides can be easily rearranged and deleted in the Slide Sorter View.

3. F6 is used to run a presentation.

4. New slides cannot be added after a presentation is saved.

5. Justified alignment arranges the document on both left and right margins.

6. The Page Preview option can be used to print a document.

C. Match the following.

1. Slide Transition	a. Runs a presentation
2. F5	b. Changes font size, type, color
3. Slide Show	c. Displays only text
4. Outline View	d. Custom Animation
5. Format ⟹ Character	e. Effects on slides

D. Answer the following questions.

1. Why do we use OpenOffice Writer?

2. Explain any two options found in the Format menu of OpenOffice Writer.

3. Describe three different ways to run a presentation.

4. What is a Slide Transition? Name any two effects.

LAB WORK

A. Create an OpenOffice document on the topic 'The importance of healthy food'. Use the internet to get some information and pictures.

B. Create a presentation on 'The Place I visited in My Summer Holidays'. Use the internet to get some information and pictures.

PROJECT WORK

Work in groups of four. All the groups need to come up with a newsletter for the school and make a group presentation in front of the class using OpenOffice Applications. Each student in the group should take up one of the below roles.

Researcher: Gathers news about various events, competitions, etc., in the school for a period of 15 days. Use OpenOffice Writer to store the research work.

Creative writer: Puts the text together in a concise and organised way using OpenOffice Writer.

Designer: Designs the layout of the newsletter in OpenOffice Impress.

Animator: Decides the text and graphics effects in OpenOffice Impress.

Introduction to OpenOffice II

SNAP RECAP

1. What is open source software?
2. Explain the difference between open and closed source software.

LEARNING OBJECTIVES

You will learn about:

- entering data in a cell in OpenOffice Calc
- formatting the cells in OpenOffice Calc
- renaming a worksheet in OpenOffice Calc
- writing functions in OpenOffice Calc
- some functions in OpenOffice Calc
- charts in OpenOffice Calc
- reasons for creating a database
- OpenOffice Base as a relational database management system
- creating a new database
- database objects and elements of tables.

OpenOffice Calc

OpenOffice Calc is part of the OpenOffice suite and is used as a spreadsheet tool. A spreadsheet tool is a common name given to a computer application that stores and displays information in a tabular form. We can also use some built-in features of the software to do calculations and analysis of the data.

The layout of the Calc window (shown on the right) is the same as that of other applications in the OpenOffice suite.

A file in OpenOffice Calc is referred to as a **workbook** with the default name as Untitled 1. It is saved with an extension of .ods. A workbook can

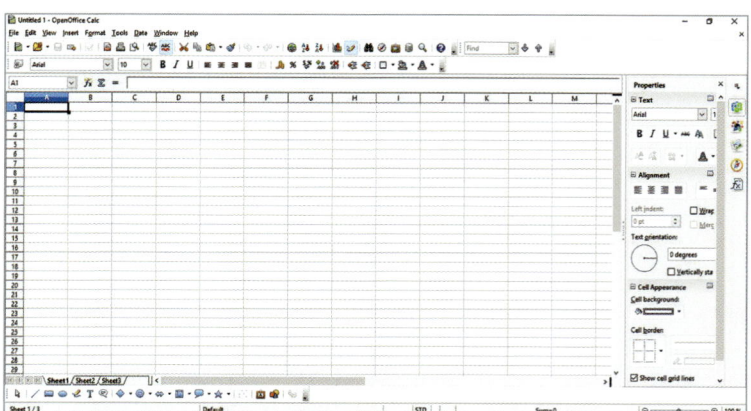

OpenOffice Calc window

have multiple sheets named Sheet1, Sheet2 and Sheet3, etc., as default. Each sheet is divided into a grid of rows (horizontal) and columns (vertical).

A **row** is labelled as numbers starting from 1, 2, 3, … with the last row as 1048576.

A **column** is labelled as letters starting from A, B, C, … with the last column as AMJ.

A **cell** is formed by the meeting of a row and a column and is referred to as A1, B6, G32, etc.

A collection of the cells together will form a **cell range**, for example, A1:A5, B1:D7.

QUICK KEY

To go to the first cell of the sheet i.e. A1	**Ctrl + Home**
To reach the last cell of the sheet i.e. AMJ1048576	**Ctrl + End**

Entering data in a cell

You can fill a workbook by entering data in the cells. Data in a cell can be in the form of text, numbers or a combination of both. The default alignment for text is left, while for numbers, it is right.

In order to enter data in a cell, follow the steps given below.

1. Select the cell where you want to enter the values.
2. Type the value that you want in a cell.
3. Press the Enter key or click on another cell to move to the next cell.

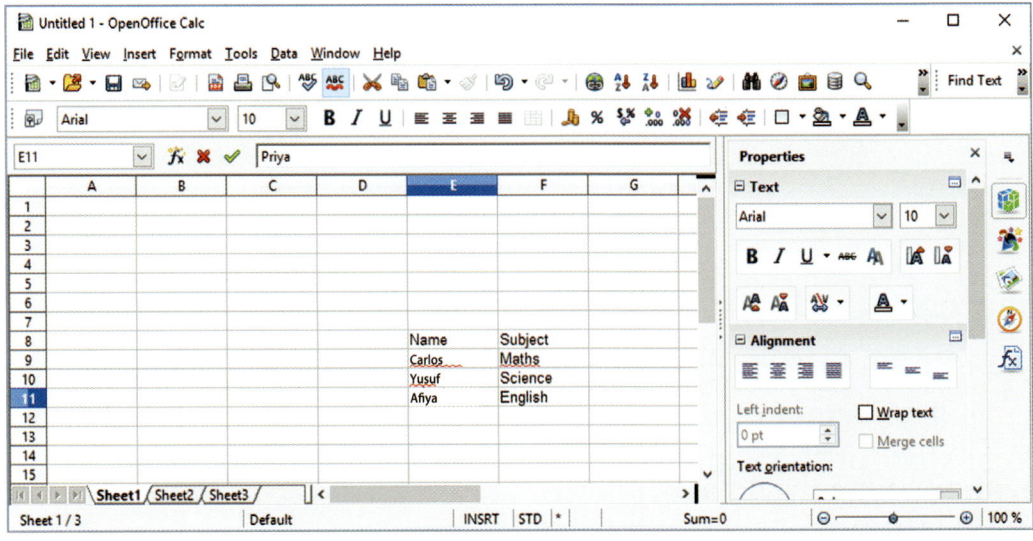

Entering data in cells of the OpenOffice Calc window

The cells can be formatted by changing their font name, size, color, etc. either by using the **Formatting** toolbar or by selecting **Format** menu ⟹ **Cell** option.

Using the AutoFill feature

In a spreadsheet, you can generate a series of number or text values by using the AutoFill handle. This process of automatically generating the series is called the AutoFill feature of a spreadsheet.

Follow these steps to generate the S.NO (Serial Number).

1. Write 1 in cell C5 and 2 in cell C6 and select them.

2. Click on the fill handle at the bottom-right corner of the selected cells. Drag the mouse as far as you want to generate the series. In the above case, drag until cell C9.

3. The series will be generated automatically as shown below.

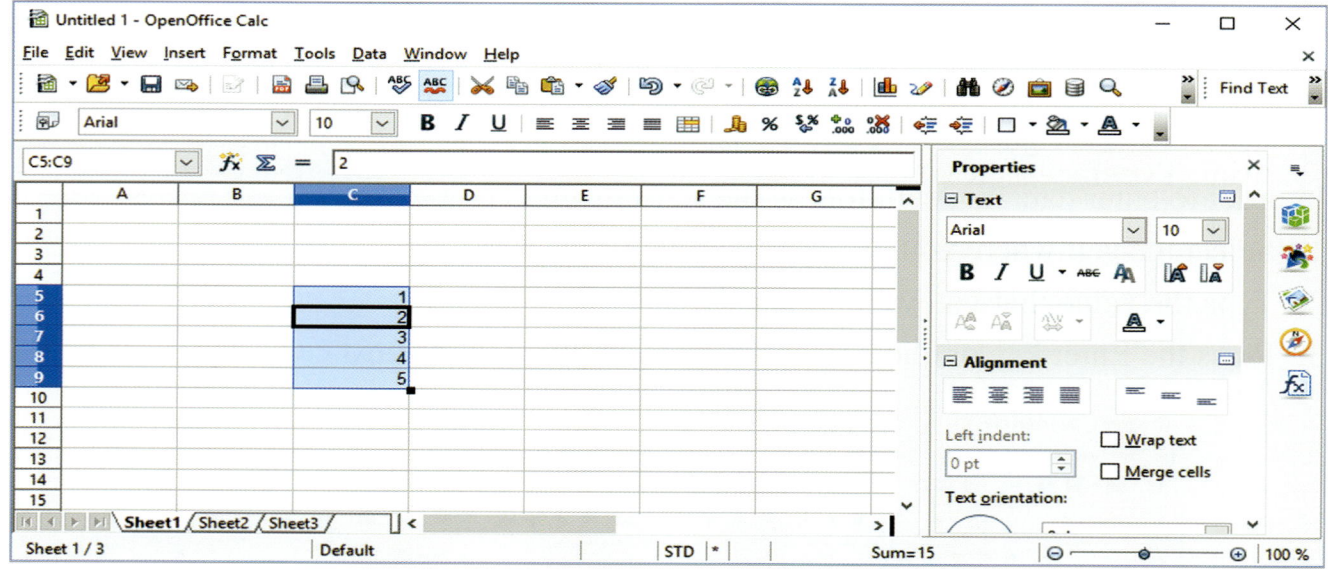

Using the AutoFill feature to generate S.NO

Formatting cells

The data in a cell can be formatted by using the tools found on the Formatting toolbar or by selecting the **Format** menu ⟹ **Cells** option. This window has a number of tabs to do different kinds of formatting. Here we will explore some of them.

1. To change the number formatting by putting a currency sign in front of amount, select the cells you want to format, then go to the **Numbers** tab in the **Cells** option and select **Currency** in **Category**, change **Format code** to dollars and **Decimal Places** as 2.

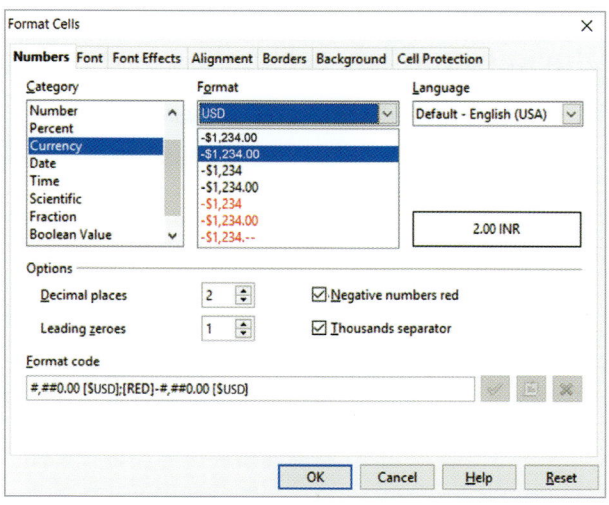

Numbers tab in the Format Cells dialog box

2. To change the font name and size of the text, select the cells you want to format, then go to the **Font** tab in the **Cells** option; select **Font** as Arial, **Typeface** as Regular and **Size** as 14.

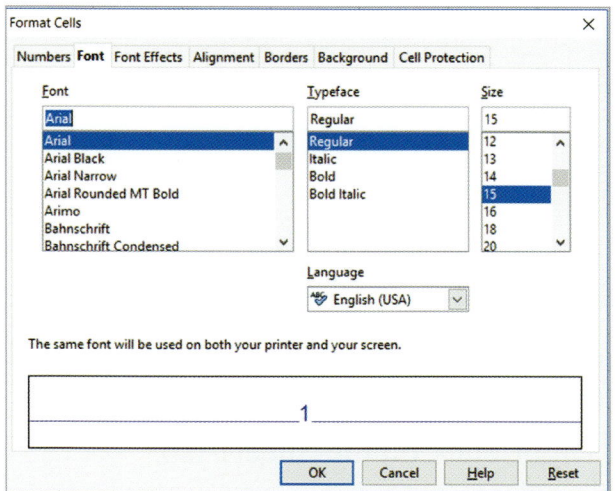

Font tab in the Format Cells dialog box

3. To change alignment of the data in the cells, select the cells, then go to **Alignment** tab (shown on the right) and change the **Horizontal** and **Vertical** alignment to align the data. Then select the checkbox **Wrap text automatically** to wrap the text on the next line in the same cell if there is too much text to fit on one line.

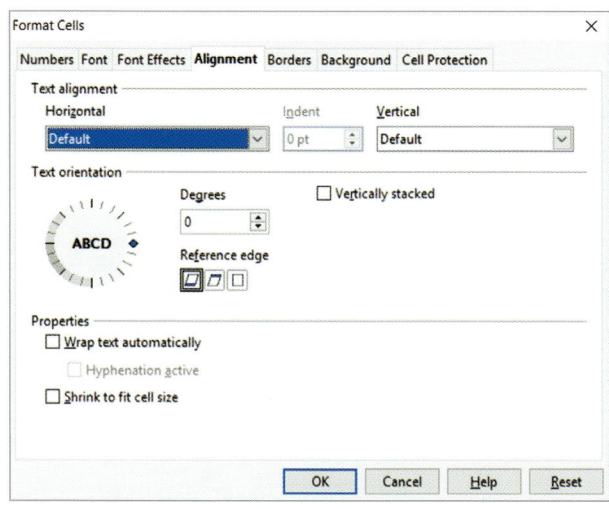

Alignment tab in the Format Cells dialog box

4. To change the cell background, select the cells you want to change, then go to the **Background** tab, select the color of your choice and click on the **OK** button.

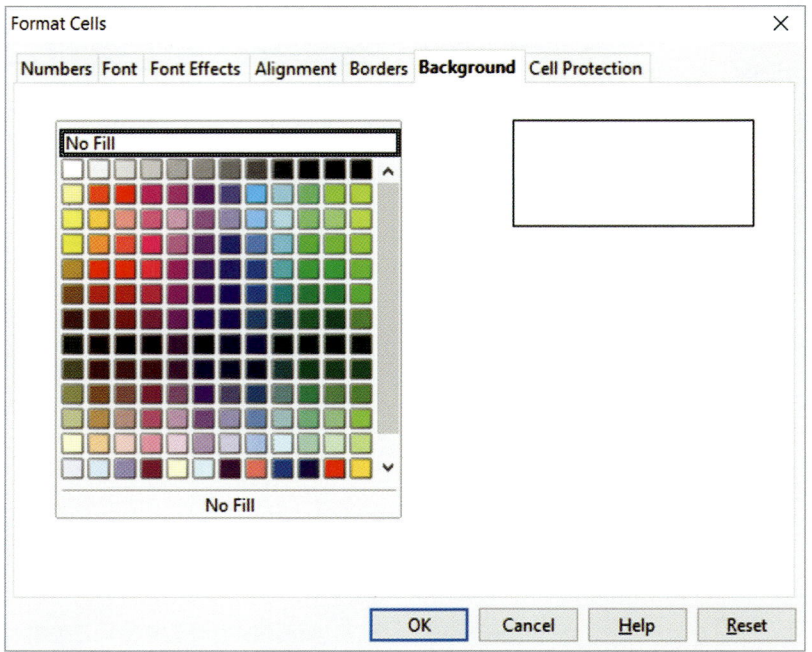

Background tab in the Format Cells dialog box

Renaming a worksheet

The worksheets are automatically named Sheet1, Sheet2, Sheet3, ... in OpenOffice Calc. If you want to change the name, follow the steps given below:

1. Right-click on the Sheet1 tab.
2. Select the **Rename Sheet** option to display the window shown below.

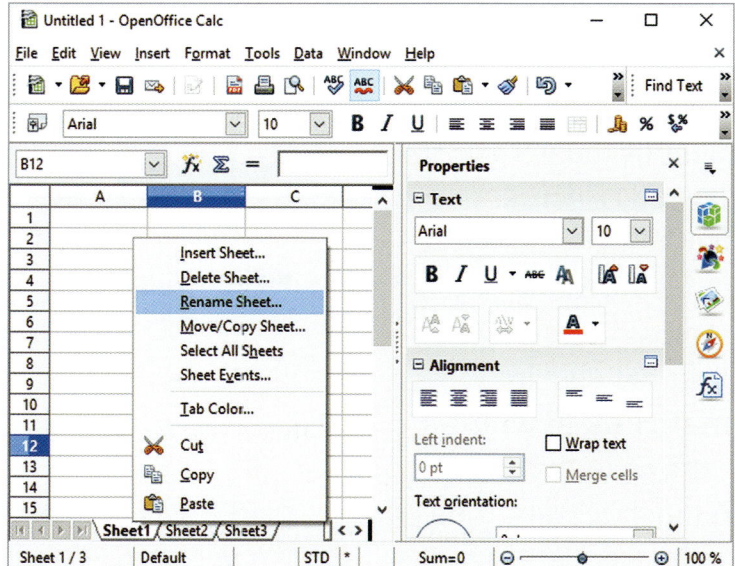

Renaming a worksheet in OpenOffice Calc

3. The **Rename Sheet** dialog box will appear as shown on the right. Change the **Name** to **MyFriends** and click on **OK**.

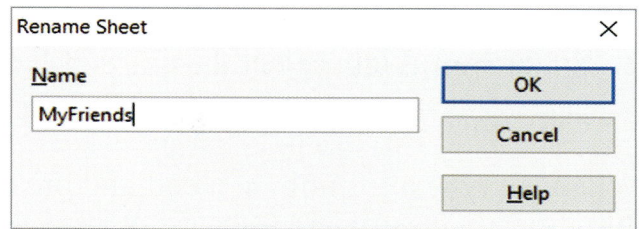

Rename Sheet dialog box

Writing functions

A formula is an expression that begins with an equal to (=) sign. You can enter a formula in a cell to do calculations on data.

Sometimes you may not remember a formula or it may be a tedious job to write the addition formula for 100 rows; in that case, you may use built-in formulae available in OpenOffice Calc to perform calculations. These formulae are called **functions**.

A function can be entered either through the Function Wizard or by typing the function, beginning with an equal to sign, with the values in a cell.

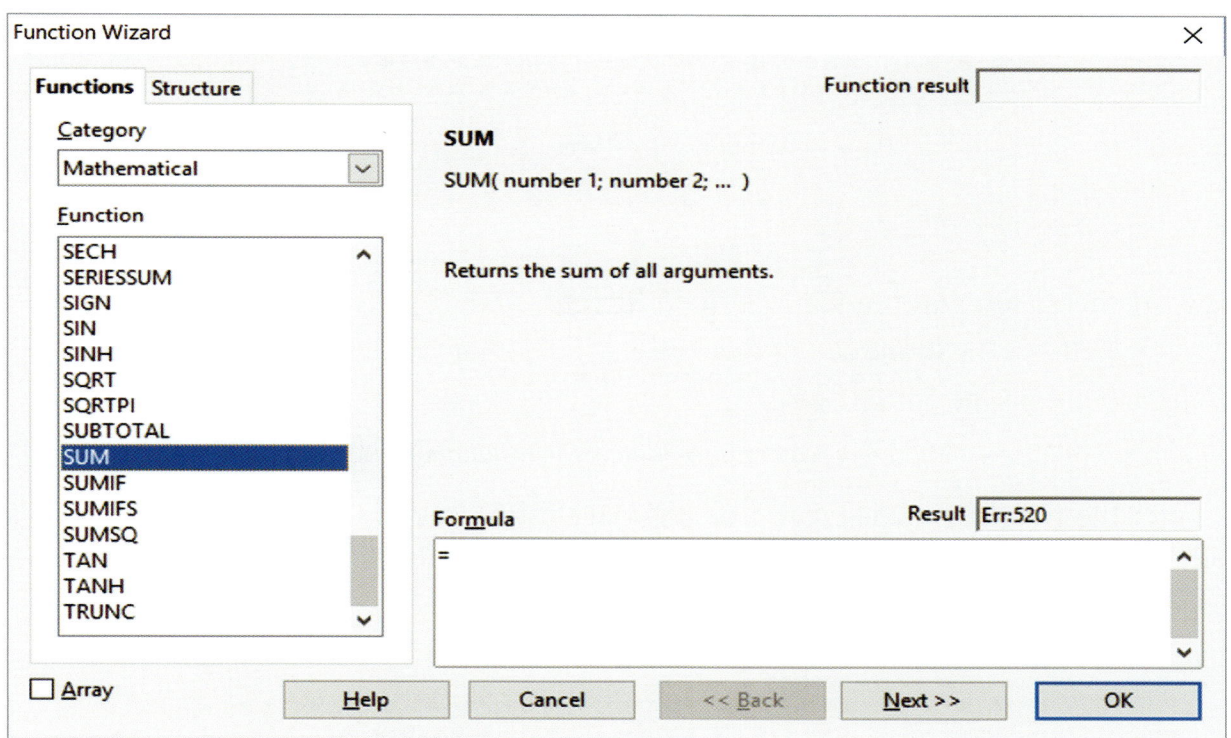

Function Wizard dialog box in OpenOffice Calc

To open the Function Wizard, select **Insert** Menu ⟹ **Function** option.

There are ten categories of functions and each category available in OpenOffice Calc includes a long list of functions for different types of calculations.

A formula or a function can contain:

- Numbers = 45 + 12
- Cell range = Sum (D2:D5)
- Cell address = A1 + B4
- Both = 34 + E6 + F6 + 25

When we type a formula in a cell and press Enter, the formula will no longer be visible. Only the result of that formula will be visible in the cell. The formula can be seen in the Input Line of the Formula bar. We can edit the formula in the Input Line of the Formula toolbar when the cell is selected or we can double-click the cell. The value changes automatically with the change in the formula.

How to use functions in a workbook

The step by step procedure to create a sample worksheet for the analysis of students' results is given below:

1. Create a worksheet with S.No, Marks 1, Marks 2, Marks 3 for result analysis.

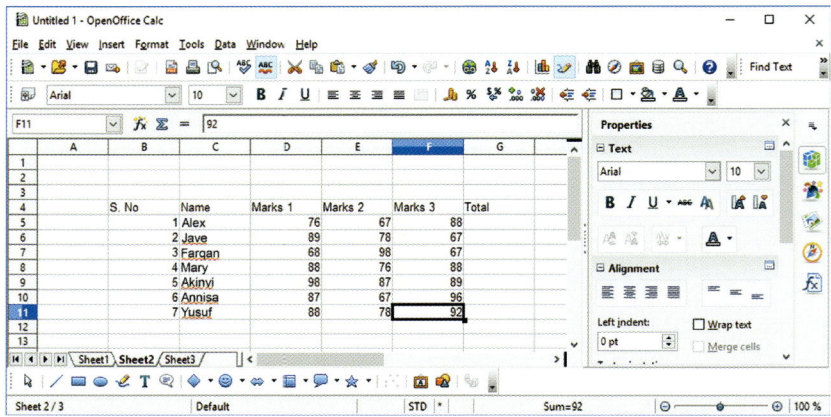

Creating a worksheet for result analysis

2. Enter the formula =D5+E5+F5 or =SUM(D5:F5) in cell G5. As soon as you press the Enter key, the formula disappears to the formula bar and the result appears in the cell.

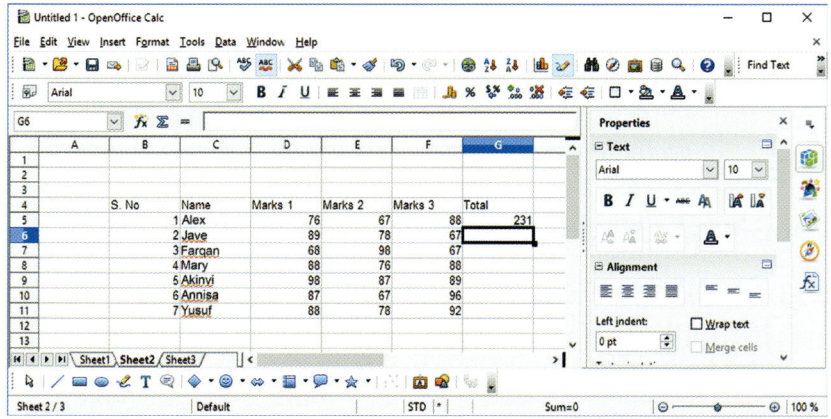

After entering the formula for Sum in a worksheet

3. Copy the formula in the rest of the cells to G11 either by dragging the Autofill handle on the right side of the selected cell G5 or by using a copy and paste option.

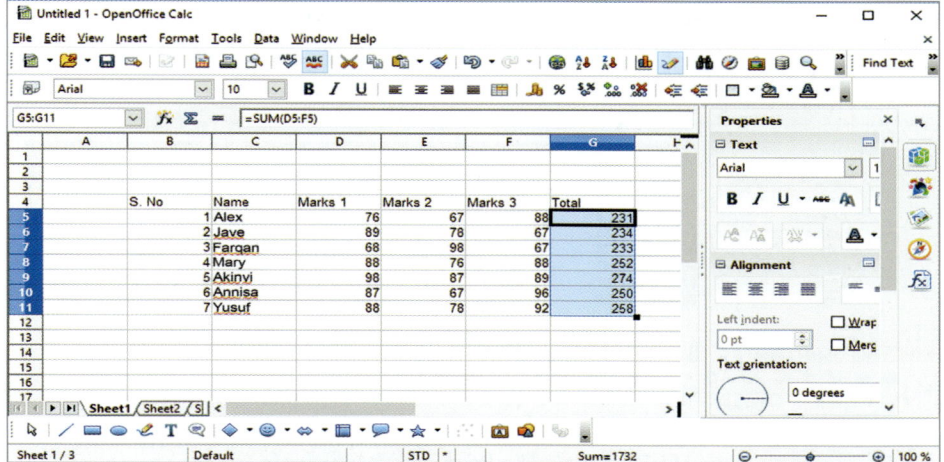

Using the Autofill option to copy the Sum formula in a worksheet

4. Next, insert the percentage column and write the formula for percentage =(G5/300)*100 in cell H5. Repeat the process of copy and paste to copy the formula from cell H5 to H11.

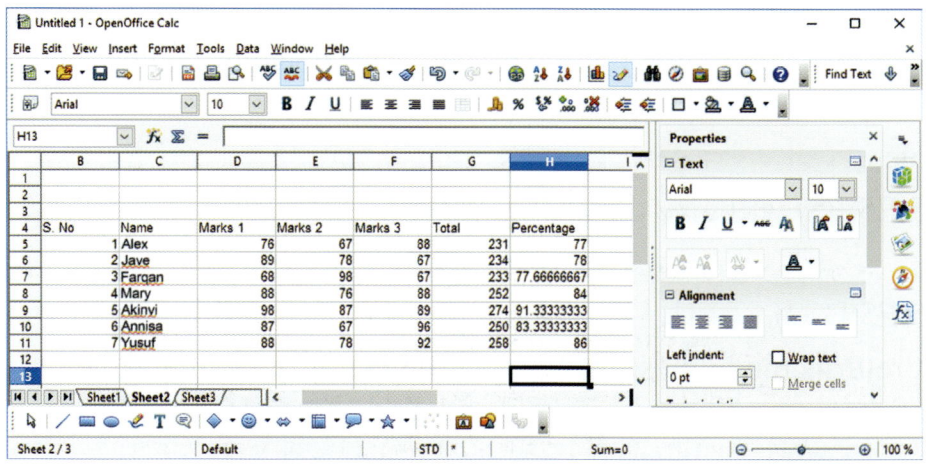

After entering the formula for Percentage in a worksheet

5. Format the number up to 2 decimal places, either by selecting **Format ⟹ Cells ⟹ Numbers ⟹ Category: Number**.

By selecting the **Number Format: Delete Decimal Place** tool found on the **Toolbar**.

6. Now insert the Grade column and write the formula =IF(H5 > 40;"PASS";"FAIL") in cell I5 to display PASS or FAIL on the basis of the percentage calculated.

7. After all the calculations are done, the spreadsheet will appear as shown below.

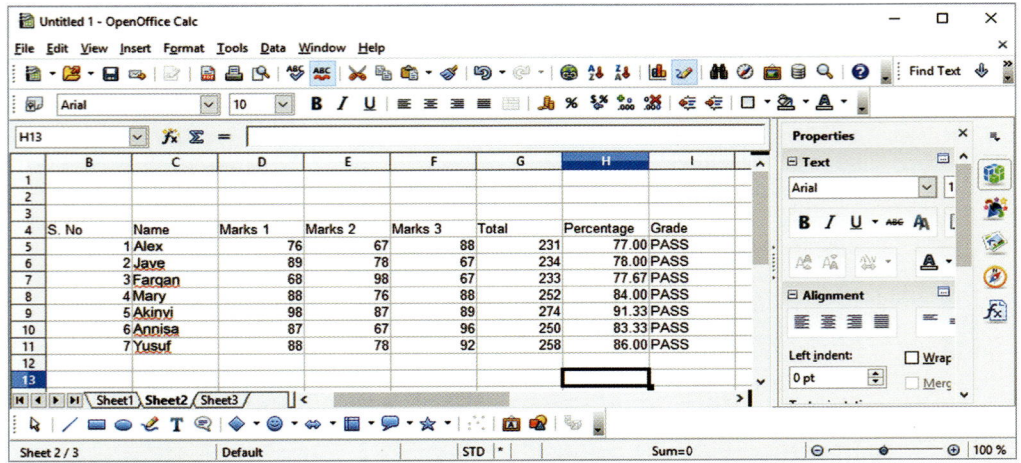

Final worksheet for result analysis

Some common functions

Some of the commonly used functions in OpenOffice Calc are given below, with examples.

- **SUM()**: It adds up the values given as parameters in the function. The parameters are separated by a semicolon (;) in between. These values can be the cell address, cell range or number.

  For example,

  =SUM(D5;E5;F5) will give the answer 231

  =SUM(D5:F5;D12)

- **MAX()**: It returns the highest value from the list of the values given as parameters in the function.

  For example, to find out the highest marks in Marks1 in the list created above:

  =MAX (D5:D11) will give the answer 98

  =MAX (D5;D6;D7)

- **MIN()**: It returns the lowest value from the list of the values given as parameters in the function.

  For example, to find out the lowest marks in Marks3 in the list created above:

  =MIN(F5:F11) will give the answer 67

  =MIN(F5;F6;F7)

- **AVERAGE()**: It calculates the average of the values given as parameters in the function.

  For example, to find out the average of Marks2, use the formula:

  =AVERAGE(D5:D11)

- **IF()**: It evaluates the condition given as the first parameter. If the condition is true, then the second parameter will be evaluated, otherwise the third parameter will be evaluated.

  For example, to display PASS or FAIL based on the condition given for the above worksheet will be:

  =IF(H5>40, "PASS","FAIL")

Charts

Charts are graphical representations of data in a spreadsheet. You can create a chart of existing data in OpenOffice Calc by using the Chart tool found on the toolbar or by selecting the **Insert** menu ⟹ **Chart** option.

It will display the Chart Wizard. In order to create a complete chart, you need to follow the four steps to select the criteria shown below.

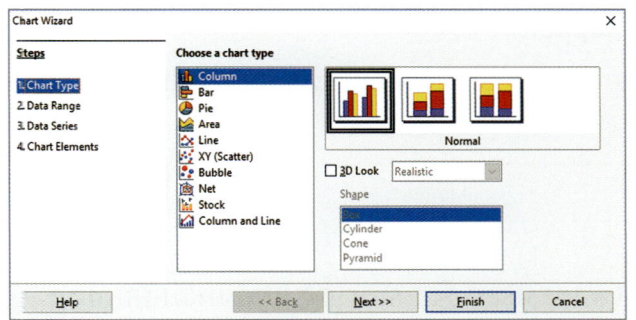

Chart Type

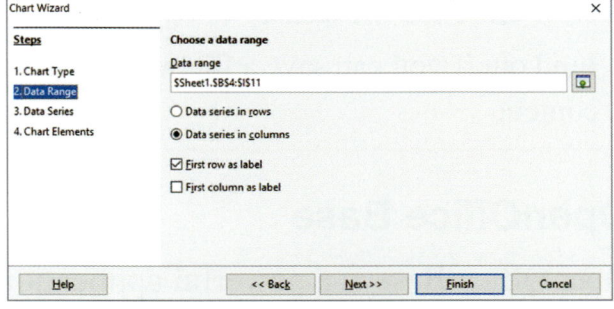

Data Range

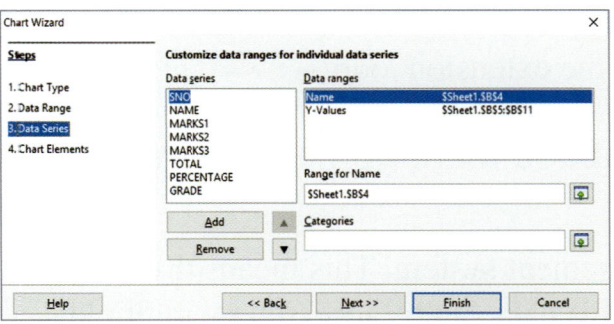

Data Series

Chart Elements

Chart Wizard in OpenOffice Calc

ACTIVITY

Complete the following activity.

1. Create a list of shopping items purchased, with the following columns – Item code, Name, Quantity purchased and Price of each item.

2. Make a new column **Amount per item** to calculate the amount purchased of each item; use the formula =Rate*Quantity.

3. Make a list of ten items purchased and calculate the Total Billing Amount. If the Billing Amount is more than $100, then give a discount of 15% or 5%.

4. Calculate the actual bill after deducting the discount.

TRY THIS

Save the file you created in the previous activity by selecting **File** ⟹ **Save As** ⟹ tick the checkbox **Save with password**. **Set password** to open file ⟹ OK.

Now close the file and try to open it. What will happen?

Find out if you can save a file with permission to open and view but cannot modify the content.

OpenOffice Base

OpenOffice Base is a powerful application software used for storing and maintaining data in the form of rows and columns. The data stored can be retrieved in the format of reports or queries.

A database is created in OpenOffice Base with the extension .odb.

OpenOffice Base as a Relational Database Management System (RDBMS)

OpenOffice Base is a relational database management system. This means that data is arranged in the form of rows and columns. This data can be accessed by multiple users, and different tables created in a database can be linked together on the basis of a common column. This feature helps to retrieve and manipulate data from multiple tables at one time. The other RDBMS available are Oracle, Microsoft Access, MYSQL, SQL Server and many more.

Creating a new database

1. Click on **File** ⟹ **New** ⟹ **Database** to create a new database. A **Database Wizard** will appear as shown below.

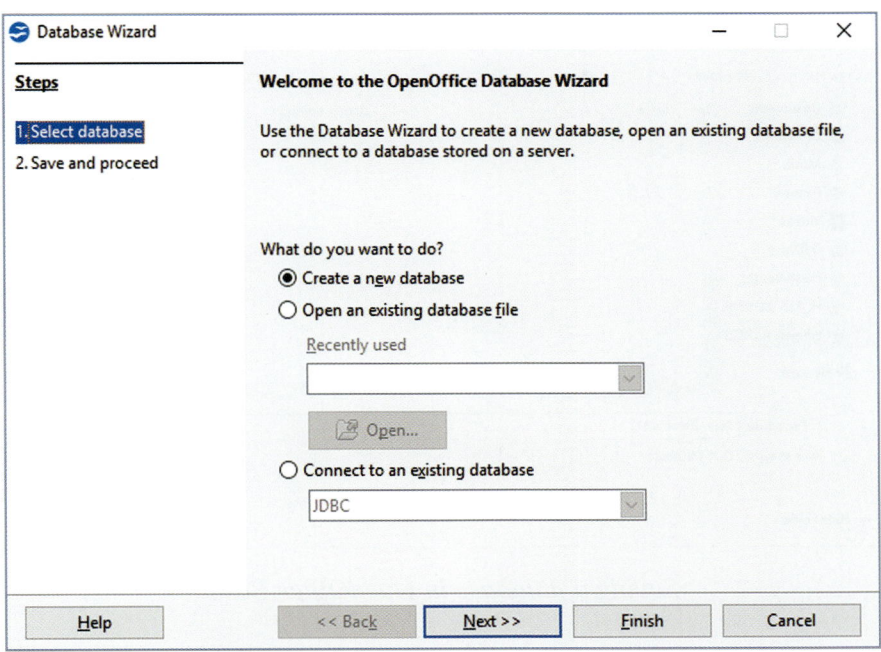

First step of Database Wizard in OpenOffice Base

2. Select **Create a new database** if a new database is required, or select **Open an existing database file** if the database has been created earlier. Click on **Next>>** to open the next step of the Database Wizard.

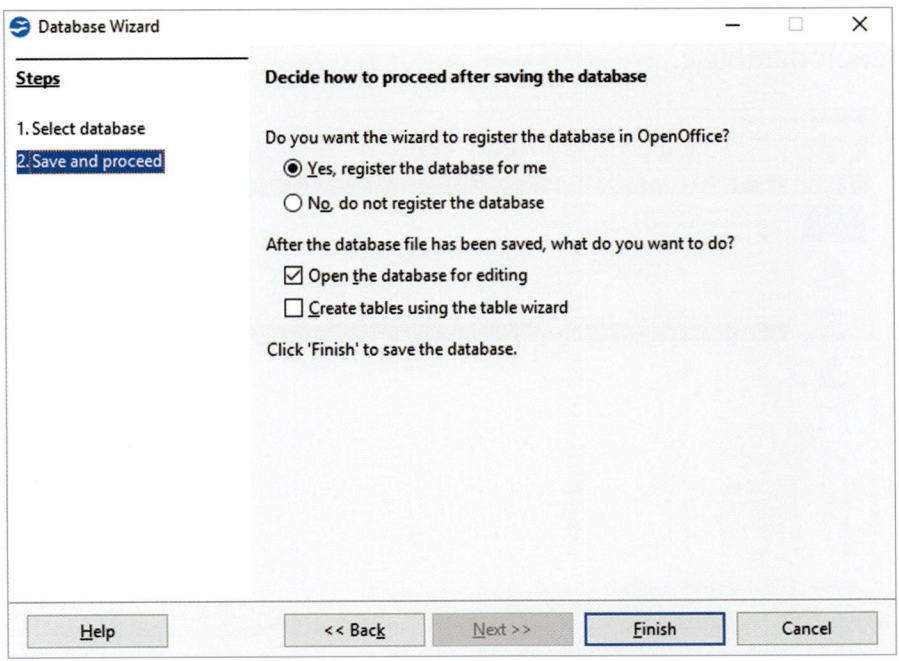

Second step of Database Wizard in OpenOffice Base

3. Select **Yes**, **register the database for me** and tick **Open the database for editing** option. Click on **Finish**. This will open the **Save As** window (see below). Assign a new name: School and click on **Save**.

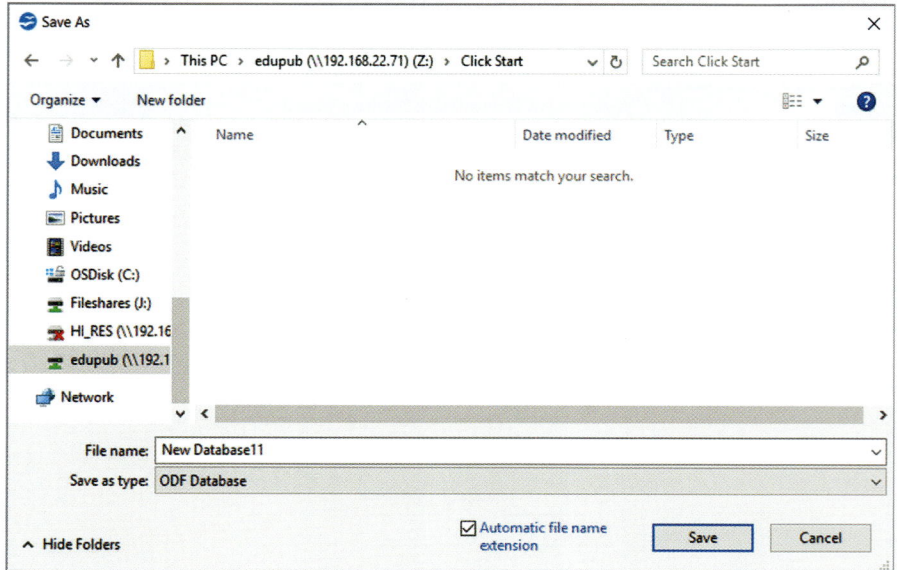

Saving a database in OpenOffice Base

4. After you save the database it will display the main window of OpenOffice Base (below). This window is divided into three parts: **Database Tables, Tasks** related to each object, and **Object Instances** created in each database.

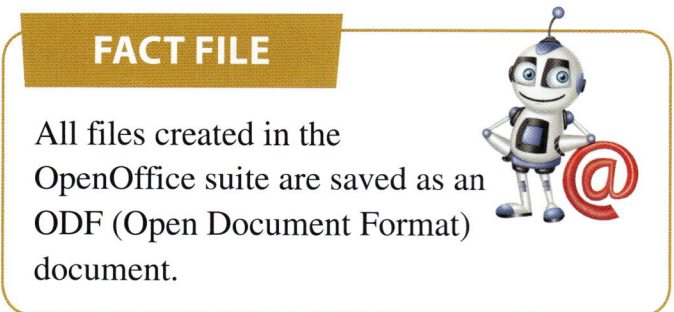

FACT FILE

All files created in the OpenOffice suite are saved as an ODF (Open Document Format) document.

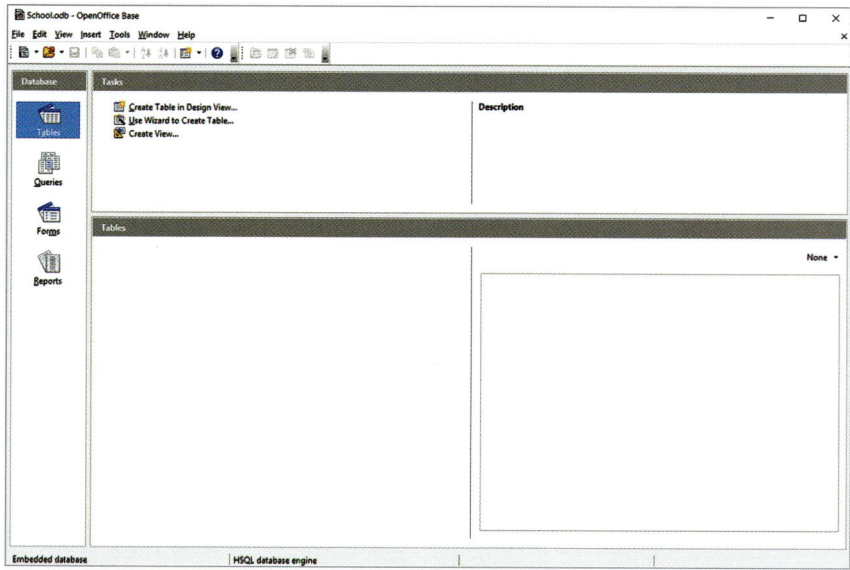

Main window of OpenOffice Base

5. Now click on **Tables** object. The **Tasks** will show three different ways of creating tables in OpenOffice base. Select **Create table in Design View**. It will open the **Table Design** window where you can design the structure of a table.

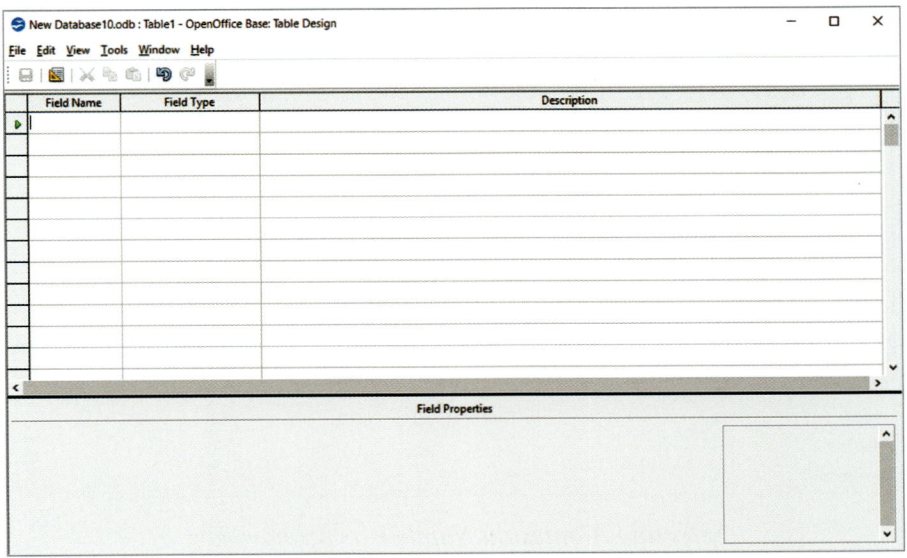

Table Design window of OpenOffice Base

6. Let us now design a Student table (see below). In the **Field Name** type **Admission Number** and **Field Type** will display the list of different data types with Text [VARCHAR] as default in the drop-down list. Select Text [VARCHAR]. Select **Description** to write a few lines to describe the column created. The description of a column is optional.

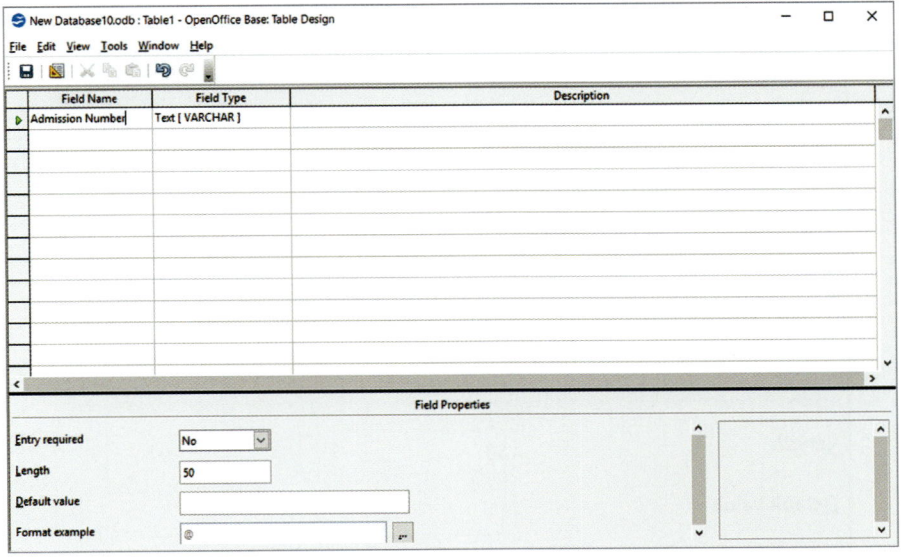

Creating a Student table in OpenOffice base

7. Right-click on the green arrow key in front of the Admission Number. This will open a shortcut menu as shown below.

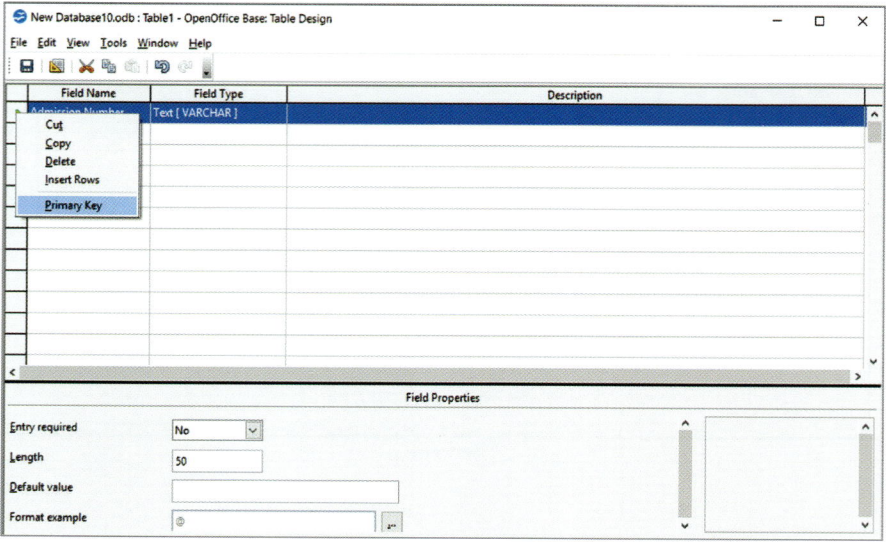

Selecting Admission Number as primary key

8. Select the option **Primary Key** from the menu to make Admission Number the primary key. A small key appears infront of the Admission Number column to show that this has been selected to save unique values in the table.

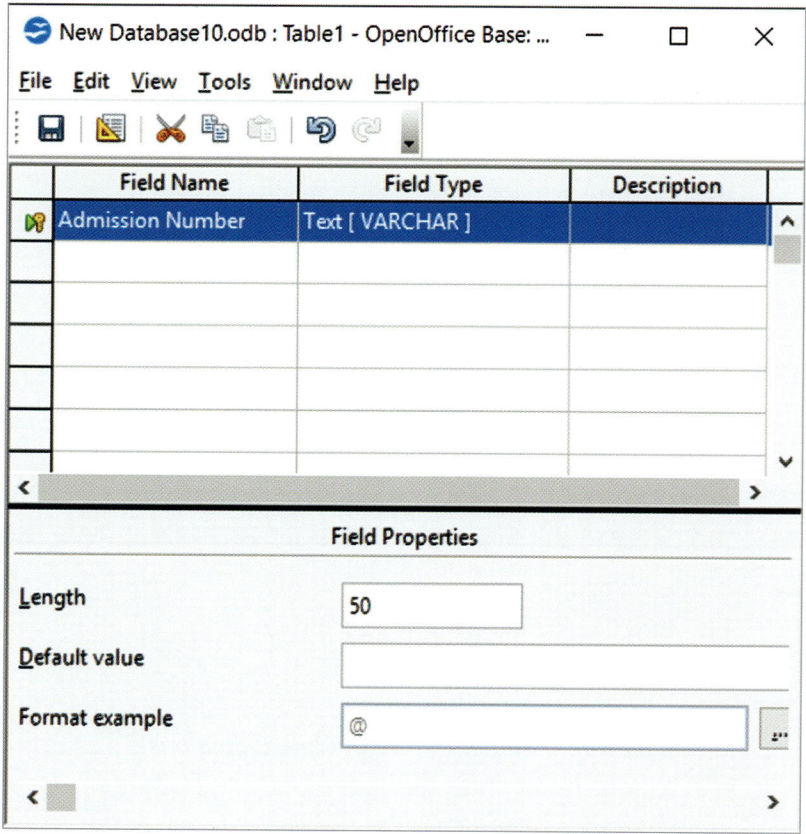

Admission Number as the primary key

9. Now create a few other columns with different data types in **Table Design** as shown below and save the table with the name **Student** and click on **OK**.

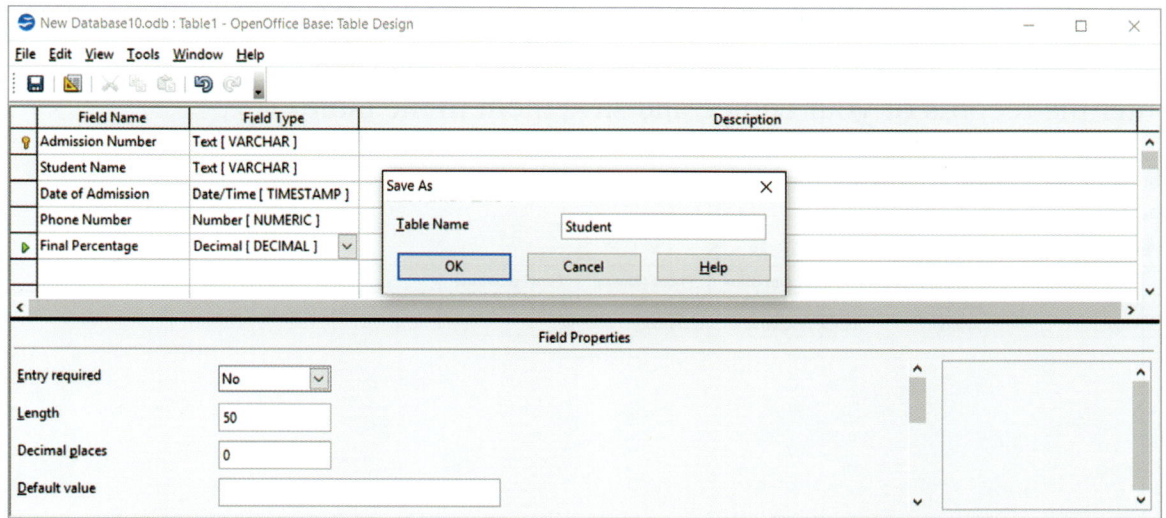

Creating more columns in the Student table

10. Close this file by selecting **File ⟹ Close** to display the window shown below. Repeat the above process to make one more table titled Library. The structure of the table can be modified by adding a new column anywhere in the structure, deleting any column and changing the existing column in the Table Design View.

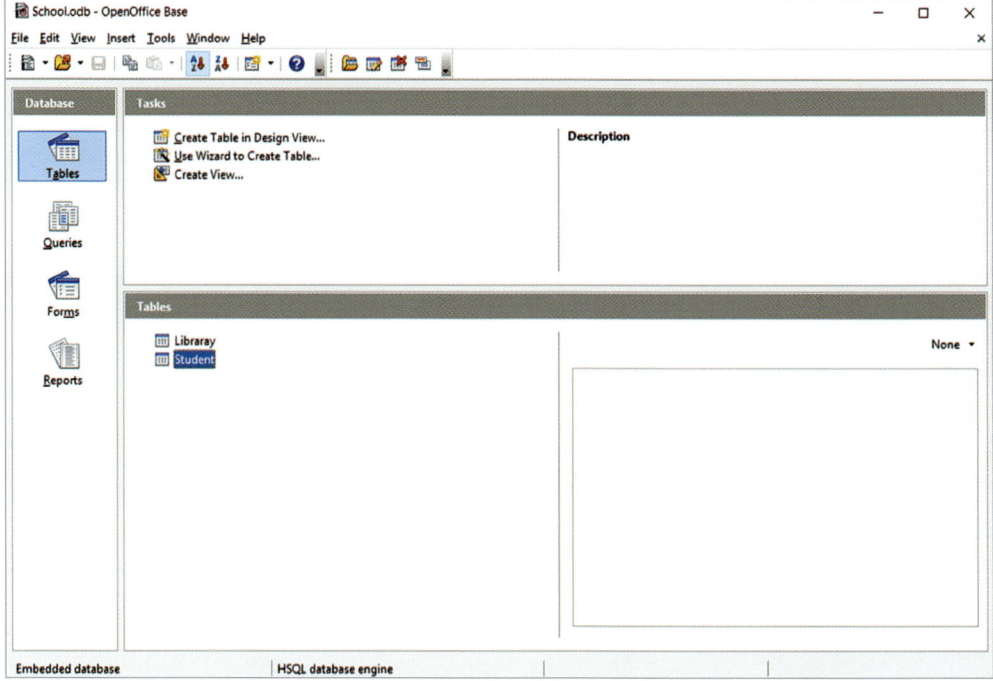

Creating a Library table

11. Either select **Open** from the Shortcut menu or double-click on the **Student Table** to open **Table Data View**. This view is used to add, modify and delete records in a table. We can only see this view after the structure of a table is designed using the **Table Design View**.

12. Enter the records of your choice and save them in the table.

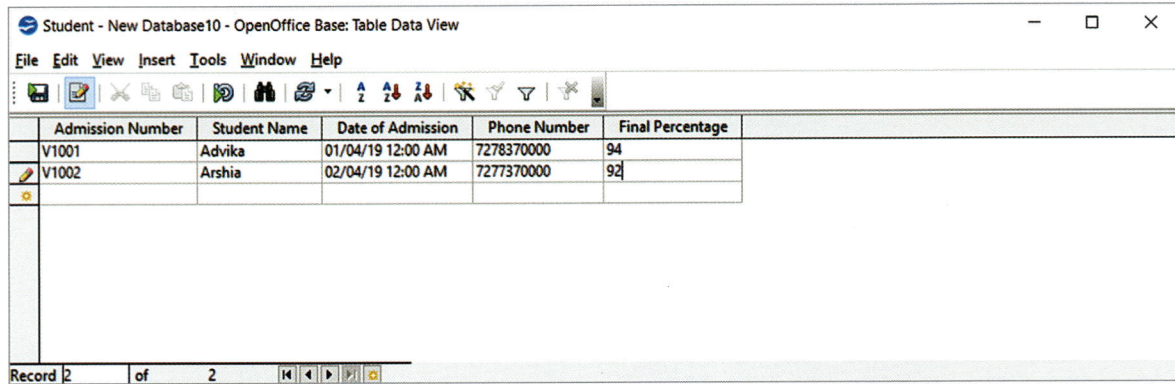

Student table in Table Data View

TRY THIS

When designing the table structure, do not select a column as primary key. Save the table. Enter the records. What did you notice? Give reasons for this.

ACTIVITY

Create a table titled **Teacher** with the columns Teacher code, Name, Subject, Classes taught by, etc., using the **Use Wizard to Create Table** option. What steps did you follow to create the structure and records in the table?

QUICK KEY

To open a new OpenOffice file	**Ctrl + N**
To open an existing OpenOffice file	**Ctrl + O**
To save an OpenOffice file	**Ctrl + S**

GLOSSARY

AVERAGE()   The function that calculates the average of the values given as parameters in the function.

Column   The arrangement of related data vertically in a table to form a field.

Data   The smallest piece of information in a table.

Database   A collection of many relevant tables together will form a database.

IF()   The function that evaluates the condition given as the first parameter. If the condition is true, then the second parameter will be evaluated, otherwise the third parameter will be evaluated.

MAX()   The function that returns the highest value from the list of the values given as parameters in the function.

MIN()   The function that returns the lowest value from the list of the values given as parameters in the function.

OpenOffice Base   A powerful software application used for storing and maintaining the data in the form of rows and columns.

OpenOffice Calc   Part of the OpenOffice suite used as a spreadsheet tool.

SUM()   The function that adds up the values given as parameters in the function.

YOU ARE HERE

3

1. A file in OpenOffice Calc is referred to as a workbook with the default name Untitled 1.

2. A spreadsheet is created in OpenOffice Calc with the extension .ods.

3. In a spreadsheet, you can generate a series of number or text values by using the AutoFill handle.

4. A function can be entered either through the Function Wizard or by typing the function beginning with an equals sign with the values in a cell.

5. Charts are graphical representation of data in a spreadsheet. You can create a chart of the existing data by using the Chart tool.

6. A database is created in OpenOffice Base with the extension .odb.

7. OpenOffice Base is a relational database management system.

EXERCISE

A. Fill in the blanks.

1. The .... object of the database displays the formatted data from the table.

2. Rows in a database are also called .... and columns are also called ....

3. A database can contain .... tables.

4. A spreadsheet is a representation of data in the form of .... and ....

5. .... is the graphical representation of data in a spreadsheet.

B. Match the following.

1. Extension of database	a. Displays the total of the values
2. Tuple	b. Forms
3. Database Objects	c. Displays the maximum values
4. Max()	d. Rows in a table
5. Sum()	e. .odb

C. True or false?

1. After a table structure is created, it cannot be modified later. ☐

2. Text in a spreadsheet is by default left-aligned. ☐

3. A cell can have any type of value in a spreadsheet. ☐

4. We can do a calculation on a text value.

5. We cannot delete a record in a table created in OpenOffice Base.

D. Answer the following questions.

1. Explain the difference between a formula and function, with an example.

2. Explain the Autofill feature, with an example.

3. Explain the different elements of a database, with an example.

4. What is a primary key? What is the advantage of creating a primary key in a table?

5. Give brief reasons for creating a database.

LAB WORK

A. Create a table in a spreadsheet (at least 10 records) with the following columns – Employee Code, Employee Name, Basic Salary, 20% Inflation Allowance, 30% Housing Rent Allowance, 20% Tax Deducted, Gross Salary (Basic + Allowance), Net Salary (Gross-deductions).

B. Use at least three different charts to represent the above data in a graphical form. Format the charts created using different colors Try swapping the rows and columns of the tables on the *x* and *y* axes of the graph to see the difference in the appearance.

PROJECT WORK

Create a database for the smooth running of a shop. Include tables like stock details, items details sold in a day, details of employees, salary calculation employees, and any other tables you can think of. Design the structure of each table and add at least five records in each.

Frames in HTML

SNAP RECAP

1. What are HTML tags and attributes?
2. How do you execute (run) a HTML script?
3. How can you create lists and tables on a web page?

LEARNING OBJECTIVES

You will learn about:

*   creating frames in HTML
*   <FRAMESET> Tag
*   <FRAME> Tag

Introduction

In this chapter, you will learn to open multiple HTML documents in a browser window. This is done by dividing the window into different blocks and then opening a different web page in each block.

Frames

Frames allow you to divide the web page into several independent parts or panes. Each of these is called a **frame**. For example, the web page shown on the right has three frames marked on it.

A web page divided into frames

The frames work as independent windows allowing multiple views at one time. They allow one part of the web page to remain static while allowing other parts to change. For example, when you click on the refresh button, you can reload one frame without having to reload the entire web page.

The following tags are used to create frames in HTML:

<FRAMESET> tag <FRAME> tag

Frameset tag <FRAMESET>

A **frameset** is defined as a set of frames inserted in a HTML web page. These frames can be in the form of rows and columns in different proportions. A frameset tells the browser how to divide the screen into split windows. The <FRAMESET> tag divides the web page into rectangular areas where an individual HTML document can be loaded for each area using the <FRAME> tag. It contains one or more frame tags.

One frameset tag can also be used within another frameset tag to form a **nested frameset**. This is required to further divide one block into small blocks that can be arranged by row or column.

The following are the attributes of the <FRAMESET> tag:

- **Cols**: Specifies the number and size of columns in a frameset. Its value can be a specific percentage of the web page or in pixels. The default value is 100% (1 column).

- **Rows**: Specifies the number and size of rows in a frameset. Its value can be a specific percentage of the web page or in pixels. The default value is 100% (1 row).

- **Border**: Specifies the thickness of the frame borders in pixels for all the frames in the outermost frameset. The default value is 5 pixels. It can be used only for the outermost frameset.

- **Bordercolor**: Specifies the color of the border of the frame.

- **Frameborder**: Specifies whether the border should be visible or not. Its value can be either Yes or No.

The <FRAMESET ...> tag is used instead of the <BODY ...> tag. The frameset file has no content of its own, so it has no need for a <BODY ...> element. For example,

<FRAMESET rows="45%, *" cols="*, 50%" frameborder="yes" border="7" bordercolor="blue">

Frame tag <FRAME>

The <FRAME> tag defines what goes into each frame of a HTML web page. This is an empty element. Each frame works as an independent browser window with its own default properties. These properties can be altered by using the frame attributes.

The following are the attributes of the <FRAME> tag:

- **Src**: Specifies the URL of the initial file to be displayed in the frame.
- **Name**: Assigns a name to the frame that may be used as a target for links.
- **Frameborder**: Specifies whether the border should be visible or not. Its value can be either Yes or No.
- **Bordercolor**: Specifies the color of the border of the frame.
- **Scrolling**: Specifies the scroll information for the frame. It can have a value Yes, No or Auto. Yes means scrollbars are displayed. No means scrollbars are never available and Auto means provides scrolling if necessary. Auto is the default value.
- **Marginheight**: Specifies, in pixels, the space to be left between the frame's contents at top and bottom margins.
- **Marginwidth**: Specifies, in pixels, the space to be left between the frame's contents at its left and right margins.

For example,

```
<FRAME src="A.HTML" name="F1" frameborder = "Yes"
bordercolor="Red" scrolling="No" marginheight="30" marginwidth="30">
```

Let us try the following examples using the frame and frameset tags.

> Before you try the following examples, make sure you have four separate HTML files, named Frame 1.HTML, Frame 2.HTML, Frame 3.HTML and Frame 4.HTML already created.
>
> These can be any other HTML files that you want to use as frames. Specify their complete path in the src attribute.

Example 1: The HTML code for creating frames in the form of two rows is given below.

```
<HTML>
<FRAMESET rows="35%,*" border="2">
<FRAME src="Frame1.HTML" name="Frame 1">
<FRAME src="Frame2.HTML" name="Frame 2">
```

Frame 1
Frame 2

```
</FRAMESET>
</HTML>
```

Example 2: The HTML code for creating frames in the form of two columns is given below.

```
<HTML>
<FRAMESET cols="50%,50%" border="1">
<FRAME src="Frame1.HTML" name="Frame 1">
<FRAME src="Frame2.HTML" name="Frame 2">
</FRAMESET>
</HTML>
```

Frame 2	Frame 2

Example 3: The HTML code for creating frames in the form of both rows and columns is given below.

```
<HTML>
<FRAMESET rows="45%, *" cols="*, 50%" frameborder="yes" border="7">
<FRAME src="Frame1.HTML" Name="F1" scrolling= No>
<FRAME src="Frame2.HTML" Name="F2" scrolling= No>
<FRAME src="Frame3.HTML" Name="F3" scrolling= No>
<FRAME src="Frame4.HTML" Name="F4" scrolling= No>
</FRAMESET>
</HTML>
```

F 1	F 2
F 3	F 4

FACT FILE

If the source file mentioned with the src attribute is not available, then a message would be displayed 'Files Not Found'.

TRY THIS

Try following the HTML codes using frames of your choice.

1.
```
<HTML>
<FRAMESET rows="50%, 50%">
<FRAME noresize="noresize" >
</FRAMESET>
</HTML>
```

2.
```
<HTML>
<FRAMESET rows="50%, 50%">
<FRAME>
</FRAMESET>
</HTML>
```

Nested frameset

Creating one frame within another frame is known as a **nested frame** set. This is done by using the nested frameset tags in the main window. One of the most popular uses for frames is nesting the frameset tags to design a complete website with the homepage on the left frame and the content, selected from the list in the homepage, on the right frame. An example is shown below of how to create a complete web page.

Example 4: The HTML code for creating three frames in the form of both rows and columns is given below.

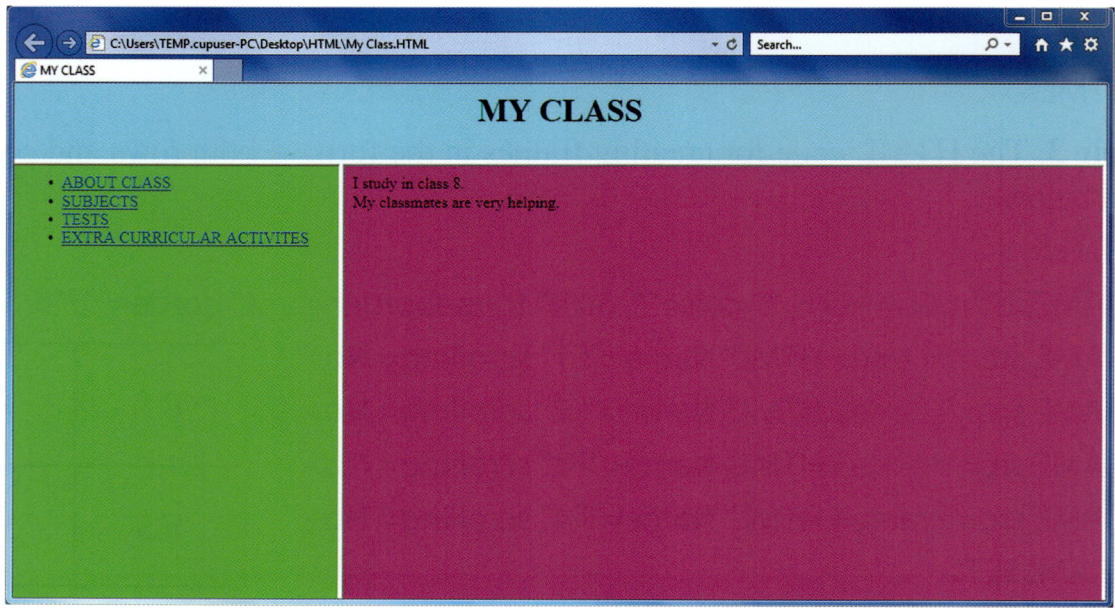

Example of a nested web page

Creating a web page My Class.HTML

```
<! This file divides the browser window into different frameset.>
<HTML>
<HEAD>
<TITLE>MY CLASS</TITLE>
</HEAD>
<FRAMESET rows="15%,*">
<FRAME src="Heading.HTML" NAME="F1" scrolling="No">
<FRAMESET cols="30%,*">
```

```
<FRAME src="Mainlist.HTML" Name="F2">
<FRAMESET cols="100%,*">
<FRAME src="Details.HTML" Name="F3">
</FRAMESET>
</FRAMESET>
</FRAMESET>
</BODY>
</HTML>
```

Creating a document for the topmost frame, Heading.HTML

```
<!This is the heading file in the topmost frame.>
<HTML>
<BODY bgcolor="cyan">
<CENTER><H1> MY CLASS
</H1></CENTER>
</BODY>
</HTML>
```

Creating a document for the second frame, Mainlist.HTML

```
<! This is the homepage displayed in the form of list in the left frame.>
<HTML>
<BODY bgcolor="lime">
<UL>
<LI><A href="DETAILS.HTML" target="MAIN">ABOUT CLASS</A>
<LI><A href="SUBJECTS.HTML" target="MAIN">SUBJECTS</A>
<LI><A href="TESTS.HTML" target="MAIN">TESTS</A>
<LI><A href="ACTIVITIES.HTML" target="MAIN">EXTRA CURRICULAR ACTIVITES
</A>
</UL>
</BODY>
</HTML>
```

Creating a document for the third frame, Details.HTML

<!This is the file displayed in the right frame when any of the list is selected in the homepage.>

<HTML>

<BODY bgcolor="#FF00FF">

I study in class 8.

My classmates are very helping.

</BODY>

</HTML>

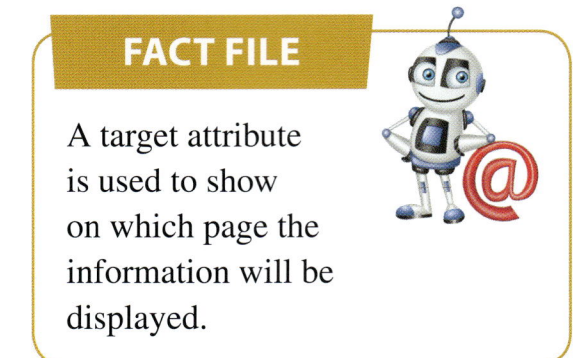

Example 5: Another example of a complex nested Frameset is given below. The HTML code for the various files created is given below.

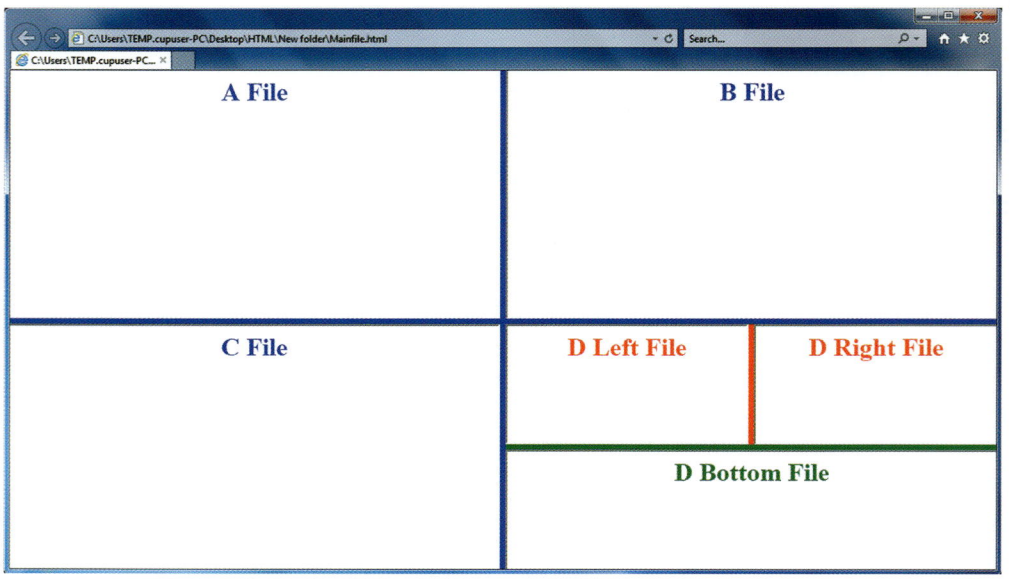

Example of a complex nested frameset

Creating document Mainfile.HTML

<! This file divides the browser window into different framesets.>

<HTML>

<FRAMESET rows="50%,50%" cols="50%,50%" border="7" bordercolor="Blue">

<FRAME src="AA.HTML" name="top_left">

<FRAME src="AB.HTML" name="top_right">

```
<FRAME src="AC.HTML" name="bottom_left">

<FRAMESET rows="50%,50%" border="7" bordercolor="green">

<FRAMESET cols="50%,50%" border="7" bordercolor="red">

<FRAME src="BCA.HTML" name="bottom_right_left" scrolling="No">

<FRAME src="BCB.HTML" name="bottom_right_right" scrolling="No">

</FRAMESET>

<FRAME src="BCC.HTML" name="bottom_right_bottom" scrolling="No">

</FRAMESET>

</FRAMESET>

</HTML>
```

Creating document AA.HTML

```
<!This file opens in the top left frame.>

<HTML>

<BODY >

<CENTER><FONT color="blue"><H1>A File</H1></CENTER></FONT>

</BODY>

</HTML>
```

Creating document AB.HTML

```
<!This file opens in the top right frame.>

<HTML>

<BODY>

<CENTER><FONT color="blue"><H1>B File</H1></CENTER></FONT>

</BODY>

</HTML>
```

Creating document AC.HTML

```
<!This file opens in the bottom left frame.>
<HTML>
<BODY>
<CENTER><FONT color="blue"><H1>C File</H1></CENTER></FONT>
</BODY>
</HTML>
```

Creating document BCA.HTML

```
<!This file opens in the bottom right left frame.>
<HTML>
<BODY>
<CENTER><FONT color=red><H1>D Left File</H1></CENTER></FONT>
</BODY>
</HTML>
```

Creating document BCB.HTML

```
<!This file opens in the bottom right frame.>
<HTML>
<BODY>
<CENTER><FONT color="red"><H1>D Right File</H1></CENTER></FONT>
</BODY>
</HTML>
```

Creating document BCC.HTML

```
<!This file opens in the bottom right bottom frame.>
<HTML>
<BODY>
<CENTER><FONT color="Green"><H1>D Bottom File</H1></CENTER></FONT>
</BODY>
</HTML>
```

A. Create the following framesets:

1.

A	A	C
		D

2.

A		
B	C	D

3.

A	B	C
D		E

4.

A	
B	C
	D
	E

B. Create a web page titled 'Book Review'. The page should be divided as shown below.

Book Review	
• Book Name 1 • Book Name 2 • Book Name 3 • Book Name 4 • Book Name 5	Details of the book selected
Made by: Student name Contact: student@email.com	

Frames   They allow us to divide the web page into several independent parts.

<FRAME> tag   The tag that defines what goes into each frame of a HTML.

Frameset   A set of frames inserted in a HTML web page.

<FRAMESET> tag   The tag that divides the web page into rectangular areas, where an individual HTML document can be loaded for each area using the <FRAME> tag.

Nested frameset   Creating one frame within another frame.

YOU ARE HERE

4

1. Attributes of a <FRAMESET> tag are Cols, Rows, Border, Bordercolor and Frameborder.
2. Attributes of a <FRAME> tag are Src, Name, Frameborder, Bordercolor, Scrolling, Marginheight and Marginwidth.

EXERCISE

A. True or false?

1. Frames allow you to divide the web page into several independent panes.

2. You need the <FRAME> and <TABLE> tags to create frames in HTML.

3. An important attribute of the <FRAME> tag is src.

4. Creating one frame within another frame is called a nested frame.

5. Scrolling in the <FRAME> tag specifies scroll information for the frame.

B. Give one word for the following.

1. The attribute that specifies the URL of the initial file to be displayed in the frame.   ....

2. The attribute that specifies the color of the border of the frame.   ....

3. The tag that is used to divide a webpage into rectangular areas.   ....

4. The attribute that specifies that a frame is not resizable.   ....

5. The tag that defines what goes into each frame of a HTML webpage.   ....

C. **Explain the difference between the following tag attributes:**

1. Cols and Rows of the <FRAMESET> tag.

2. Border and Bordercolor of the <FRAMESET> tag.

3. Src and Name of the <FRAME> tag.

4. Marginheight and marginwidth of the <FRAME> tag.

D. **Answer the following questions.**

1. Why do you need to create frames in a HTML window?

2. Discuss the <FRAMESET> tag and its attributes.

3. Discuss different attributes of the <FRAME> tag.

4. What is a nested frameset? Give an example.

LAB WORK

A. Create a website on the topic 'Football World Cup 2018'. The browser window should be divided into three frames: heading frame; list of matches as hyperlink in the left frame; the list of participating countries in the right frame. The information should be displayed only when a hyperlink is selected.

B. Design a website about the importance of hygiene.

PROJECT WORK

Create a web page about electric cars. It should contain information using bullets, tables, images and backgrounds. The web page should contain frames. Use the internet to gather information.

JavaScript in HTML Documents

SNAP RECAP

1. List the elements of HTML you have learnt so far.
2. What do you think is a limitation of HTML script?

LEARNING OBJECTIVES

You will learn about:

* the importance of JavaScript
* writing a JavaScript program
* using an external JavaScript file
* the object model in JavaScript
* the document.write() method
* JavaScript variables and operators
* using the window.alert() and window.confirm() methods
* using parseInt() and parseFloat( ) to do arithmetic calculations.

Introduction

HTML is a very limited document formatting language. It is based on tags that instruct the browser how to display text or an image. As such, HTML is limited to a static, one-way interaction with the user.

To add functionality to your web page you need a scripting language. JavaScript is one of the most popular scripting languages for the internet. It works in all major browsers such as Internet Explorer, Firefox, Chrome, Opera and Safari. In this chapter, you will learn to add functionality to your web pages by using JavaScript.

JavaScript

JavaScript is a scripting language with a very simple syntax. It is used to add interactivity

FACT FILE

Do not confuse JavaScript with Java language. Both share similar names but are different in most aspects.

84

to your web pages. JavaScript is set to execute when changes need to be reflected on the web page, such as, when a page has finished loading or when a user clicks on a HTML element. This type of interaction requires knowledge of constructs such as **IF statements** and **FOR loops** which are not part of the HTML syntax.

JavaScript provides web page authors with the power to reach a very high level of interaction between the user and the document.

The importance of JavaScript

JavaScript is used because:

*   It helps to add interactive elements to HTML pages.
*   It is a scripting language which is also a lightweight programming language.
*   Everyone can use JavaScript without purchasing a licence.
*   It is supported by all major browsers, such as Internet Explorer, Firefox, Chrome, Opera and Safari.

Writing a JavaScript program

JavaScript is lines of executable computer code usually embedded directly in HTML pages.

JavaScript statements can be included in HTML documents by enclosing the statements between an opening <SCRIPT> tag and a closing </SCRIPT> tag.

The section between the opening <SCRIPT> tag and the closing </SCRIPT> tag is called the **script block**. For example,

```
<SCRIPT language="JavaScript">

....

[JavaScript statements]

....

</SCRIPT>
```

The <SCRIPT> tag may be placed in either the head or body of a HTML document. The script code can be broken into smaller parts and placed in different sections of the HTML document. To have different script sections, start each with the <SCRIPT> tag and close it with the closing tag </SCRIPT>. However, it is recommended to keep all the JavaScript code together in one single section of the document. This is done for better readability and understanding.

```
<HTML>                              <BODY>
<HEAD>                              <SCRIPT language="JavaScript">
<language="JavaScript">             ....
....                                </SCRIPT>
</SCRIPT>                           </BODY>
</HEAD>                             </HTML>
```

Using an external JavaScript file

If you want to run the same JavaScript on several pages without having to write the same script on every page, you can write a JavaScript in an external file. The external file is simply a text file containing JavaScript code with a .js file extension.

To use the external script, point to the .js file in the 'src' attribute of the <SCRIPT> tag.

For example,

```
<SCRIPT language="JavaScript"
src="scriptFile.js">
[additional JavaScript statements]
</SCRIPT>
```

> **FACT FILE**
>
> JavaScript files have an extension of .js, and are identified by an icon $. These files contain just the code, and no <SCRIPT> tag is required.

The Object Model in JavaScript

Like most other programming languages of its generation, JavaScript is characterised by the Object Model. This means that you think about your JavaScript program in terms of the objects you want to work with. For programming purposes, the browser window, the HTML document, forms, etc., are the objects which in turn are formed of other objects such as Text Boxes and Radio buttons.

You can access information about the objects with the help of **methods**. Methods are functions associated with objects. In other words, the actions you can perform on or with objects are called methods. Here, you will learn to use simple objects and methods to write programs in JavaScript.

For any object that has a method, type the name of the object, followed by a dot (.), then the name of the method and a set of parenthesis. In other words, **object.method**(). For example, if you have an object named Car and you want to define a method, say Travel, you would type:

```
Car.Travel()
```

Let us study some simple codes for JavaScript.

document.write( ) method

The document.write() method is used for displaying the text on the browser window. It uses an object called 'document', which refers to the current document on the browser window.

This object manages many of the instructions that JavaScript can handle for HTML. One of the methods, write(), of this object is to display a string or text on the screen. For example, document.write("Welcome to JavaScript")

This will display the message "Hello friends!" on the browser window.

A simple JavaScript program

To display a simple text on the browser window as shown below, the following script has to be written.

```
<HTML>
<HEAD>
<TITLE>Welcome</TITLE>
</HEAD>
<BODY>

<SCRIPT language="JavaScript">
document.write("Welcome to JavaScript");
</SCRIPT>
</BODY>
</HTML>
```

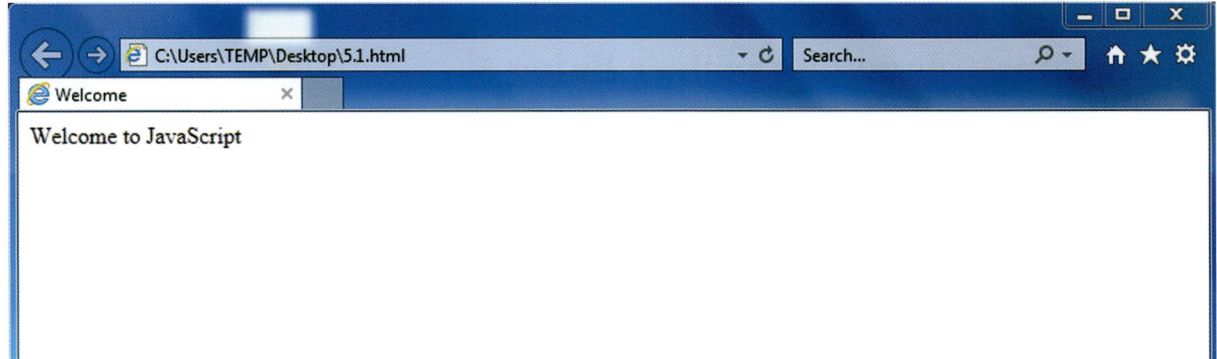

Displaying text

Using HTML tags in JavaScript

HTML tags can also be included in the JavaScript code to generate HTML elements that will be displayed in the browser window. All HTML tags are valid in JavaScript. Once the browser receives a string from the document.write( ) method, the

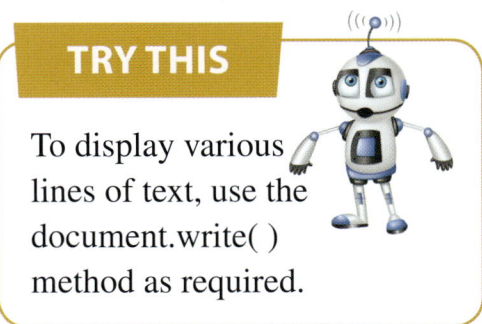

TRY THIS

To display various lines of text, use the document.write( ) method as required.

browser accepts the string enclosed within the parentheses and double-quotes, and treats it as HTML code. The string without the HTML tags is accepted as a simple text. The browser treats each HTML tag accordingly.

For example, here is the script for the output as shown in the screen below.

```
<HTML>
<HEAD> <TITLE> Using HTML Tags</TITLE> </HEAD>
<BODY>
<SCRIPT language="JavaScript">
document.write("<H1>Every dark cloud has a silver lining</H1>");
document.write("<H2><U>Fortune favours the brave</U></H2>");
document.write("<B>An apple a day keeps the doctor away</B><BR>");
document.write("A friend in need is a friend indeed");
</SCRIPT>
</BODY>
</HTML>
```

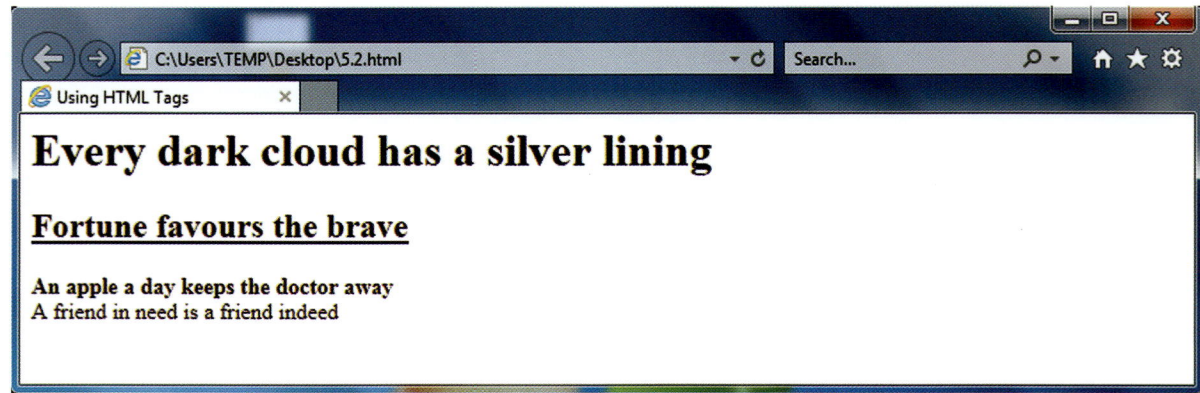

Using HTML tags with JavaScript

Rules for writing a JavaScript program

You should follow the rules given below when writing a program using JavaScript:

- The scripting language has to be written within <SCRIPT> ... </SCRIPT> tags in a HTML document.
- The <SCRIPT> ... </SCRIPT> tags can either be written in the <HEAD> or <BODY> of a HTML document.

- A program can have more than one of the <SCRIPT> ... </SCRIPT> tags.
- JavaScript is a case sensitive language.
- Using a semicolon at the end of the statement is optional. Using semicolons makes it possible to write multiple statements on one line.

Before you learn more about methods in JavaScript, you will learn how to add comments to the JavaScript code.

Adding comments to JavaScript code

A **comment** is a line of code that is not interpreted by the browser. The browser ignores any text that is written as a comment. Comments can be added to make the code more readable.

There are two different types of comments in JavaScript:

- **Single line comments**: These are used when the comment entry has to be given in one line. These comments begin with double slash (//). For example,

  // This is comment line 1

- **Multiple line comments**: These are used when the comments extend beyond one line. The comment block is enclosed between /* and */. For example,

  /* This is comment line 1

  This is comment line 2 */

> **FACT FILE**
>
> If you do not wish to use a part of a code, you should make that part a comment rather than deleting it. It is then not executed but can be read and used when needed.

Some examples of JavaScript are given below.

The script for the output shown in the screen on the next page, is given below:

```
<HTML>

<BODY>

<SCRIPT language="JavaScript">
document.write("<H1>This is a heading</H1>");
```

```
document.write("<P>This is a paragraph.</P>");

document.write("<P>This is another paragraph.</P>");

</SCRIPT>

</BODY>

</HTML>
```

An example of output using JavaScript

The script for the output as shown in the screen on the next page is given below:

```
<HTML>

<HEAD>

<SCRIPT language="JavaScript">

document.write("<H3>This is a script written in head part</H3>");

</SCRIPT>

</HEAD>

<BODY>

<SCRIPT language="JavaScript">

document.write("<H3>This is a script written in body part</H3>");

</SCRIPT>

<H3>This is a text written using HTML without scripting </H3>
```

```
</BODY>

</HTML>
```

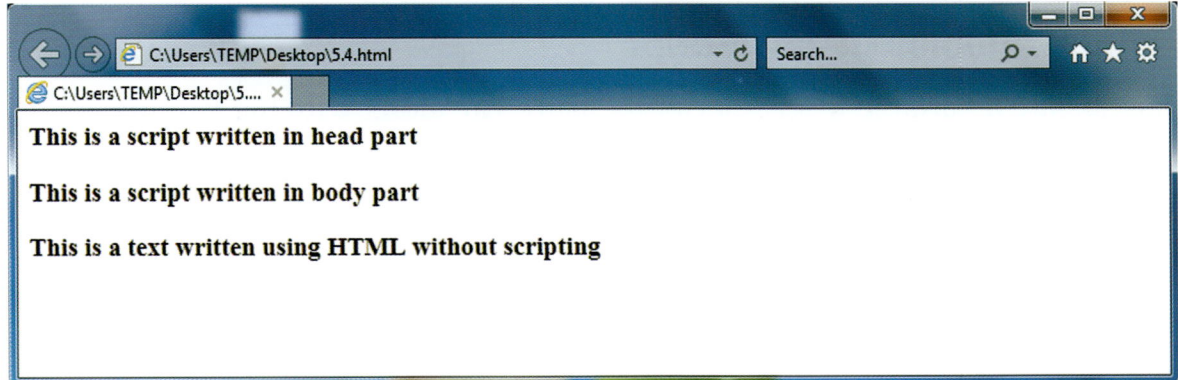

An example of output using JavaScript

ACTIVITY

Create a webpage including the following:

1. Display a 'Hello' message using the heading level of your choice. It should be bold and underlined.

2. Display your name in the centre of the web page in blue.

3. Display the heading 'I am learning JavaScript' in a bigger font size, centre aligned and underlined. Now write its definition on a separate line using different colors.

JavaScript variables

Variables are the names assigned to a memory location that can be used for storing data. Its value can change during the execution of a script. A variable can have a short name, like x, or a more descriptive name, like Fname. These variables, by default, hold only one value at a time. If you try to assign another value then the previous one is overwritten.

The rules below should be followed when assigning a name to a variable:

- A variable name is case sensitive (y and Y are two different variables).
- It can contain letters (A...Z, a...z), digits (0...9), and underscores (_) only.
- It must start with a letter or an underscore character.

- It cannot contain empty space (white space).
- It cannot have more than 255 characters.
- It cannot be one of the language's reserved words (keyword), such as var, alert, etc.

Declaring variables in JavaScript

You can declare a variable in JavaScript by using **var** along with the variable name.

For example, variables n1, fname and age are declared below. These variables are empty by default with no value:

```
var n1, result
var fname
var age
```

Values can be assigned to variables at the time of declaring them or later. In the example below, the value "Putri" (i.e. a first name) is assigned to the variable fname.

```
var n1=2
var fname="Putri"
```

> Use double quotes to assign a text value to a variable.

Let us write a small program to see how variables are used. The output of this program is shown below.

```
<HTML>
<BODY>
<SCRIPT language="JavaScript">
var fname="Daniel"
document.write("Hello " + fname + "<BR> Welcome to Lab");
</SCRIPT>
</BODY>
</HTML>
```

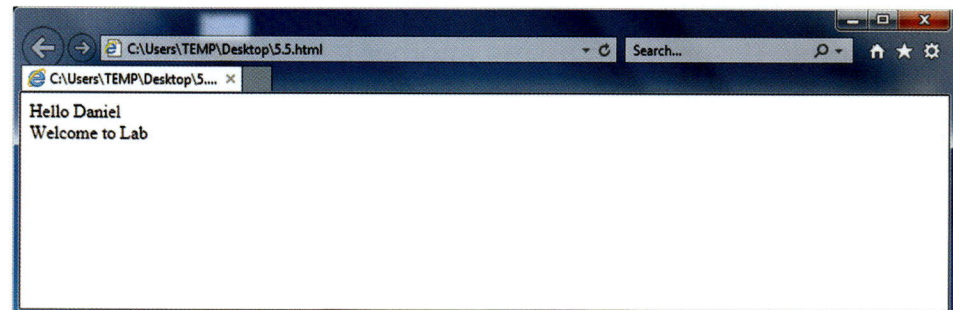

Using variables in JavaScript

JavaScript operators

An operator is a symbol applied to data values like variables and constants that causes the computer to carry out a specific operation on that data. The different types of operators available in JavaScript are:

- Arithmetic operators
- Comparison/Relational operators
- Logical operators
- String operator

Arithmetic operators

Arithmetic operators are used to perform arithmetic calculations using variables or constants. Different types of arithmetic operators are given in the table below.

Operator	Description	Example	Result
+	Addition	2 + 4	6
–	Subtraction	6 – 2	4
*	Multiplication	5 * 3	15
/	Division	15 / 3	5
%	Modulus	10 %3	1

Types of arithmetic operators

The HTML code using arithmetic operators to give the output as shown in the screen on the next page is given below:

```
<HTML>
<BODY>
<SCRIPT language="JavaScript">
var a=2
var b=10
document.write("The addition of two numbers is = ");
var result = a + b
document.write(result);
document.write("<BR> The multiplication of two numbers is = ");
```

```
result = a * b

document.write(result);

</SCRIPT>

</BODY>

</HTML>
```

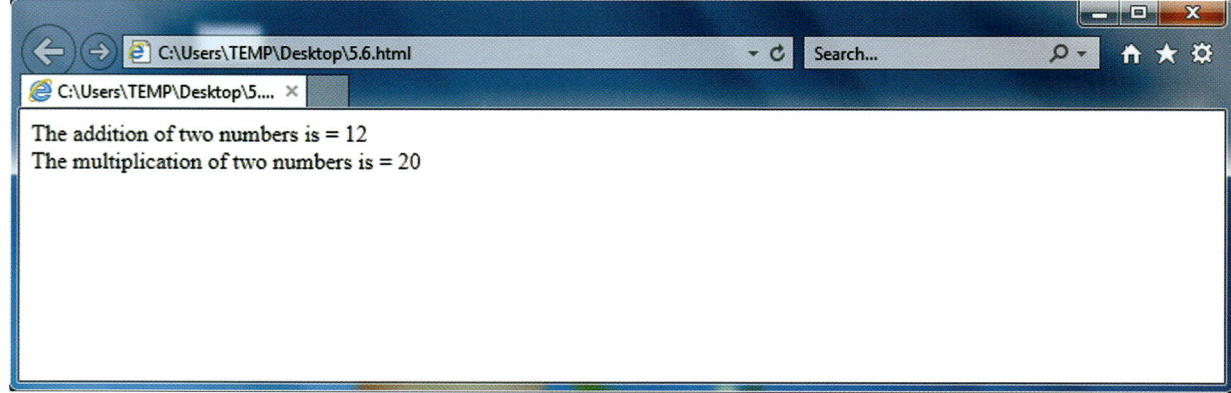

Using arithmetic operators

Comparison operators

Comparison operators are used to test if two variables relate to each other in the specified way. These return values which are either True or False.

Operator	Description	Example
==	is equal to (equality operator)	10==20 returns False
!=	is not equal	10!=20 returns True
>	is greater than	10>20 returns False
<	is less than	10<20 returns True
>=	is greater than or equal to	10>=20 returns False
<=	is less than or equal to	10<=20 returns True

Comparison operators

Logical operators

The logical operators perform logical operations on variables.

Operator	Description	Example
&&	and	x=2 y=3 (x < 10 && y > 1) returns True
||	or	x=12 y=3 (x==5 || y==5) returns False
!	not	x=12 y=3 !(x==y) returns True

Logical operators

String operators

A string is a set of characters. To join two or more string values together, you use the plus '+' operator. This is also known as the **string concatenation operator**.

For example, a HTML code using the string concatenation operator for the output in the screen on the next page is given below:

```
<HTML>
<HEAD>
<BODY>
<SCRIPT language = "JavaScript">
var str1,str2
str1="Hello"
str2="Friends"
document.write(str1+str2+" </Br>");
//to add a space in between
document.write(str1+ " " +str2);
```

```
</SCRIPT>
</BODY>
</HEAD>
</HTML>
```

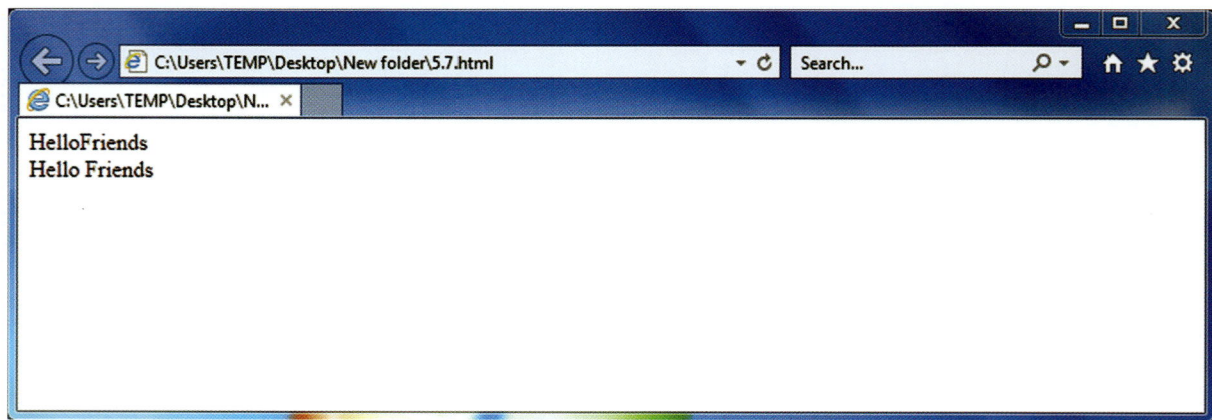

Output using string operators

Methods for the window object

Let us now learn to write some more JavaScripts using various methods for the window object.

window.alert () method

window.alert () is a method of the window object. It is the simplest dialog box used to display a short message to the user in a separate small window. The dialog box contains the text given as a parameter to the alert( ) method and a button labelled **OK**.

The syntax for the alert box is:

window.alert (message)

alert (message)

> It is not necessary to specify the window object, you can leave it out of the code.

96

For example, the HTML code using the window.alert () method for the output shown in the screen below is as follows:

```
<HTML>
<HEAD>
<TITLE>Using window.alert()</TITLE>
</HEAD>
<BODY>
<H2>alert window demo</H2>
<SCRIPT language="JavaScript">
alert("Hi! \n JavaScript is very interesting")
</SCRIPT>
</BODY>
</HTML>
```

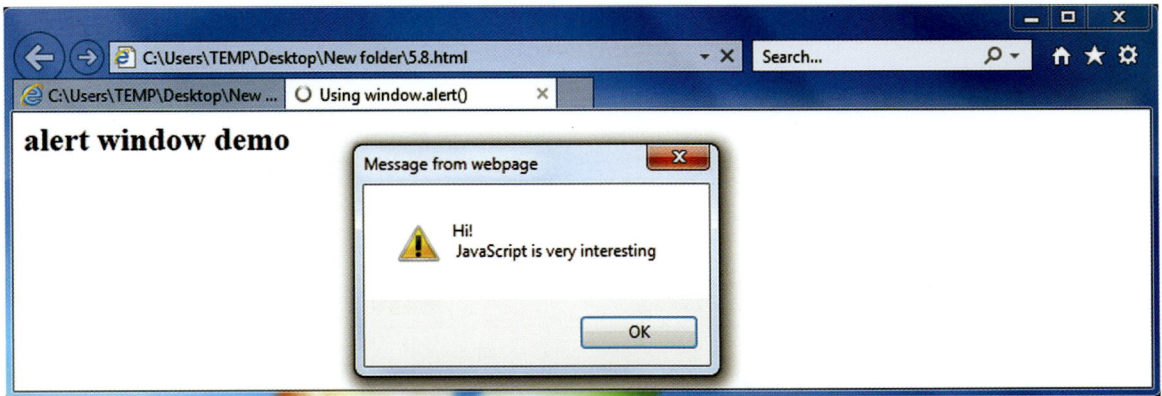

Output using the window.alert() method

In the above code \n or newline is used instead of the
 HTML tag. HTML tags are not supported with the object window because it opens as a separate pop up window, not as a separate web page.

window.confirm() method

The confirm dialog box is also a method of the window object. The confirm box includes both **OK** and **Cancel** buttons. This method returns the value True if OK is pressed and False if Cancel is pressed. Confirm boxes are different from alert boxes because they evaluate a value, based on a decision made by the user.

The syntax for the confirm box is:

window.confirm(message)

confirm(message)

For example, the HTML code using the window.confirm() method for the output shown in the screen below is shown here:

```
<HTML>

<BODY>

<SCRIPT language="JavaScript">

var reply = confirm("You must always follow the traffic rules")

document.write(reply);

</SCRIPT>

</BODY>

</HTML>
```

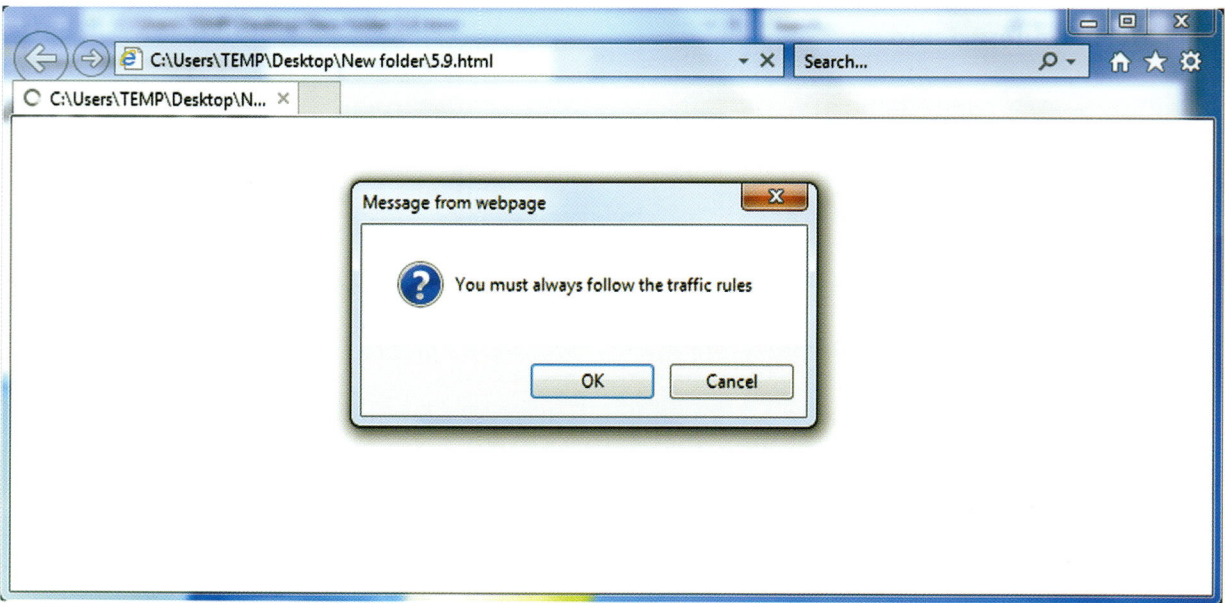

Output using the confirm() method

In the above example, the value returned when **OK** is clicked is True, but whereas when **Cancel** is clicked the value, is False.

window.prompt() method

The prompt dialog box is another method of the window object. This method is used for obtaining input from the user. It displays an **Explorer User Prompt** dialog box with a message and an input field.

It is similar to the confirm box, except that it returns the value of the input field, rather than True or False.

The syntax for the prompt box is:

window.prompt (message, default value)

prompt(message, default value)

where

message: This can be any text to be displayed in the prompt window.

default value: This can be any default value given in an input box before the user enters a value.

For example, the HTML code using the window.prompt() method for the prompt box (see below) and the output shown below is given here:

```
<HTML>

<BODY>

<SCRIPT language="JavaScript">
var name1

name1=prompt("Enter your
friend's name","abc")

document.write("<FONT
color='blue' size='6'> Hello
"+name1+"!<BR> Which book
did you read today?
</FONT><BR>");

</SCRIPT>

</BODY>

</HTML>
```

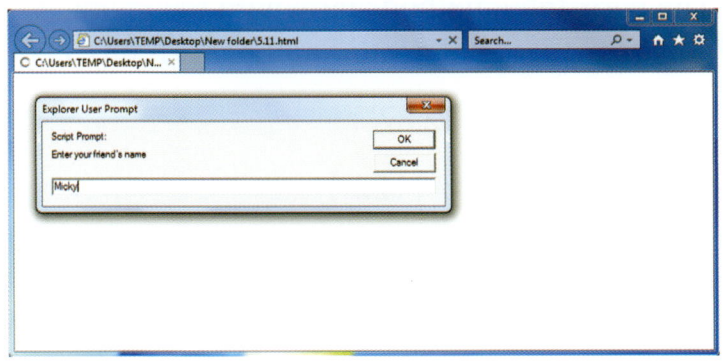

Prompt box

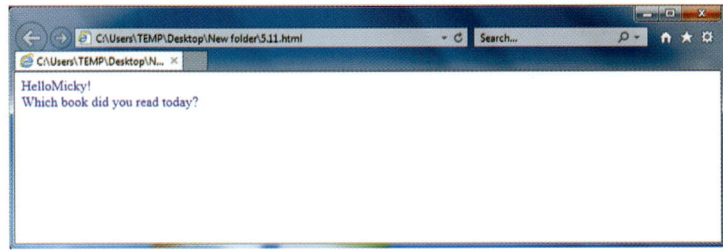

Output to the program

If you click on the Cancel Button for the prompt box, the value returned will be null.

ACTIVITY

A. Input a name, class and section from the user. Display the message "Hi, <name>.
 you study in class <class> section <section>." Choose colors of your choice.

B. Accept the radius of a circle and display the area and circumference in an alert box.

parseInt() and parseFloat() methods

parseInt() and parseFloat() methods in JavaScript are used to convert a non-number value into numbers. parseInt() converts a string value into integers (numbers without decimal places) and parseFloat() converts a string value into floating numbers (numbers with decimal values).

The parseInt() method starts with the character in position 0 and checks that it is a valid number, if it is not a valid number it returns **NaN**. For example,

var x= parseInt("32.87")   // returns 32

var y= parseInt("B-1122")   // returns NaN

var z= parseInt("14square")   // returns 14

A HTML code using the parseInt() method is given below:

// This is to display the sum of two numbers entered by the user.

<HTML>

<BODY>

<SCRIPT language="JavaScript">

var n1,n2,tot

n1=prompt(Enter first number , 0)

n2=prompt(Enter second number , 0)

tot=parseInt(n1) + parseInt(n2) document.write(The total is +tot);

100

```
</SCRIPT>
</BODY>
</HTML>
```

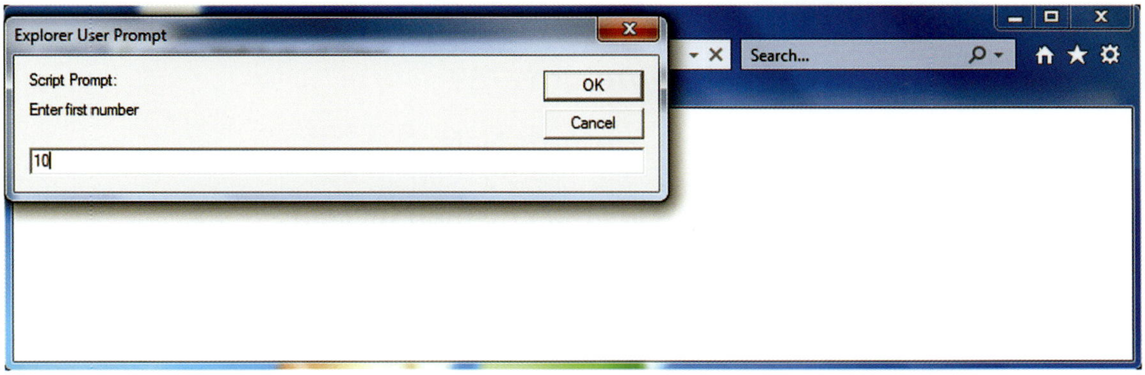

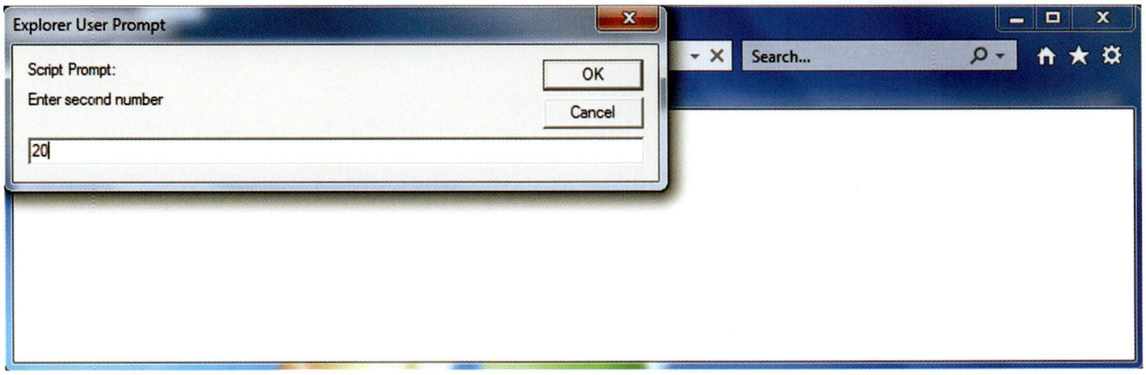

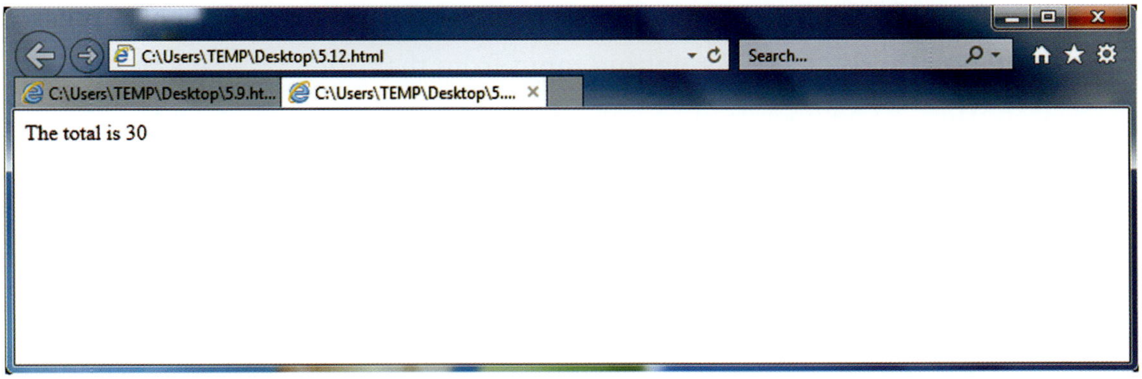

Using the parseInt() method

The parseFloat() method works in a similar way to parseInt(). It starts looking at each character string in position 0 and continues until it finds the first invalid character. The decimal point is a valid character the first time it appears. If there are two decimal points, the second is considered as invalid and the parseFloat() method converts the string until the first decimal point.

For example,

```
var a= parseFloat("32.45.98")      //returns 32.45
var b= parseFloat("14square")      //returns 14.0
var c = parseFloat("32.76")        //returns 32.76
var d = parseFloat("0789")         //returns 789
var e = parseFloat("Vijay")        //returns NaN
```

Try the above HTML code using the parseInt() method instead.

GLOSSARY

document.write() method   Used for displaying the text on the browser window.

parseFloat()   Converts the input into a numeric value.

parseInt()   Converts a text value into an integer value.

Script block   The section between the opening <SCRIPT> tag and the closing </SCRIPT> tag.

window.alert() method   Displays a short message to the user in a small window.

window.confirm() method   Returns true if OK is pressed and false if Cancel is pressed.

window.prompt() method   Used for getting input from the user.

String concatenation   The operation of joining character strings end-to-end.

YOU ARE HERE

5

1. JavaScript is a scripting language with a very simple syntax. It is used to add interactivity to a web page.

2. The <SCRIPT> tag may be placed either at the head or body of a HTML document. The script code can be broken into smaller parts and placed in different sections of the HTML document.

3. If you want to run the same JavaScript on several pages, without having to write the same script on every page, you can write a JavaScript in an external file with .js extension.

4. JavaScript is characterised by the object model. This means that you think about your JavaScript program in terms of the objects (the things you want to work with).

5. HTML tags can also be included in the JavaScript code to generate HTML elements that will be displayed in the browser window.

6. Comments can be added to make the code more readable.

7. You can declare a variable in JavaScript by using var.

8. A string is a set of characters. To join two or more string values together you use the + operator. This is also known as the string concatenation operator.

9. The confirm dialog box is another method of the window object. This method returns a True, if OK is pressed, and False if Cancel is pressed.

10. The prompt dialog box is also a method of the window object. This method is used for getting input from the user. It displays a prompt dialog box with a message and an input field.

EXERCISE

A. True or false?

1. JavaScript is a very complex scripting language.

2. The actions you can perform on or with objects are called methods.

3. A program can have more than one <SCRIPT> ... </SCRIPT> tags.

4. Single line comments end with a double-slash (//).

5. JavaScript helps to add interactive elements to HTML pages.

B. Give JavaScript statements to perform the following tasks.

1. Concatenating (joining) two strings: "Click" and "Start".
2. Using single line and multiple line comments.
3. Declaring four variables: length, breadth, height and volume.
4. Display a confirm dialog box with the message "Plant more trees".

C. **Describe the use of the following methods in JavaScript.**

1. document.write()   2. window.prompt()

3. window.alert()   4. window.confirm()

5. parseInt()   6. parseFloat()

D. **Answer the following questions.**

1. What is JavaScript? Why is it important?

2. Discuss object model in JavaScript.

3. How can you use HTML tags in JavaScript?

4. How do you declare variables in JavaScript?

5. Discuss various types of operators in JavaScript.

LAB WORK

A. Write a JavaScript program to input marks of all your subjects and then calculate the average.

B. Write a JavaScript program to take user inputs of sides of a rectangle and calculate its area.

C. Input the first name and last name from the user and display a message "The name you entered is <first name><last name>".

D. Input your school name and display it in red and in a bigger font size.

PROJECT WORK

A. Write a JavaScript program which takes a random integer between 1 to 10, and the user is then prompted to input a guess number. If the user input matches the random number, the program will display a message "Good Work" or otherwise display a message "Not matched".

B. Write a JavaScript program to convert temperatures to and from Celsius and Fahrenheit.

HTML5 – Introduction

SNAP RECAP

1. List the various tags of HTML you have learnt so far.

LEARNING OBJECTIVES

You will learn about:

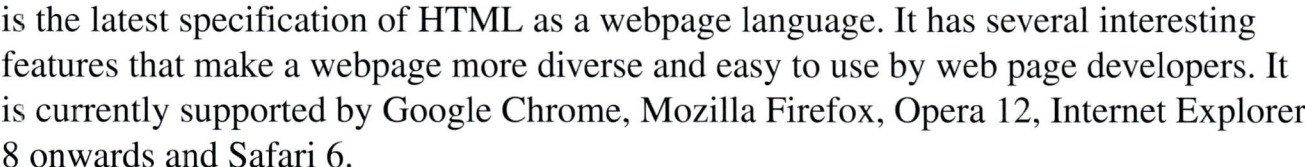

- new features in HTML5
- backward compatibility
- points to remember for writing HTML5 codes
- tags in HTML5
- attributes in HTML5
- inserting pictures in HTML5
- inserting audio and video files in HTML5.

Introduction

HTML stands for Hyper Text Markup Language. You have already learned that it is used to create webpages with hypertext and hyperlinks that can be viewed by using any web browser. There are several versions of HTML. HTML5 is the latest specification of HTML as a webpage language. It has several interesting features that make a webpage more diverse and easy to use by web page developers. It is currently supported by Google Chrome, Mozilla Firefox, Opera 12, Internet Explorer 8 onwards and Safari 6.

New features

The reasons for launching HTML5 are listed below:

- HTML5 is an independent markup language and is no longer a part of SGML.
- It can be used on desktop as well as mobile devices like tablets and smartphones.

- A web page is treated as a web document having a specific structure with new tags like <header>, <footer>, <article>, <nav>, <sections>, <aside>, <figure>.
- A web page can be made more interactive by adding audio and video files by using new tags <audio>, <video>.
- It has <menus>, <commands>, <details>,<datagrid> to help a web application developer with the designing of a dynamic webpage.
- It has a new <canvas> tag for drawing graphics. It also has several methods to draw paths, boxes, circles, text, and add images. You need to use JavaScript to support this tag in a web page.

Backward compatibility

Backward compatibility means the compatibility of the new HTML5 with the older versions of the markup language features to run in older versions of web browsers, along with new features supported by latest web browsers. For example, a web page created with the older version can be edited by adding new tags of HTML5 that can run in a later web browser that supports HTML5, and also in older browsers which will treat all unrecognised elements as inline elements. HTML5 is designed to have maximum backward compatibility with the existing browsers.

Points to remember for writing HTML5 codes

- Tags are not case sensitive. We can write a code in upper, lower or mixed case.
- Quotes are optional for attributes as well as attribute values.
- The first line of the document should be <!doctype html>.This tells the browser about the version of the HTML.
- The <html> tag and the <body> tag can be omitted.
- It is advisable to write:

  <meta charset="UTF-8">

  This will tell the browser about the type of character set used to convert bits to character. Here we are using UTF-8 encoding, which is necessary for HTML5.
- We can use any text editor to write HTML code. Some examples of text editors are Sublime Text, Notepad, Notepad++ and Netbeans.

Sample Code

```
<!doctype html>
<html>
  <head>
    <meta charset="UTF-8">
    <title>HTML5 document</title>
  </head>
  <body>
    <h1><u>My first web page in HTML5</u></h1>
  </body>
</html>
```

Tags in HTML5

There are a lot of new tags in HTML5. Here, we will discuss some of the most important of these:

Structural elements

These are a group of elements which are used to create the structure of HTML5 documents. Each of these elements are also called section elements.

Some of these are explained below:

- **header** – This tag defines the header of a web page document. We can use it to set the main title section of the webpage.

- **nav** – This tag defines the section in the document with the navigation links to other webpages or to the same webpage.

- **article** – This tag defines a section of the document which can be an independent block in the whole document. We can use this tag to create articles of newspapers or blogs.

- **section** – This tag defines a portion of a document as one section.

- **aside** – This tag defines a portion of content that can be set aside as a sidebar or extra information in the webpage.

- **footer** – This tag defines the footer of a webpage. It generally contains information about the author, copyright, company logo, etc.

Let us now design a webpage using the above structural tags:

```html
<!DOCTYPE html>
<html>
 <head>
  <meta charset="utf-8">
  <title>MY FIRST HTML5 PROGRAM</title>
 </head>

 <body>
  <header>
   <h1>SAVE FOREST SAVE TIGERS</h1>
   <p>Tiger is a beautiful animal but it is also the indicator of the
      forest's health. Saving the tiger means we save the forest since
      tiger cannot live in places where trees have vanished and in turn
      secure food and water for all.
   </header>

  <nav>
   <ul>
     <li><a href="http://www.Tigertruth.com">Bitter Truth</a></li>
     <li><a href="http://www.tigernumber.com">Where are the Few?</a></li>
     <li><a href="http://www.tutorialspoint.com/javascript">Can they be
         saved?</a></li>
   </ul>
  </nav>

  <article>
   <section>
     <h3>Oct 2018 - "eye on the tiger" </h3>
     <p >World's largest ever professional tiger photographic
        exhibition held at the Royal Albert Hall, London.
        Over 35 of the world's best photographers featuring
```

```
        87 stunning photos to help raise awareness regarding
        the plight facing wild tigers in 2018.</p>
    </section>
  </article>

  <aside>
    <h4>Save Wild Tigers</h4>
    <p> International Tiger Day is observed on 29 July every year to raise
        awareness about the conservation of tiger and to promote the
        protection of natural habitat of tigers.</p>
  </aside>

  <footer>
    <br><br><br>
    <hr>
    <b><u>Created by Authors of Click Start</u></b>
  </footer>
 </body>
</html>
```

The output for the above code is:

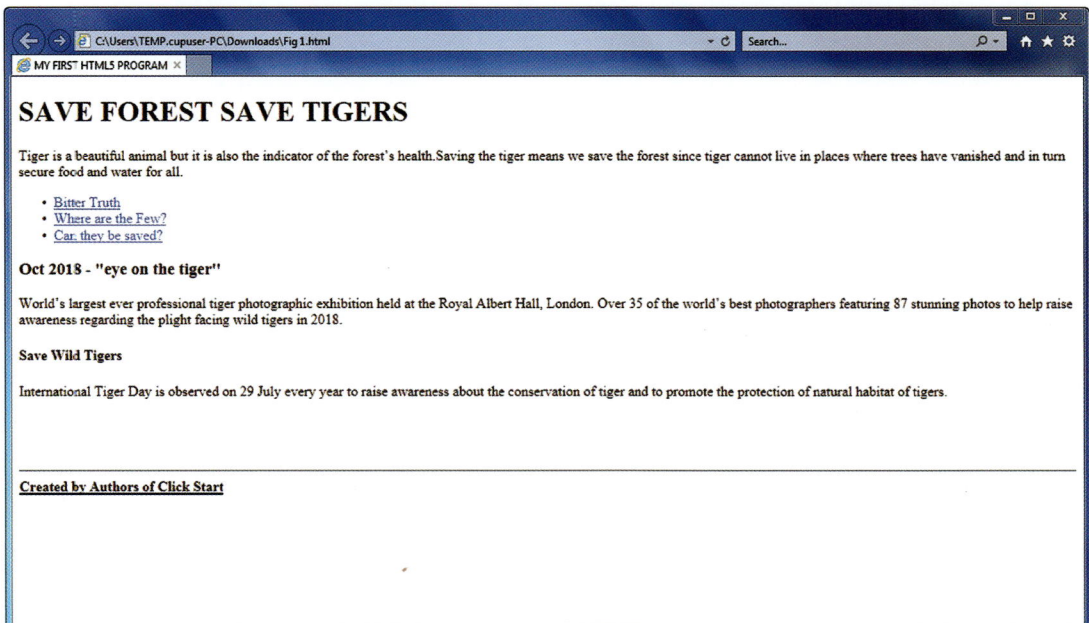

Some of the tags and attributes used in the earlier versions of HTML can also be used in HTML5 as listed below:

TAGS	ATTRIBUTES	EXAMPLES
<BODY>	• bgcolor="any color" Sets the background color of the webpage • background="any picture file" • text="any color" for the text used	<body bgcolor=red text=blue>
<title>		<title> My first webpage</tilte>
HEADING TAGS	• From <h1> level to <h6> with <h1> as highest and <h6>as lowest level	<h2> this is heading level 2</h2> <h3>This is heading level3</h3>
<font>	• face=name of the font • size=size of the font • color=color of the font	<font face="Algerian" size=4 color=green> HTML5 is a markup language</font>
<OL>	Defines an ordered list • type=1/A/a/I/i • start=any number to start the list	Creates the list of subjects <ol> <li> English <li>Maths <li>Science </ol>
<UL>	Defines unordered list • type=square/disc/circle	Shopping list of stationary items <ul> <li> pens <li>pencil <li> eraser </ul>

`<table>`
  `<tr>`
    `<th>`
    `<td>`
  `</tr>`
`</table>`
	It creates a table with the specific rows and columns	`<table>`
		  `<tr>`
		    `<th>subjects</th>`
		    `<th>marks1 </th>`
		    `<th>marks2</th>`
		  `</tr>`
		  `<tr>`
		    `<td>english</td>`
		    `<td>87</td>`
		    `<td>89</td>`
		  `</tr>`
		  `<tr>`
		    `<td>science</td>`
		    `<td>91</td>`
		    `<td>92</td>`
		  `</tr>`
		`</table>`

`<A>`	Anchor tag used to create a hyperlink	`<a href="file.html">Click here to open file </a>`

Attributes in HTML5

Elements in HTML work with default settings. We can alter the default setting by using attributes with or without values. The value assigned to an attribute can be enclosed in double or single quotes. For example `<body bgcolor="red">`.

There are two different types of attributes used with HTML5 elements.

Standard attributes

These are also called global attributes, and are supported by almost all the elements in HTML. Some of these attributes are listed below:

Attributes	Use	Example
background	Used to place an image as a background for the element it is used with.	\<table background="image1.jpg"\> \<body background="image2.jpg"\>
accesskey	Gives the shortcut keys to access the element.	\<a href="file1.html" accesskey="f"\>
align	Horizontally aligns the elements as left, right or center.	\<table align=left\> \<img align=right\> \<p align=center\>
valign	Vertically aligns the elements as top, middle, bottom.	\<tr valign=top\>
bgcolor	Sets the background color of the element used.	\<body bgcolor=red\> \<tr bgcolor=green\> \<td bgcolor=blue\>
height	Sets the height of the element.	\<img height=200\> \<table height=300\>
width	Sets the width of the element.	\<img width=300\> \<table width=400\>

Custom attributes

These attributes are created by the user for a specific element. To create a custom attribute we use "data-", followed by the desired custom attribute name and then set to the desired string value.

For example:

\<p data-author="Click Start"\> This is an example of custom attributes created by the authors of the click start series \</p\>

The best use of custom attributes is in cascading style sheets or JavaScript in HTML5 documents, but these are not covered in this book.

Inserting images

We can insert images in HTML5 in two ways:

1. Using the <img> tag

The <img> tag is used to insert simple or animated images in a webpage. The image formats supported by this tag are JPG, GIF and PNG.

The attributes used with the <img> tag are:

- **Src** – the source file name of an image file to be displayed on the webpage.
- **Alt** – displays the alternative text if the image is not displayed on the webpage due to any reason.
- **Height** – the height (pixels) of the image displayed on the webpage.
- **Width** – the width (pixels) of the image displayed on the webpage.
- **Border** – changes the thickness of the border.
- **Align** – aligns the image to the left, right, middle, top, bottom.

For example:

```
<html>
 <body>
   <img src="flowers.jpg" height=300 width=400 border=3 align=right alt="Sorry!
Image cannot be displayed">
</body>
</html>
```

2. Using the <picture> tag

This tag is new in HTML5 and gives more flexibility in specifying picture resources. It is used to display the same or different images for different screen sizes.

The <source> tag is used as a child element (e.g. an element that is found nested within another 'parent' element) with in the <picture> tag to specify different versions of an image source for different viewports. If the screen size displayed in a browser is not within the given options specified with the <source> tag then the image given with the <img> tag, as the child element of the <picture> tag, will be displayed.

113

For example:

```
<html>
 <body>
<picture>
    <source media="(min-width:500px) and (max-width:700px)" src="flower1.
    jpg">
    <source media="(min-width:701px) and (max-width:1000px)" src="flower22.
    jpg">
    <img src="flower3.jpg" height=200 width=300>
  </picture>
  </body>
</html>
```

The example given above will display the image depending on the screen size. If the screen size is between 500px and 700px, then the image of flower1 will be displayed. If the screen size is between 701px and 1000px, then the image of flower2 will be displayed. If the screen size is not any of the above two, then the flower3 image will be displayed.

QUICK KEY

Ctrl + Scroll Up/Scroll Down	Adjusts the screen size to see the difference in the image displayed.

TRY THIS

<a href="file2.html><img src="picture.jpg" height=30% width=40% border=3></a>. This code will create an image as a hyperlink. When we click on the image, file2 will open.

Inserting audio and video files

In earlier versions of HTML, audio and video files were supported by the browser only through plugins. This problem is solved in HTML5 by using the inline tags <audio> and <video>.

The **<audio>** tag is used to add audio files in a webpage. The three different audio files supported by the browsers Chrome, Firefox and Opera are MP3, WAV, and OGG.

Some of the attributes of the <audio> tag are:

- **Control** – displays the audio control buttons – play, pause, volume on the webpage.
- **Loop** – keeps on playing the audio file in a loop.
- **Autoplay** – automatically plays the audio file added with the <source> tag.
- **Muted** – mutes the audio file played with the <source> tag.

The **<source> tag** with **src** attribute specifies the URL source of the audio file which will be played on the web page.

For example:

```
<!DOCTYPE html>
<html>
 <body>
    <h4> This is a demo to show audio support in HTML5</h4>
    <audio controls>
   <source src="audiofile1.ogg" type="audio/ogg">
      If audio controls not visible. No worries. Some browsers do not support audio
      files.
    </audio>
 </body>
</html>
```

The output of the above code will be:

This is a demo to show audio support in HTML5

The **<video> tag** is used to insert video files in a HTML5 webpage. The three different video files supported by the browsers Chrome, Firefox and Opera are MP4, WEBM and OGG.

Some of the attributes of the <video> tag are:

- **Control** – displays the video control buttons – play, pause, volume on the webpage.
- **Autoplay** – automatically plays the video file added with the <source> tag.
- **Muted** – mutes the audio in the video file played with the <source> tag.
- **Height** – sets the height (pixels) of the video on the webpage.
- **Width** – sets the width (pixels) of the video on the webpage.
- **Loop** – keeps on playing the video file in a loop.
- **Poster** – loads the image to show before the video actually starts playing.

The **<source>** tag with src attribute specifies the URL source of the video file which will be played on the web page.

For example:

```
<!DOCTYPE html>
<html>
 <body>
   <h3> This is a video of Tiger</h3>
   <video height=400 width=500 controls poster>
      <source src="tigerjumping.webm" type="video/webm">
      <source src="tiger.mp4" type="video/mp4">
      Sorry! Your browser does not support video file format
   </video>
 </body>
</html>
```

FACT FILE

Multiple <source src="file"> can be included in <audio> and <video> tags to give multiple alternatives to the browser to run the audio or video file.

116

Create a webpage about a book you've recently read or any of your favourite books. Include images of the characters, favourite text from the book, etc. Record an audio reflection about the book using any audio recording software and insert that on the webpage using relevant HTML Tags. The webpage should be created with an aim to inspire your fellow classmates to read that book.

GLOSSARY

<audio> This tag is used to add audio files in a webpage.

Custom attributes These attributes are created by the user for a specific element.

<!doctype html> This tag tells the browser about the version of the HTML.

<meta charset="UTF-8"> This tag tells the browser about the type of character set used to convert bits to character.

Standard attributes These are also called global attributes, which are supported by almost all the elements in HTML.

Structural elements These are a group of elements which are used to create the structure of a HTML5 document.

<source> This tag with src attribute specifies the URL source of the audio file which will be played on the web page.

<video> This tag is used to insert video files in a HTML5 webpage.

YOU ARE HERE

6

1. HTML5 is the latest specification of HTML as a webpage language.
2. HTML5 is an independent markup Language and is no longer a part of SGML.
3. HTML5 is designed to have maximum backward compatibility with existing browsers.

4. Some of the tags and attributes used in the earlier versions of HTML can also be used in HTML5. For example, <body>, <title>, <table>, etc.
5. Default settings can be altered by using attributes with or without values.
6. Images in HTML5 can be inserted either by using either the <img> tag or the <picture> tag.
7. The three different audio files supported by the browsers Chrome, Firefox and Opera are MP3, WAV, and OGG.
8. The three different video files supported by the browsers Chrome, Firefox and Opera are MP4, WEBM and OGG.

EXERCISE

A. Write a one-line code to do the following.

1. Give the title of a webpage as "HTML5 – SUMMARY".
2. Use bgcolor to set the background color of the whole webpage.
3. Change the font color of a text to blue and font to "Old Bookman Style".
4. Set the audio file "guitar.mp3" to play automatically on the webpage.
5. Set the image "school.jpg" on the right side with border 5.

B. What happens when?

1. "Data" keyword in front of the custom attribute is not written.
2. HTML file saved with extension .txt is opened in any browser.
3. <font> tag is not closed after use.
4. <source> child element is not included in <picture> tag.
5. <!DOCTYPE html> is not written as the first line of a HTML5 document.

C. True or false?

1. HTML5 is not backwards compatible.

2. Attributes can be created with or without values.

3. We can write HTML code only in Notepad.

4. <audio> tag can work without controls attribute.

5. <img> cannot be used to insert animated images.

D. Answer the following questions.

1. Give three important points to remember for writing HTML5 code.

2. Give two different ways of inserting an image in HTML5. Give a short code to support your answer.

3. What are standard attributes? Name any three.

4. What is backward compatibility? Is HTML5 backward compatible?

5. What are structural elements? Name any three.

LAB WORK

A. Create a webpage on 'Digital Civility'. The webpage must have relevant text, graphics and other multimedia elements to make it impactful.

B. Create a webpage on 'My Favourite Pastime'.

Use all the tags you have learnt so far to create the above two webpages.

PROJECT WORK

Create a four-page website on 'Artificial Intelligence'. The pages should be linked with each other and the website should be easily navigable. Use different HTML tags learnt so far to make the website resourceful and attractive.

Introduction to Python

SNAP RECAP

1. What do you understand by programming?
2. Why do you need programming languages?

LEARNING OBJECTIVES

You will learn about:

- features of Python
- writing and executing commands in Python
- how to exit the Python Shell
- operators in Python
- variables in Python
- using the input() function for user input
- conditional constructs.

Introduction

Python is a high-level programming language which is open source and object-oriented. Python was developed by Guido Van Rossum in 1991. It is currently owned by Python Software Foundation (PSF).

Python is an interactive language with simple syntax that allows developers to write robust programs easily and efficiently. Python is an interpreter-based scripting language which can be used:

- to create web-based applications
- to handle large amounts of data
- to perform complex calculations
- to connect to database systems and to read and modify files.

Features of Python

Some important features of Python are listed below:

- Python source code is freely available.
- It is a loosely typed object-oriented programming language with few keywords and simple English-like structure, and therefore easy to learn.
- It supports Graphical User Interface (GUI).

Writing and executing commands in Python

To write and run Python programs interactively, you can either use the command line window or the Python IDLE. IDLE is a simple Integrated Development Learning Environment that comes with Python. It allows you to edit, run, browse and debug a Python program from a single interface.

Python Shell

You can launch Python IDLE by downloading it and then clicking on its icon created on the desktop, or by clicking on the **START ⟹ IDLE (Python 3.7 32-bit)** option. It always starts up in the Python Shell.

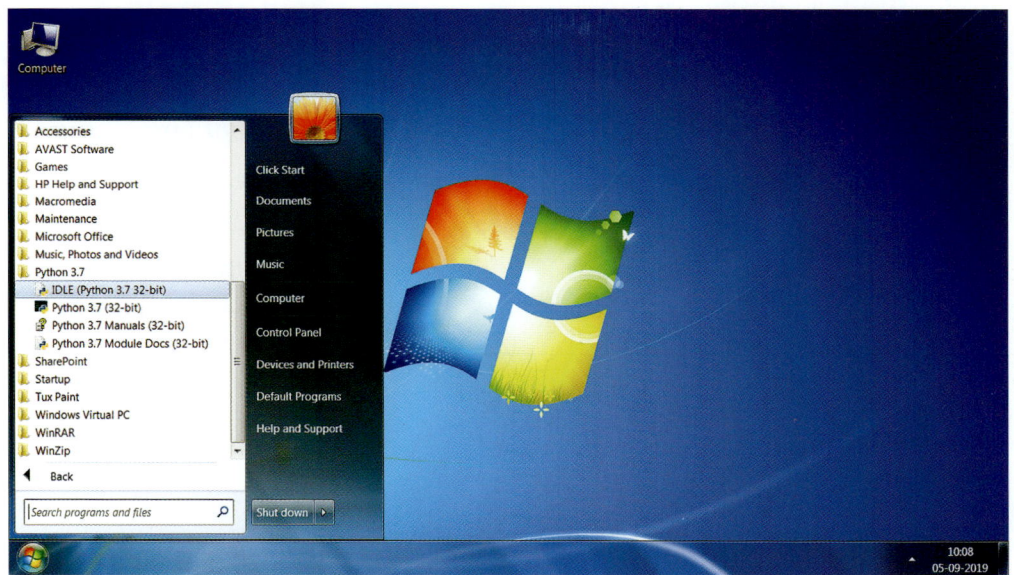

Launching Python using the Start menu

When commands are entered directly in IDLE from the keyboard, the interpreter/IDLE is said to be in **interactive mode**. In this mode, type the command "Hello" in front of the prompt (>>>) and press Enter. This will print 'Hello' on the desktop (see the next page).

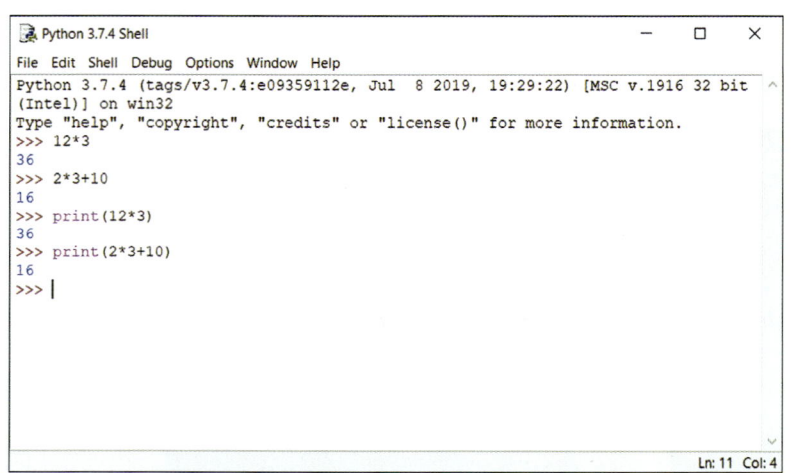

Writing commands in the Python Shell

Similarly, you can perform mathematical calculations by directly typing the commands. You can also use the print() function to evaluate these commands.

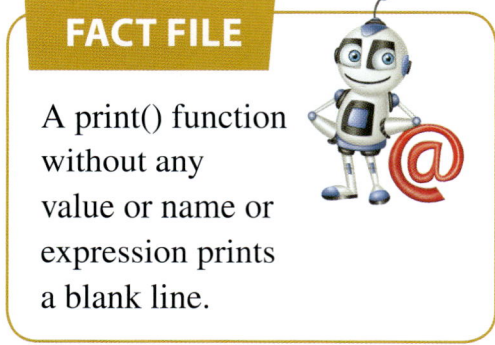

FACT FILE

A print() function without any value or name or expression prints a blank line.

Writing commands using print( ) in the Python Shell

Python IDLE

In Python IDLE you can get the same results as you get while using the Python Shell.

1. In the Python Shell, select **File ⟹ New File** to open the Python script editor.

2. Write the statements to be executed.

3. Save the file by selecting **File ⟹ Save/Save As** option.

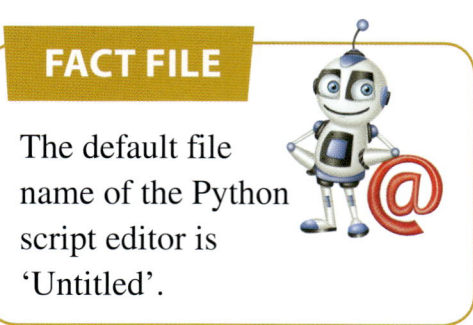

FACT FILE

The default file name of the Python script editor is 'Untitled'.

4. Execute the code by selecting **Run** $\Longrightarrow$ **Run Module** OR press **F5**.

5. The output will be visible in the previously opened Python Shell.

How to exit the Python Shell

To exit the Python Shell, simply type >>> quit() or >>> exit(). A dialog box will appear asking you "Your program is still running! Do you want to kill it?" Click on the **OK** button if you want to quit, otherwise click on **Cancel** button.

Select **File** → **Exit** option

Operators in Python

Operators are special symbols used in a programming language to operate on values and variables.

Python divides the operators into four categories.

Arithmetic operators

These are used with numeric values to perform common arithmetic calculations. Arithmetic operators with their syntax and examples are given in the table below.

Operator	Name	Syntax	Example
+	Addition	x+y	>>>5+4 9
–	Subtraction	x–y	>>>5–4 1
*	Multiplication	x*y	>>>3*6 18
/	Division	x/y	>>>8/2 4
%	Modulus	x%y	>>>5%2 1
**	Exponentiation	x**y	>>>5*3 125
//	Floor division	x//y	>>>15//4 3

Arithmetic operators in Python

Assignment operators

These operators are used to assign values to variables. Assignment operators with their syntax and examples are given in the table below.

Operator	Syntax	Description	Example
=	Num=5	Variable Num is assigned a value 5	>>>Num=5
+=	Num+=5 OR Num=Num+5	Increases the value of Num by 5	Num=17 >>>Num+=5 22
-=	Num−=5 OR Num=Num−5	Decreases the value of Num by 5	Num=20 >>>Num−=5 15
*=	Num*=5 OR Num=Num*5	Multiplies the value of Num by 5	Num=20 >>>Num*=5 100
/=	Num/=5 OR Num=Num/5	Divides the value of Num by 5	Num=100 >>>Num/=5 20
%=	Num%=5 OR Num=Num%5	Displays the remainder by dividing the value of Num by 5	Num=25 >>>Num%3 1
//=	Num//=5 OR Num=Num//5	Variable Num is assigned floor value of division of Num by 5	Num=35 >>>Num//3 11
**=	Num**=5 OR Num=Num**5	Num is assigned a value of last value of Num raised to the power of 5	Num=10 >>>Num**=2 100

Assignment operators in Python

Relational operators

These operators are used to compare two values and return a logical value which is either True or False. Relational operators with their syntax and examples are given in the table below.

124

Operator	Syntax	Description	Example
==	x==y	Equal to	x=16;y=20 >>>x==y False
!=	x!=y	Not equal to	x=15;y=25 >>x!=y True
>	x>y	Greater than	x=6;y=10 >>x>y False
<	x<y	Less than	x=10;y=15 >>>x<y True
>=	x>=y	Greater than or equal to	x=13;y=14 >>>x>=y False
<=	x<=y	Less than or equal to	x=16;y=15 >>>x<=y False

Relational operators in Python

Logical operators

These operators are used to combine conditional statements and return a result as either True or False. Logical operators with their syntax and examples are given in the table below.

Operator	Syntax	Description	Example
and	x>5 and x<=10	Returns True if both the conditions are True	>>>print("10<25 and 5>6:", 10<25 and 5>6) False
or	Alpha="A" or Alpha="a"	Returns True if any one of the conditions is True	>>>print("10<25 or 5>6:", 10<25 or 5>6) True
not	not (Num % 10 == 0)	Reverses the result, returns False if the result is True	>>>print("not 35<60", not 35<60) False

Logical operators in Python

Variables in Python

Variables are named memory locations whose value may change during the execution of the program. Some rules for naming variables in Python are given below.

- A variable name can consist of letters, digits and underscore (_).

- A variable name can start with a letter or an underscore (_) but not with a digit.

- A variable name cannot have space in it.

- Keywords are not allowed as a variable name.

- Python is a case-sensitive language, so variables in upper case are different to those in lower case.

FACT FILE

Keywords are reserved words in Python. Some examples of Python keywords are print, and, not.

Declaring variables

Every variable has a type and this type defines the format and behaviour of the variable.

For example, if we write x=3

It means value 3 will be assigned to the integer variable x automatically.

FACT FILE

An integer in Python can be of any length.

Similarly, if we write x=15 (>>>x=15) and then write >>>x and press the Enter key, value 15 will be displayed as output in the Python Shell.

Assigning multiple values to multiple variables

Multiple variables can be assigned values using a single Python assignment statement as in the following example:

x, y, z = 15, 18.5, "Hello"

The above code assigns value 15 to variable x, 18.5 to y and "Hello" to z.

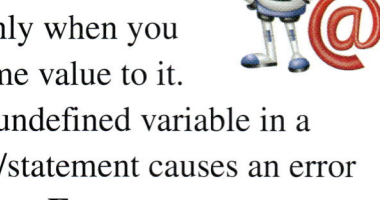

FACT FILE

A variable is said to be defined only when you assign some value to it.
Using an undefined variable in a command/statement causes an error called **Name Error**.

Assigning the same value to multiple variables

Multiple variables can be assigned the same values using a single Python assignment statement as in the following example:

x = y = z = 25

The above code assigns the same value 25 to the three variables x, y, z.

Using input() function for user input

In a variable, value can be stored in two ways. It can either be declared in a variable within the program or can be accepted from the user. To fetch an input from the user, the **input()** function is used.

This function is used to get data from the user while working with the script mode. It enables us to accept an input string from the user without evaluating its value.

> **Syntax**
>
> input(<Prompt>)

The input() function in Python works as explained below:

- When the input() function is executed, the program flow stops until the user submits an input value.

- The prompt is displayed on the output screen to ask a user to enter an input value. However, this prompt is optional.

- Whatever value is entered by the user as an input, the input() function converts it into a string. If any numeric value is entered, the input() function converts it into a string. To treat the users input as a numeric value, an explicit conversion is needed, either into an integer or float.

```
Num1=int(input("Enter first number"))
Num2=int(input("Enter second number"))
Sum=Num1+Num2
print("The sum of two numbers is", Sum)
```

```
Python 3.7.4 (tags/v3.7.4:e09359112e, Jul  8 2019, 19:29:22
) [MSC v.1916 32 bit (Intel)] on win32
Type "help", "copyright", "credits" or "license()" for more
information.
>>>
============================ RESTART: Z:/s.py ===========
====================
Enter first number5
Enter second number8
The sum of two numbers is 13
>>>
```

Using input() to accept user input in Python

For example, consider the sample code given on the right.

In the example on the previous page, when the user enters a number, if that needs to be treated as a number, then an int() function is used to convert the string into a number. But if we do not use the int() function, the + operator will concatenate (join) the two strings as shown below.

```
s.py - Z:/s.py (3.7.4)                                  —   □   ×
File  Edit  Format  Run  Options  Window  Help
First=input("Enter the first name")
Last=input("Enter the second name")
FullName=First+Last
print("The full name is", FullName)

                                              Ln: 4  Col: 34
```

```
Python 3.7.4 Shell                                      —   □   ×
File  Edit  Shell  Debug  Options  Window  Help
Python 3.7.4 (tags/v3.7.4:e09359112e, Jul  8 2019, 19:29:22) [MS
C v.1916 32 bit (Intel)] on win32
Type "help", "copyright", "credits" or "license()" for more info
rmation.
>>>
============================ RESTART: Z:/s.py =================
==============
Enter the first nameRay
Enter the second nameJohnson
The full name is RayJohnson
>>> |

                                               Ln: 8  Col: 4
```

Using + operator to concatenate two strings

Conditional constructs

The order of execution of the statements in a program is known as the **flow of control**. By default, the flow of control is sequential which means the statements written first are executed first in the sequence. However, to change the flow of control based on a condition, conditional statements are used.

There are three types of conditional statements in Python.

if statement	if - else statement	if - elif ladder

If statement

The if statement checks if the condition given after if is true, then the statement(s) following the if condition is/are executed. If the condition is false, then the flow of control is transferred to the next un-indented statement(s).

> **Syntax**
>
> if <condition>:
>
>   statement(s)

Some rules need to be followed while using the if condition in the program. They are:

- an if statement must end with a colon (:)
- statements within the 'if' that need to be executed if the condition is true should be indented, otherwise the control skips the block of statements inside it
- the if condition can also be written in parenthesis () but it is not mandatory
- there is no limit to the number of statements that can appear under an if block.

Program 1: Consider the program given below. This program takes age as an input. If the age entered is greater than or equal to 18, the output will be "Eligible for voting", otherwise the program will terminate.

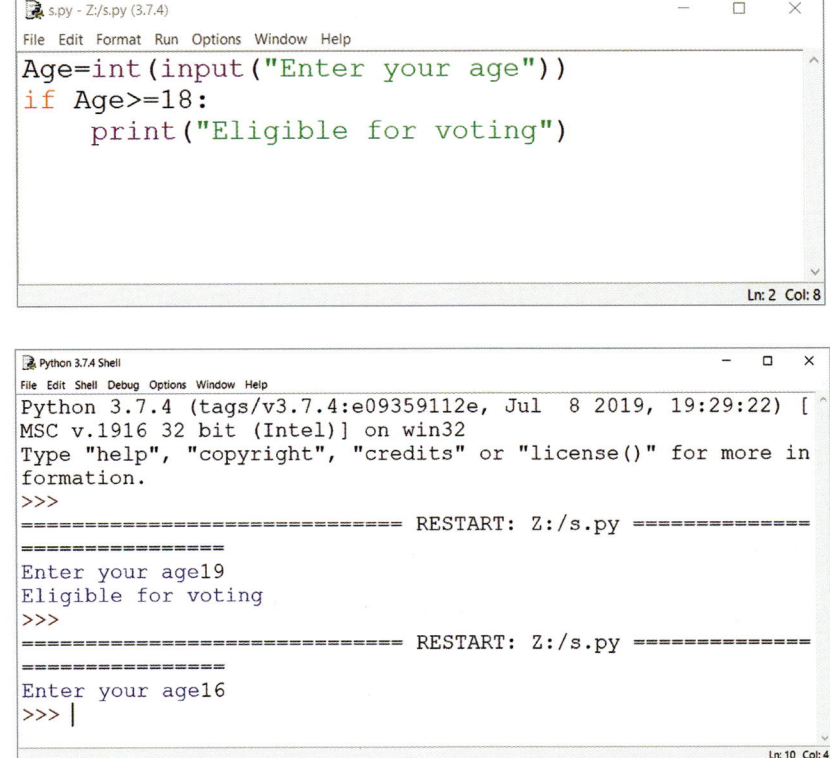

Using an if statement

If-else statement

In the code given in the code shown on the previous page, the statements after if will not be executed unless the condition given is true. So in such cases we can use *else* statement with *if* statement to execute a block of code when the condition is false.

> **Syntax**
>
> if <condition>:
>
>   statement(s)
>
> else:
>
>   statement(s)

Program 2: Consider the program given below. This program is the modified version of Program 1. Here, if the age entered is greater than or equal to 18, the output will be "Eligible for voting", otherwise the output will be "Not eligible for voting". In the end it will display "Program over".

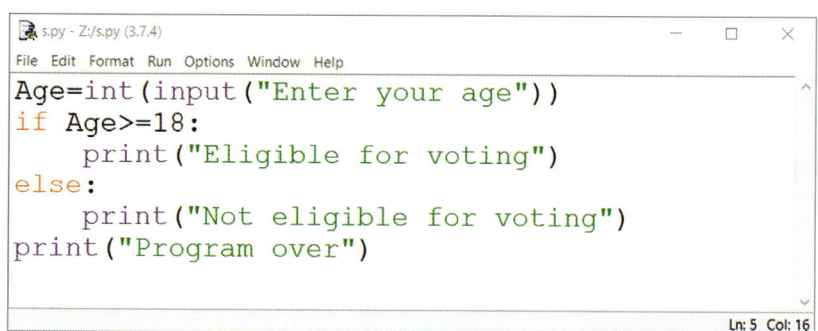

Using an if-else statement

If-elif-else statement

This construct is used in situations where a user can decide among multiple conditions. As soon as one of the conditions controlling the '*if*' is true, then the statement(s) associated with that '*if*' are executed, and the rest of the ladder is bypassed. If none of the conditions is true, then the final '*else*' statement will be executed.

Syntax

if <condition>:

        statement(s)

elif <condition>:

        statement(s)

elif <condition>:

        statement(s)

else:

        statement(s)

Program 3: Accept marks in 5 subjects from the user, calculate the percentage and display the grades based on the following criteria.

Percentage	Grade
>85	A
>70 and <=80	B
>60 but <=70	C
>45 but <=60	D
<=45	E

```
Eng=int(input("Enter marks of English:"))
Mat=int(input("Enter marks of Maths:"))
Sci=int(input("Enter marks of Science:"))
Com=int(input("Enter marks of Computer:"))
Hin=int(input("Enter marks of Hindi:"))
Per=(Eng+Mat+Sci+Com+Hin)/5
if Per>85:
    print("Grade A")
elif Per>70 and Per<=80:
    print("Grade B")
elif Per>60 and Per<=70:
    print("Grade C")
elif Per>45 and Per<=60:
    print("Grade D")
else:
    print("Grade E")
```

```
Python 3.7.4 (tags/v3.7.4:e09359112e, Jul  8 2019, 19:29:22)
[MSC v.1916 32 bit (Intel)] on win32
Type "help", "copyright", "credits" or "license()" for more
information.
>>>
========================= RESTART: Z:/s.py =============
====================
Enter marks of English:90
Enter marks of Maths:88
Enter marks of Science:78
Enter marks of Computer:92
Enter marks of Hindi:85
Grade A
>>>
```

Using the if-elif-else statement

131

Find the output of the following programs.

A. p=10

   q=20

   p*=q//3

   q+=p+q**2

   print(p,q)

B. Name="Vikas"

   Age=21

   print(Name,"you are ",21, "now but")

   print("you will be", Age+1,"next year")

C. X=10

   X=X+10

   X=X–5

   print(X)

   Y = 20

   X,Y=Y–2,22

   print(X,Y)

QUICK KEY

To exit the Python command prompt	**Ctrl + Q** **OR** **Type quit() or exit() and press Enter key**

GLOSSARY

Arithmetic operators   These operators are used with numeric values to perform common arithmetic calculations.

Assignment operators   These operators are used to assign values to variables.

Conditional statements   These are used to change the flow of control based on a condition.

Flow of control   Shows the order of execution of the statements in a program.

IDLE   A simple Integrated Development Learning Environment that comes with Python.

input()   This function is used to fetch an input from the user.

Logical operators   These operators are used to combine conditional statements and return a result as either True or False.

Relational operators   These operators are used to compare two values and return a logical value which is either True or False.

Variables   These are named memory locations whose value may change during the execution of the program.

YOU ARE HERE

7

1. Python is a high-level programming language which is also open source and object-oriented.
2. To exit the Python Shell, simply type >>>quit() or select **File → Exit** option.
3. Every variable has a type and this type defines the format and behaviour of the variable.
4. Multiple variables can be assigned values using a single Python assignment statement.
5. In a variable, value can be stored in two ways. It can either be declared in a variable within the program or can be accepted from the user.
6. There are three types of conditional statements in Python: if statement, if-else statement and if-elif-else ladder.

EXERCISE

A.   Fill in the blanks.

1. .... construct is used in situations where a user can decide among multiple conditions.

2. An "if" statement must end with a ....

3. The statement X+=1 is equivalent to ....

4. The statement 5%2 will evaluate to .... and 5/2 will evaluate to ....

5. .... is used to exit the Python Shell.

B. **Spot and correct the errors in the following programs.**

1. Value=40

   If Value>=25

   print("Smaller Value)

   print "Program Over"

2. A=10,B=20

   if (15==A)

   print("A=";A,"B=";B)

3. input('Entera number',A)

   Print ('The number is ' A)

4. Num1=input()

   Num2=int(input())

   print(Num1+Num2)

C. **Write a program in Python to execute the following instructions.**

1. Accept the length and the breadth of a rectangle from the user and calculate its area and perimeter.

2. Accept three numbers from the user and display the largest number.

3. Accept a number from the user and check if it is an odd or even number.

D. **Answer the following questions.**

1. Give any two features of the Python language.

2. Explain the difference between = and ==. Explain with the help of an example.

3. What are relational operators? Give examples.

4. Identify which of the following are valid or invalid variable names. Give reasons for any invalid names.

   a. Num%　　b. First Name　　c. Value1　　d. Int　　e. Stock

5. How do you accept data in a variable from the user? Give the syntax of the command along with an example.

LAB WORK

A. Accept a number from the user and display if it is a positive or a negative number.

B. Accept the year of birth from the user and check if it is a leap year or not.

PROJECT WORK

Write a Python program to accept two numbers and an operator from the user. The user must be given a menu of operators to choose from:

1. Addition (+)   2. Subtraction (–)   3. Multiplication (*)   4. Division (/)

5. Remainder (%)   6. Power (**)   7. Exit

Accept the user's choice. Depending upon the menu option selected, perform the required mathematical function on the two numbers accepted.

WHO AM I?

I was born on 31 January 1956 in the Netherlands.

I am known as the author of Python programming.

I have received an award for the Advancement of Free Software in 2001.

I was made a fellow of the Computer History Museum in 2018.

I am …………..

More About Python

Loops in Python

Sometimes there may be a need to repeat a set of statements more than once based on a certain condition. This process of repetition is called a **loop** or **iteration** in programming.

A loop is used to repeat a block of statements a specific number of times. The following loops are available in Python:

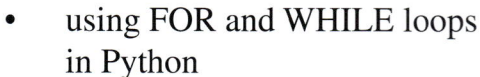

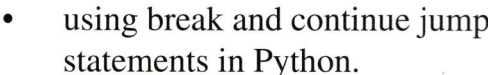

FOR... loop   WHILE... loop

FOR loop

The FOR… structure is used to repeat a loop a specific number of times. It uses a counter variable which is incremented (increased by a discrete value) or decremented (decreased by a discrete value) with each repetition of the loop.

FOR loop syntax 1

for counter_variable in(<collection>):
    statement(s)

Here,

- The counter_variable is assigned the first value in the sequence for the statement at the beginning of the loop.
- The range() function is used to create a list containing a sequence of numbers starting from **start** and ending with one less than the **stop**.

$$range([start], stop,[step])$$

The start and step parameters are optional. By default, the list starts from 0 and in every iteration, it is incremented by one, but we can specify a different increment by using the **step** parameter.

For example, different commands for range and their corresponding outputs are given in the table below.

Command	Output
>>>range(10)	[0,1,2,3,4,5,6,7,8,9]
>>>range(1,11)	[1,2,3,4,5,6,7,8,9,10]
>>>range(0,30,5)	[0,5,10,15,20,25]
>>>range(0,–9,–1)	[0,–1,–2,–3,–4,–5,–6,–7,–8]

Commands for range and their output

Program 1: Write a program using the FOR loop to print the first ten natural numbers.

```
for i in range(1,11):
    print (i)
```

```
1
2
3
4
5
6
7
8
9
10
>>>
```

Program 2: Write a program using the FOR loop to print the first ten multiples of 2.

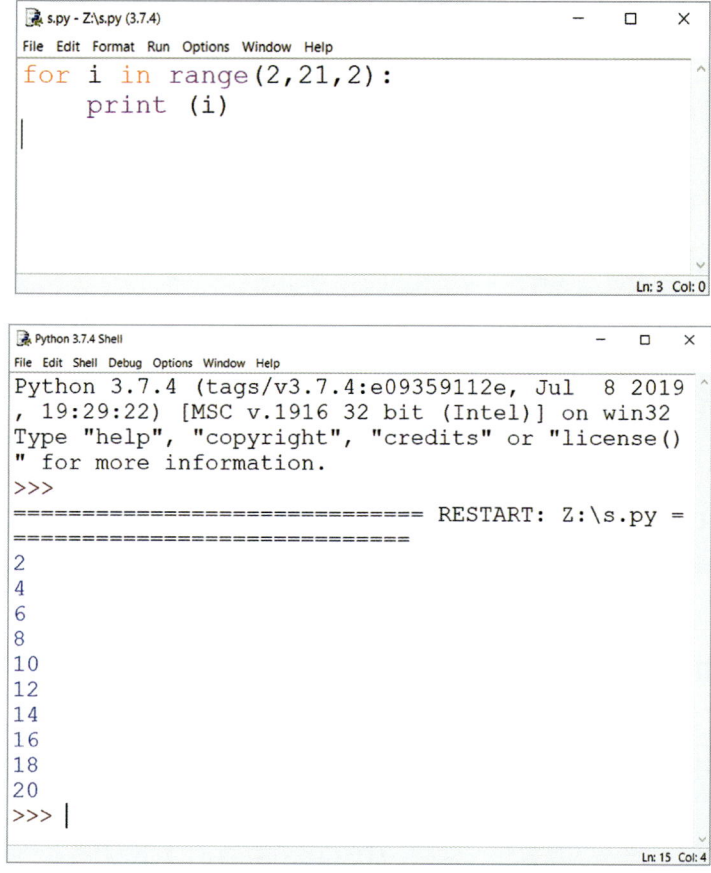

Program 3: Write a program using the FOR loop to print the first ten natural numbers in reverse order.

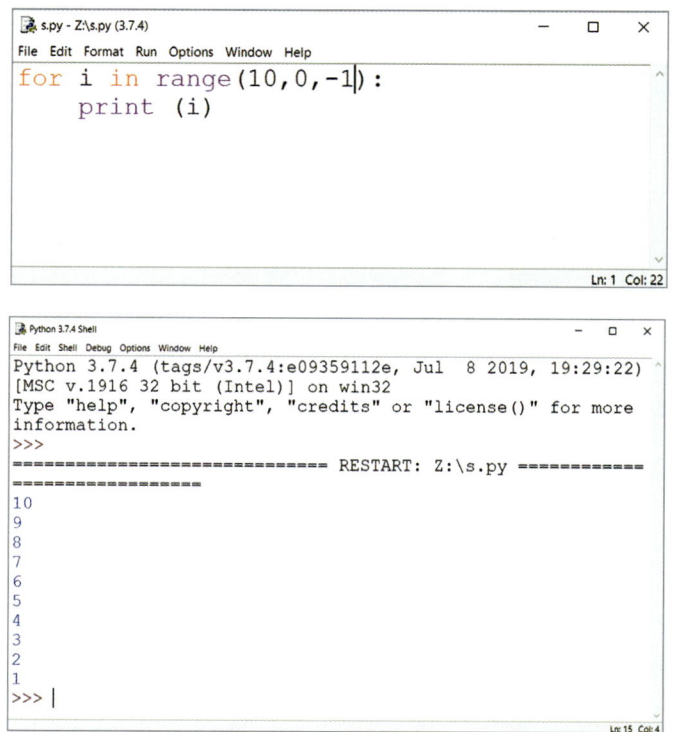

Program 4: Write a program using the FOR loop to print the multiplication table of a number N.

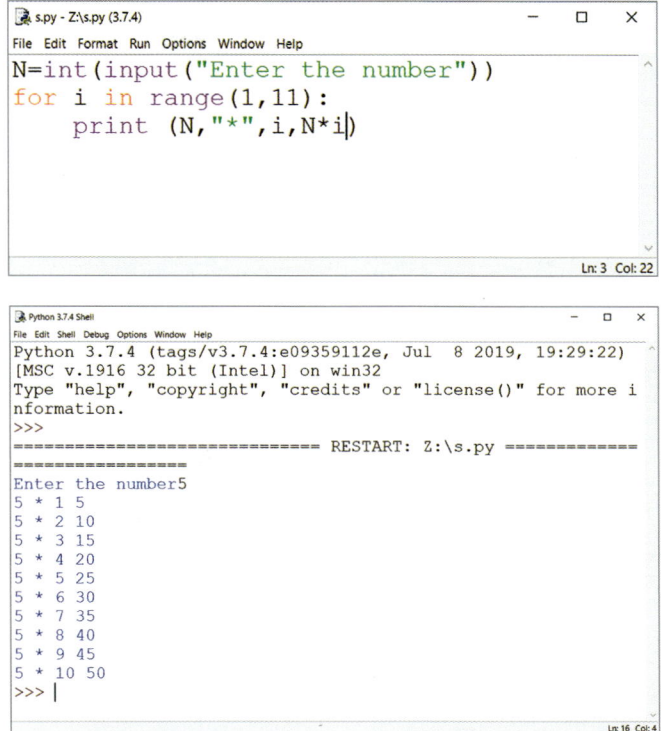

In the above example, the value of the variable N is accepted from the user. The sample program is executed for the input value N=5.

Program 5: Write a program using the FOR loop to print X raised to the power of Y.

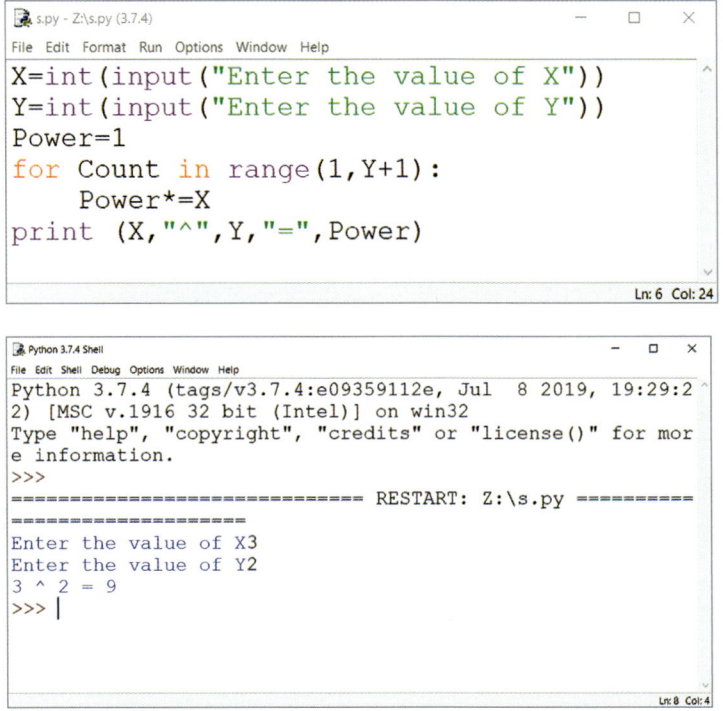

Program 6: Write a program using the FOR loop to accept ten numbers from the user and display their sum.

```python
Sum=0
for i in range(1,11):
    N=int(input("Enter a number:"))
    Sum+=N
print("The sum of 10 numbers is:",Sum)
```

```
Python 3.7.4 (tags/v3.7.4:e09359112e, Jul  8 2019, 19:29:22)
[MSC v.1916 32 bit (Intel)] on win32
Type "help", "copyright", "credits" or "license()" for more
information.
>>>
============================= RESTART: Z:\s.py =============
====================
Enter a number:1
Enter a number:2
Enter a number:3
Enter a number:4
Enter a number:5
Enter a number:6
Enter a number:7
Enter a number:8
Enter a number:9
Enter a number:10
The sum of 10 numbers is: 55
>>>
```

Program 7: Write a program using the FOR loop to display factors of number N.

```python
N=int(input("N="))
Fact=1
for Count in range(1,N+1):
    Fact*=Count
print(N,'!=',Fact)
```

```
Python 3.7.4 (tags/v3.7.4:e09359112e, Jul  8 2019, 19:29:22
) [MSC v.1916 32 bit (Intel)] on win32
Type "help", "copyright", "credits" or "license()" for more
information.
>>>
============================= RESTART: Z:\s.py ===========
====================
N=5
5 != 120
>>>
```

FOR loop syntax 2

for <Counter_Variable> in <Collection>:

<statement(s)>

else:

<statement(s)>

Here,

- Collection may be a list, a string or a tuple (you won't learn about tuples in this book).
- The 'else' statement will be executed only when the FOR loop completes all its iteration. If the **FOR** loop terminates in between, the else statement will not execute.
- Counter_Variable is a variable that takes a new value from the range each time a loop is executed.

Program 8: Write a program using the FOR loop with strings.

```
s.py - Z:\s.py (3.7.4)
File  Edit  Format  Run  Options  Window  Help
for Counter in ("Python"):
    print(Counter)

Ln: 3  Col: 0
```

```
Python 3.7.4 Shell
File  Edit  Shell  Debug  Options  Window  Help
Python 3.7.4 (tags/v3.7.4:e09359112e, Jul  8 2019, 19:29:2
2) [MSC v.1916 32 bit (Intel)] on win32
Type "help", "copyright", "credits" or "license()" for mor
e information.
>>>
============================== RESTART: Z:\s.py ==========
====================
P
y
t
h
o
n
>>>
Ln: 9  Col: 1
```

Program 9: Write a program using the FOR loop with **else** to print multiples of 2.

```python
for Count in range(2,20,2):
    print(Count,end=",")
else:
    print("All Done!")
```

```
Python 3.7.4 (tags/v3.7.4:e09359112e, Jul  8 2019, 19:2
9:22) [MSC v.1916 32 bit (Intel)] on win32
Type "help", "copyright", "credits" or "license()" for
more information.
>>>
============================= RESTART: D:/s.py =======
========================
2,4,6,8,10,12,14,16,18,All Done!
>>>
```

WHILE loop

A WHILE loop executes a block of code repeatedly as long as the test/control condition of the loop is true. It is useful when the number of iterations are not known prior to the execution of the loop.

> **WHILE loop syntax 1**
>
> while <condition>:
>
>   statement(s)

Here,

- 'while' is a reserved word (remember, a reserved word means a word with a predefined meaning and syntax in Python – you can't use 'while' as an identifier for variables and functions etc.).

- Condition is checked for true or false; the statements are executed only if the condition is true.

- At least one statement must be in the body of the loop.

Program 10: Write a program using the WHILE loop to print the first five natural numbers.

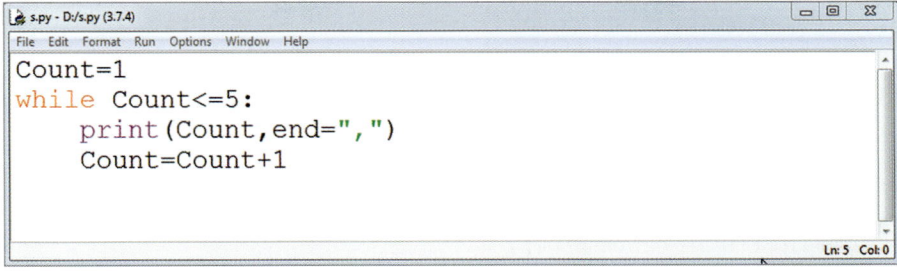

Program 11: Write a program using the WHILE loop to display the digits of a number in reverse order.

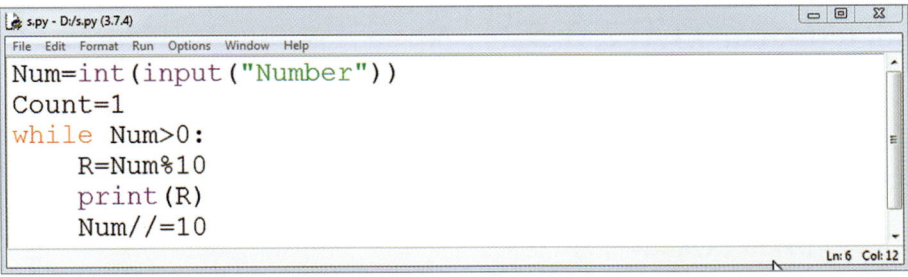

To display the last digit of any number, display the remainder after dividing the number by 10. The number can be then reduced by dividing the number by 10 and storing the integer part only.

Program 12: Write a program using the WHILE loop to display the factors of a number.

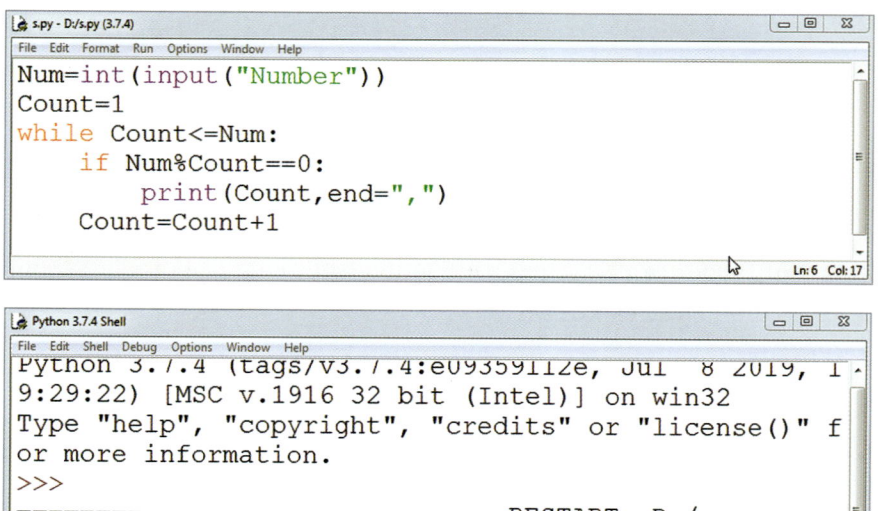

```
Num=int(input("Number"))
Count=1
while Count<=Num:
    if Num%Count==0:
        print(Count,end=",")
    Count=Count+1
```

```
Python 3.7.4 (tags/v3.7.4:e09359112e, Jul  8 2019, 1
9:29:22) [MSC v.1916 32 bit (Intel)] on win32
Type "help", "copyright", "credits" or "license()" f
or more information.
>>>
============================== RESTART: D:/s.py ====
==========================
Number16
1,2,4,8,16,
>>>
```

Program 13: Write a program using the WHILE loop to display the Fibonacci series to the Nth term, i.e. 0,1,1, 2, 3, 5, …, N.

```
Num=int(input("Number"))
A=0;B=1
Count=1
while Count<=Num:
    print(A,end=",")
    A,B=B,A+B
    Count=Count+1
```

```
Python 3.7.4 (tags/v3.7.4:e09359112e, Jul  8 2019, 1
9:29:22) [MSC v.1916 32 bit (Intel)] on win32
Type "help", "copyright", "credits" or "license()" f
or more information.
>>>
============================== RESTART: D:/s.py ====
==========================
Number7
0,1,1,2,3,5,8,
>>>
```

WHILE loop syntax 2

```
while <condition>:
        statement(s)
else:
        statement(s)
```

Here,

The else part of the WHILE loop is executed only when the WHILE loop completes all its iterations. If the WHILE loop terminates in between, the **else** part is not executed.

Program 14: Write a program using the WHILE loop with **else** to check if a number is a prime number.

```
Num=int(input("Number="))
I=2
while I<Num:
    if Num%I==0:
        print(Num,"is not a prime number")
        break
    I+=1
else:
        print(Num,"is a prime number")
```

```
Python 3.7.4 (tags/v3.7.4:e09359112e, Jul  8 2019, 19:29
:22) [MSC v.1916 32 bit (Intel)] on win32
Type "help", "copyright", "credits" or "license()" for m
ore information.
>>>
============================ RESTART: D:/s.py ========
=====================
Number=11
11 is a prime number
>>>
============================ RESTART: D:/s.py ========
=====================
Number=9
9 is not a prime number
>>>
```

Jump statements in Python

Python offers two 'jump' statements to be used within loops to jump out of loop iterations. These are 'break' and 'continue' statements. They are used to alter the flow of control in a loop.

The break statement

The break statement enables a program to skip over a part of the code. This statement terminates the current loop and resumes execution at the statement immediately after the body of the loop.

Program 15: Write a program to implement the WHILE loop with **break**.

```
i=1
while i<=5:
    print(i)
    if i==3:
        break
    i=i+1
print('The end')
```

```
Python 3.7.4 (tags/v3.7.4:e09359112e, Jul  8 2019, 19:
29:22) [MSC v.1916 32 bit (Intel)] on win32
Type "help", "copyright", "credits" or "license()" for
more information.
>>>
============================= RESTART: D:/s.py ======
==========================
1
2
3
The end
>>>
```

```
while <test_condition> :
        statement 1
        if <condition> :
            break
Loop    statement 2
Terminates statement 3
statement 4
statement 5
```

```
for <var> in <sequence> :
        statement 1
        if <condition> :
            break
        statement 2    Loop
        statement 3    Terminates
statement 4
statement 5
```

The continue statement

The continue statement skips the rest of the loop statements and executes the next iteration of the loop. This statement executes the next iteration by updating the loop variable with the next value in the sequence.

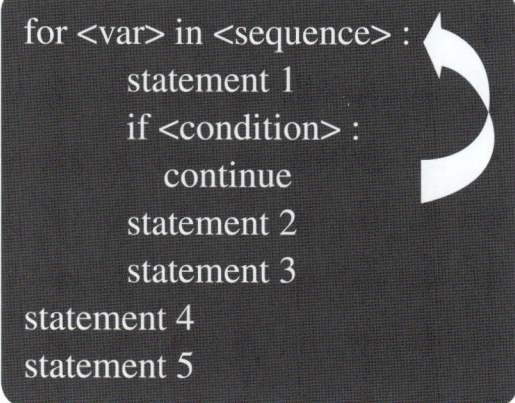

Continue would skip statement 2 and statement 3, and would cause the next iteration to start.

Program 16: Write a program to implement the WHILE loop with **continue**.

```
i=1
while i<5:
    i+=1
    if i==3:
        continue
    print(i)
print('The end')
```

```
Python 3.7.4 (tags/v3.7.4:e09359112e, Jul  8 2019, 19:29:22
) [MSC v.1916 32 bit (Intel)] on win32
Type "help", "copyright", "credits" or "license()" for more
information.
>>>
============================= RESTART: D:/s.py ============
====================
2
4
5
The end
>>>
```

TRY THIS

Write programs to implement the FOR loop with break and continue.

ACTIVITY

Spot and correct any errors in the following programs.

1. For x in range(1,11)

      Print x

   End

2. Num==1

   While

   Num<=5)

      print(Num*5)

      Num+1=Num

3. Num=int("Enter Num=")

      for I in range[0,11]

         if x=y

            print x+y

      else

            print x−y

GLOSSARY

break   This statement enables a program to skip over a part of the code.

continue   This statement skips the rest of the loop statements and executes the next iteration of the loop.

FOR loop   The loop that uses a counter variable which is incremented (increased by a discrete value) or decremented (decreased by a discrete value) with each repetition of the loop.

jump statement   This statement alters the flow of control in a loop.

loop   Repeats a block of statements a specific number of times.

WHILE loop   The loop that executes a block of code repeatedly as long as the test/control condition of the loop is true.

1. Two types of loops used in Python are: FOR loop and WHILE loop.

2. The WHILE loop is helpful when the number of iterations are not known prior to the execution of the loop.

3. Python offers two jump statements to be used within loops to jump out of loop iterations. These are break and continue statements.

4. The break statement terminates the current loop and resumes execution at the statement immediately after the body of the loop.

5. The continue statement executes the next iteration by updating the loop variable with the next value in sequence.

EXERCISE

A. Fill in the blanks.

1. The .... statement skips the rest of the loop statements and causes the next iteration of the loop to take place.

2. The .... statement enables a program to skip over a part of the code.

3. The .... part of the while loop is executed only when the while loop completes all its iterations.

4. Condition is checked for True or False, and the statements are executed only if the condition is ....

5. The .... loop is helpful when the number of iterations are not known prior to the execution of the loop.

B. Convert the following loops as directed.

1. while => for

```
x=5
while(x<10):
        print(x+10)
        x+=2
```

2. for => while

```
for x in range(5,20,5):
        print(x)
```

C. Give the output for the following codes.

1.
```
Num=0
while (Num<10):
    Num+=1
    if Num==5:
        break
    print(Num,end=",")
```

2.
```
for val in "String":
    if val=="I":
        break
    print(val)
print("Over")
```

D. Write Python programs for the following.

1. Write a program to accept a number from the user and display if it is a palindrome or not. [**Hint**: A palindrome number is where the reverse of the number is the same as the number itself.]

Input	Output
Num=1221	Palindrome Number
Num=231	Not a Palindrome Number

2. Write a program to accept a number and find out whether it is a perfect number or not. [**Hint**: A perfect number is a positive integer that is equal to the sum of its proper divisors. The smallest perfect number is 6.]

3. Write a program to accept a number from the user and check if it ends with 4 or 8. If it ends with 4, print **"Ends with 4"**, if it ends with 8, print **"Ends with 8"**, otherwise print **"Ends with neither"**.

4. Write a program to calculate and print the sum of even and odd integers of the first N natural numbers.

E. Answer the following questions.

1. What is the significance of using iterations in Python?
2. Explain the range() function with the help of an example.
3. Explain the difference between FOR and WHILE loops.
4. What are jump statements?

LAB WORK

Write a program to print the sum of the following series:

1. 2+4+6+....Nth term
2. 10,20,30,...Nth term
3. $X+X^2+X^3+X^4+.....$Nth term
4. 1!+2 !+3!+....Nth term
5. $X+X^{2/2}!+X^{3/3}!+....$Nth term

PROJECT WORK

A. Write a Python program to create a histogram from a given list of integers.

B. Write a Python program to print all even numbers from a given numbers list in the same order and stop the printing if any number comes after 237 in the sequence.

Sample numbers list:

numbers = [386, 462, 47, 418, 907, 344, 236, 375, 823, 566, 597, 978, 328, 615, 953, 345, 399, 162, 758, 219, 918, 237, 412, 566, 826, 248, 866, 950, 626, 949, 687, 217, 815, 67, 104, 58, 512, 24, 892, 894, 767, 553, 81, 379, 843, 831, 445, 742, 717, 958, 743, 527]

Introduction to Artificial Intelligence

9

LEARNING OBJECTIVES

You will learn about:

- the definition of artificial intelligence
- goals of AI
- application areas of AI
- domains of AI
- tools used for AI
- problem solving by AI
- limitations of AI.

Introduction

Artificial Intelligence (AI) has become important across applications in our personal computing lives. The question 'Can a machine think and behave like humans do?' led to the concept of artificial intelligence. The development of AI started with the intention of creating human intelligence in machines.

Artificial intelligence is composed of two words, **artificial** and **intelligence**, where artificial defines '*man-made*,' and intelligence defines '*thinking power*'. Hence AI means '*man-made thinking power*'.

Interpretation of Artificial Intelligence

According to the creator of the term 'Artificial Intelligence', John McCarthy, it is 'the science and engineering of making intelligent machines, especially intelligent computer programs'.

AI is a form of intelligence, a type of technology and a field of study. AI theory and development of computer systems are able to perform tasks that normally require human intelligence. AI covers a broad range of domains and applications and is expected to impact every area of our lives.

AI can also be used to extend machine capabilities to accomplish tasks like perceiving, learning, thinking, decision-making and problem-solving. These are referred to as **cognitive tasks**.

Intelligence is the ability of a system to reason, learn from experience, solve complex problems, comprehend new ideas, use natural language fluently, adapt to new situations, and store and retrieve information.

Intelligence is composed of:

- Reasoning
- Learning
- Problem-solving
- Perception
- Linguistic intelligence

An **intelligent system** is a machine which can carry out one or more of the above tasks (e.g. reasoning, learning etc.) Some examples of intelligent systems are Siri on iPhone and Alexa by Amazon, which use combinations of the components of intelligence to give relevant answers.

Goals of AI

The main goal of an intelligent system is to enable the system to think and behave like humans do, in order to solve a problem. The purpose of AI is to:

1. Implement human intelligence in machines by creating systems that can think, act, learn and behave like humans.

2. Create expert systems that can behave intelligently, learn, explain, demonstrate and give suggestions to its users.

3. Enable a system to understand and process natural language.

4. Empower a system to perform intellectual tasks that a human can perform.

Applications of AI

AI is used in various fields such as:

- **Intelligent robots**: Robots are capable of performing all the tasks that a human can do. In addition, they are programmed to learn from their mistakes and adapt to changes.

- **Expert systems**: Applications which include machines and programs that provide explanation and advice to humans.

- **Gaming**: AI plays an important role in gaming, where machines can think of a large number of possible options based on the data acquired, such as chess, tic-tac-toe, etc.

- **Vision systems**: Using AI, systems can understand and comprehend the visual input on the computer.

- **Natural language processing**: AI has gained competency in natural languages spoken by humans.

- **Handwriting recognition**: AI-enabled software can read handwritten text on paper or screen. It can also convert it to editable text.

- **Speech recognition**: AI is also capable of handling speech-related data. It can comprehend commands in different accents. It can also handle background noise and voice modulation.

ACTIVITY

Imagine the world in 2030 and write to your future self. Mention things that you think you would probably be doing and experiencing in daily life using what you have learned so far about AI.

Domains of AI

AI can be used for different purposes. There are three types of tasks that we use AI to carry out:

1. **Mundane tasks**: These are tasks that humans do on a routine basis without any special training. Common sense, planning and reasoning are common characteristics of this task.

2. **Formal tasks**: These are tasks that require formal training like verifications and theorems. For example, games like chess requires logic based on theorems.

3. **Expert tasks**: These require educational qualifications such as engineering to make functional expert systems needed for manufacturing planning, medical diagnosis, etc.

AI tools

The following tools are used to develop artificial intelligence in computers.

Logic

Different forms of logic are used in AI research. Logic is used for concept representation and problem-solving. Logic programs are used by programmers to verify their correctness. Proportional Logic involves truth functions such as 'or' and 'not'. First Order Logic can express facts about objects, their properties and their relations with each other.

Search and optimisation

Problems in AI can be solved when we search through the best possible solutions. Simple **exhaustive** search methods are used for solving AI problems. To find solutions, many search techniques use **rules of thumb** to prioritise choices in favour of those that are more likely to reach the goal in the minimum number of steps, thus optimising the search techniques.

Classifiers and statistical learning methods

Classifiers are patterns or observations, where each observation belongs to a class (i.e. decision to be made). All the classes together form a dataset. When a new observation is received, it is based on previous observations in the dataset. Classifiers can be organised or trained in many ways using various statistical learning approaches.

Probabilistic methods for unrealistic reasoning

Problems in AI may involve working with assumed data and circumstances. AI researchers have devised a number of powerful tools to solve these problems using probability theory and economics. Precise mathematical tools have been developed that analyse how an agent can make choices and plan using various theories and techniques.

Artificial neural network

A neural network inspired by the human nervous system, that enables a machine to find patterns in the input which are complex for a human programmer to identify.

It resembles the human nervous system in the following ways:

- The human brain uses 86 billion nerve cells called neurons, which are connected through thousands of **axons**.
- The information is received in the form of **stimuli** through the sensory organs and accepted by dendrites. These stimuli create electric impulses, which travel through the neural system.

In the neural network, a neuron can forward the message to other neuron to take care of the issue.

Artificial neural methods follow the same concept, receiving the input of data, with a hidden layer which processes the information in a way which the output layer can use. The nodes (neurals) are connected through links and each link has a weight (like the weighted average). The data is processed using these weights and the output is passed on to other nodes. The output can be altered by changing the weight value. The artificial neural method enables a machine to find patterns in the input which are complex for a human programmer to identify.

Problem-solving by AI

We are surrounded by problems, big or small. We may become so used to a problem that it becomes a part of our life. Identifying such a problem and finding a way to solve it, is what problem-solving is about.

Problem-solving in games like **Sudoku** can be done by building an artificial intelligent system to solve the problem. To do so, we need to define the problem first and then generate the solution, keeping in mind the conditions.

The process of problem-solving consists of five steps:

1. **Defining the problem**: The problem must be defined explicitly and precisely. It should contain a number of possible situations to achieve an acceptable solution.

2. **Analysing the problem**: Problem analysis and its requirements must be done to have an impact on the resulting solution.

3. **Identification of solutions**: This step generates a number of solutions to the given problem falling in a particular range.

4. **Choosing a solution**: The best solution is chosen from the identified solutions to achieve the target.

5. **Implementing**: After choosing the best solution, you need to implement the chosen solution to solve the problem.

State space search

This is the process of considering states or successive configurations of an instance to find the **goal state** from the **current state**. The given problem is a set of states, where a state contains all of the information necessary to determine if it is a goal state. The effect of action determines states and moves from the start state to the goal state.

For example, if a delivery drone is to go from the warehouse address to the delivery address, it would use the state space search model to achieve this.

Games are an integral part of our culture. People across the world participate in different kinds of online games as a form of social interaction, competition and enjoyment. The basic principle of every game is rule-setting and following the rules.

Some games that use the AI concept are discussed below.

Rock-Paper-Scissors: A game based on data where the machine tries to predict the next move of the participant. The machine tries to win by learning from the participant's previous moves.

Mystery Animal: A game based on natural language processing where the participant has to guess the animal name by asking a maximum 20 questions to an AI system. The animal randomly gets selected for each game by using an AI system and the machine replies either Yes or No.

Emoji Scavenger Hunt: A game based on computer vision where the machine initiates the game by showing an emoji. The participant is expected to show a similar object in front of the camera while the machine keeps on guessing what is being shown to it.

Limitations of AI

Despite its advantages, every technology also has some limitations as well. The following limitations can be found when creating AI systems:

1. Developing AI enabled systems is very expensive.
2. Programming or training these systems can be very difficult.
3. There is a lack of feelings, emotions and creativity in these systems.
4. Dependency on machines increases as AI develops.

ACTIVITY

A. List the instances from your daily life where you may have experienced problems related to a topic of your choice. Go online and research around your chosen topic.

Theme ⟶ Topic ⟶ List of problems

After listing the problems determine the goals for solving these problems.

B. Write down three rules in the spaces below that you would set before playing any game.

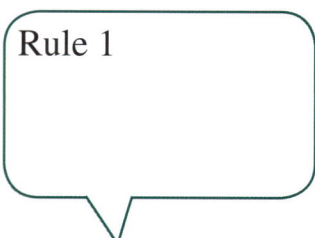
Rule 1

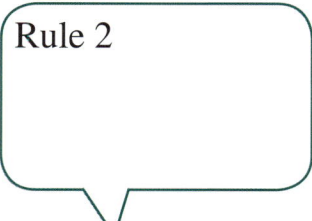
Rule 2

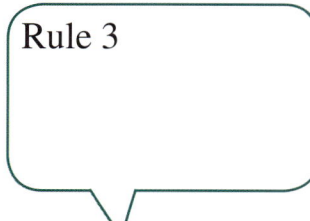
Rule 3

GLOSSARY

Artificial Intelligence   A form of intelligence; a type of technology and a field of study.

Expert systems   Applications which includes machines and programs that provide explanation and advice to humans.

State space search   The process of considering states or successive configurations of an instance to find the goal state from the current state.

1. AI theory and development of computer systems are able to perform tasks that normally require human intelligence.

2. AI can be used to extend machine capabilities to accomplish tasks like perceiving, learning, thinking, decision-making and problem-solving, referred to as cognitive tasks.

3. Intelligence is composed of reasoning, learning, problem-solving, perception and linguistic intelligence.

4. The main goal of an intelligent system is to enable a system to think and behave like humans in order to solve a problem.

5. Application areas of AI include intelligent robots, expert systems, gaming, vision systems, natural language processing, handwriting and speech recognition.

6. The tools used for AI are logic, search and optimisation, classifiers and statistical learning methods, probabilistic methods for unrealistic reasoning and artificial neural network.

7. The process of problem-solving consists of five steps: defining a problem, analysing the problem, identification of solutions, choosing a solution and implementing the chosen solution.

EXERCISE

A. Fill in the blanks with the correct word.

1. .... is the last step in problem-solving after choosing the best solution.

2. Tasks that humans do on a routine basis without any special training are called ....

3. In .... using AI, the systems can understand and comprehend the visual input on the computer.

4. .... is the science and engineering of making intelligent machines, especially intelligent computer programs.

5. In .... AI is capable of handling speech-related data.

B. **Match the following.**

1. Gaming	a. Tools used for AI
2. Alexa	b. Natural language processing
3. Mystery Animal	c. Medical diagnosis
4. Expert tasks	d. Chess
5. Artificial neural network	e. Intelligent system

C. **Number the following steps used for problem-solving in AI.**

a. Identification of solutions   b. Implementing

c. Defining a problem   d. Analysing the problem

e. Choosing a solution

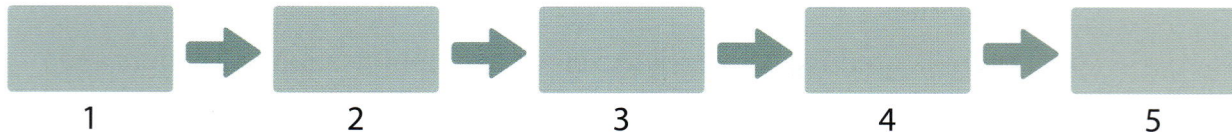

1   2   3   4   5

D. **Answer the following questions.**

1. Define AI.

2. What are the tools used for AI?

3. What are the goals of AI?

4. What are the limitations of using AI?

LAB WORK

A. Think about at least five job roles that do not exist today but may exist in 20 years, given the advancements in the field of technology and AI. Write them down in your notebook.

B. Create a job advertisement in any suitable software application for one of the job roles you have identified. Mention the top ten skills that the candidates need to possess. Make a presentation on the limitations of using AI in this scenario. Give examples from your daily life to support it.

PROJECT WORK

Create a floor plan of your dream home. Include AI-related features which will convert your home into a smart home.

You can either use an A4 sheet and draw the plan using colored pens, or you can create this on the computer using Paint.

WHO AM I?

I was the first person to use the term 'Artificial Intelligence' and I am one of the founders of the AI discipline.

In 1971, I was given the Turing award for my contributions to the field of AI.

I am also known as the Father of AI.

I am ....

Virus and Anti-virus

Introduction

Information Technology has made huge changes to our society. There are many software developers that support the growth of IT by contributing to it in positive ways. They develop tools and applications to help us work better. But there are also software developers that contribute in a destructive way, causing damage to the IT industry by designing and spreading destructive computer programs. In this chapter you will learn more about these destructive programs, and their different types.

FACT FILE

You could remember the meaning of 'virus' with the sentence 'Vital Information Resources Under Siege'.

Computer viruses

A computer virus is a destructive software program. All computer viruses are man-made. They can spread from one computer to another through disks, networks, email links, etc. A computer virus may corrupt or delete data on a computer. It may even delete everything on the hard disk and can interfere with computer operations.

Some viruses remain active even when you shut down the computer, while some become active only when the infected program or application is executed, or you have started your computer from a disk that has infected system files. Once a virus is active, it loads onto the computer's memory and is saved there. It then replicates (makes copies of itself) in your hard drive or applications or system files on the disks you use.

Some viruses are programmed specifically to damage the data on your computer. Many viruses are not very harmful as they only display a message, or produce sound when active. Other viruses make your computer system behave erratically, corrupt programs, delete files or crash the computer system frequently.

It is interesting to know how the computer virus got this name. Let us draw an analogy between a computer virus and a biological virus.

- A biological virus destroys the cells of the body. A computer virus is a program that is secretly put onto a computer in order to destroy the information that is stored in it.

- Like a biological virus, it can form multiple copies of itself inside another computer. It needs some other program or document in order to launch. Once it is running, it can infect other programs and documents.

- Like a biological virus, you do not realise the presence of a computer virus until your computer has already been affected.

> If your computer is not operating properly, it is good practice to check for a virus with an up-to-date virus-checking program.

What a virus cannot do

Look at the following to see when the computer system is not affected by a virus.

- Computer viruses cannot infect write-protected discs (CD–ROMs) or infect written documents.

- Viruses do not infect compressed files, unless the file was infected prior to compression.

- A virus cannot do physical damage to computer hardware, such as chips, boards and monitors.

- Macintosh viruses do not infect DOS/Windows computer software and vice versa. For example, the Melissa virus of 1998 worked only on Windows-based machines and could not operate on Macintosh computers.

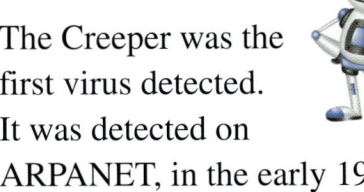

FACT FILE

The Creeper was the first virus detected. It was detected on ARPANET, in the early 1970s.

How does a computer virus spread?

Computer viruses can spread in several ways, as explained below:

- A computer virus begins to work and spread whenever you start up the infected program or application. For example, any word-processing application that contains the virus will place the virus in the memory every time the program is run.

- Once the virus is copied onto the computer memory it may get programmed to attach to other applications, disks or folders. It may also infect a network.

- Viruses behave in different ways. Some stay active only until the infected application is running. They become inactive when the computer shuts down. Other viruses operate every time you start your computer after they have infected a system file or network.

FACT FILE

Before the easy accessibility of the internet, viruses were typically spread by infected floppy disks.

Symptoms of a computer virus

You can detect the presence of a virus in your computer. The following are some of the primary indicators that a computer may be infected.

- The computer runs more slowly than usual.
- The computer stops responding, or it locks up frequently.
- The computer crashes and restarts every few minutes.
- Applications on the computer do not work correctly.
- Disks or disk drives are inaccessible.
- You see unusual error messages.
- You see distorted menus and dialog boxes.
- You cannot print items correctly.
- There is a double extension on an attachment that you recently opened, such as a .jpg, .gif or .exe extension.
- New icons appear on the desktop that you did not place there, or the icons are not associated with any recently installed programs.
- Strange sounds or music plays from the speakers unexpectedly.
- A program disappears from the computer even though you did not intentionally remove the program.

Kanjna is making a science project on her computer. She is having some trouble while accessing her computer. Tick (✓) the symptoms you think indicate the presence of a computer virus.

1. The computer is running more slowly than usual.

2. She is unable to access write-protected discs.

3. She is having problems while printing.

4. The brightness of her monitor is too low.

5. She is getting error messages.

6. Strange music plays from her speakers unexpectedly.

Types of computer viruses

Computer viruses are classified depending upon the infection methods. A few of them are discussed here.

Boot sector virus

The **boot sector** is that area of the computer that is accessed when the computer starts. A boot sector virus infects this part. This allows the virus to spread fast and cause damage. Once the boot sector is infected, the virus is loaded onto the memory when the computer starts. This virus then infects boot sectors on removable media – these commonly used to be on floppy disks. Boot sector viruses have become less common as floppy disks have become rarer.

FACT FILE

The first PC virus was a boot sector virus named Brain, created in 1986 by the Farooq Alvi Brothers.

The best way of avoiding boot sector viruses is to ensure that floppy disks are write-protected and you never start your computer with an unknown floppy disk in the disk drive. A few examples of boot sector viruses are Polyboot.B, Form, Disk Killer, Michelangelo and Stoned.

Program virus

The file infector virus infects files that contain executable codes like .exe, .com, .dll, .bin, .sys and many more. Some file infectors are **memory resident**. This means that the virus will stay in the memory, and continue to infect other programs. Other file infector viruses only infect the files when they are executed.

The file infector virus can cause irreversible damage to the files. By overwriting the files, it permanently destroys the content. Some file viruses also operate as email, worm virus and Trojan horse. You will learn about these later.

The only way to disinfect files from the file virus is to ensure that the infected files are deleted and restored if they have been taken from the back-up.

Examples of known file infector viruses include Jerusalem and Cascade.

Macro computer virus

Macro is a set of commands written by the user to be executed later. Macros can be created in application software such as Word, Excel, Access, etc. This virus infects the macro files and whenever any macro is executed they alter the macro code.

The existence of the **autoexec macro** makes it possible to create many macro viruses. The **autoexec** macro is executed in response to some event and does not depend on the user command. Other existing macro viruses are those which replace command names like Save, Open, etc. with their code. Unlike the auto macros which can be disabled, commands cannot be disabled. Once the macro virus uses these commands, it can copy itself to other files and even delete those files.

The auto macros are disabled if you use the **Disable Auto Macros** command in any macro that is written. It can also be disabled by holding down the Shift key while opening a document.

A Word document cannot contain macros, but word templates can. You can mask a template as a document file to prevent it from infection.

Examples of macro viruses include W97M.Melissa, WM.NiceDay and W97M.Groov.

Multipartite virus

Some computer viruses appear to behave like many other viruses and sometimes more than one type. These are **hybrids** and are called multipartite computer viruses.

Multipartite viruses infect both boot records and program files. These are particularly difficult to repair. If the boot area has been sanitised but not the files, the infection would recur in the boot area. The same holds true for sanitising the program files. If the virus has not been removed from the boot area, any file that you have sanitised will be infected again.

Examples of a multipartite virus include One_Half, Emperor, Anthrax and Tequilla.

Polymorphic virus

Polymorphic viruses are written in such a way that they change their code whenever they pass to another machine. Polymorphic viruses infect the computer with encrypted copies of it, making it difficult for an anti-virus scanner to locate them. Flaws in the program code make it easy to track down this virus.

FACT FILE

Any destructive program written for causing damage to the computer and the network is also known as malware. Viruses, worms, Trojan horse, etc. are all examples of malware.

Other harmful programs

Malware stands for Malicious Software. It is used or programmed to infiltrate a computer, gather secret information and disrupt its functioning. Malware includes Viruses, Worms, Trojan horses, etc.

Worms

Computer worms are destructive software programs designed to spread through computer networks. Anyone can install the worm inadvertently by opening an email attachment or message that contains executable scripts.

A virus is dependent upon the host file or boot sector and transfer of files between computers to spread. However, a computer worm can execute independently and spread on its own through network connections. They replicate themselves from system to system without the use of a host file and can lead to negative effects on your system. Unlike a computer virus, worms do not corrupt files and folders.

Being embedded inside everyday network software, computer worms easily penetrate most firewalls and other network security measures. Due to their high replication rate, worms consume a large part of the system memory and network bandwidth. This in turn leads to a significant slowdown in the speed of web servers, network servers and individual computers.

You might have heard of specific computer worms, such as Sasser worm, the Blaster worm and the Conficker worm.

Trojan horses

Trojan horses are harmful programs that, unlike a computer virus, do not reproduce by infecting other files, nor do they self-replicate like worms. They claim to be something desirable. Trojan horses contain malicious code. The code when triggered causes loss or even theft of data. Trojan horses can spread when you open an email attachment or download and run a file from the internet.

The name of the virus comes from Greek mythology. It is based on the Trojan War where the Greeks fooled the Trojans by presenting a wooden horse as a gesture of goodwill. But this horse actually brought the downfall of Troy because the horse was filled with Greek soldiers who then fought with the Trojans. Similarly, the code pretends to be friendly but has the harmful code inside. It acts in this way to get control and do damage, such as ruining the file allocation table on your hard disk. Vundo is a very common example of a Trojan horse.

Logic bombs

A logic bomb is a destructive program which lies dormant until a specific piece of program logic is activated. They are different from viruses as they do not replicate. They are not even programs in their own right but rather camouflaged segments of other programs.

In some ways, a logic bomb is the least harmful programmed threat, because a logic bomb must be targeted against a specific victim. Their objective is to destroy data on the computer once certain conditions have been met.

Spyware

Spyware is a software that secretly gathers information about a person or an organisation without their knowledge. It passes on this information to advertisers or third parties.

Spyware can be installed when a user downloads something from the internet or clicks on something leading to a pop-up window opening up. It uses a lot of the computer memory and slows it down. It also steals the personal information of the user and sends it to its source.

Adware and tracking cookies are examples of spyware.

ACTIVITY

Check out the latest list of known viruses and the anti-virus software available on the internet.

Protection against computer viruses

Anti-virus software

Anti-virus software is used to prevent, detect, and remove destructive programs, including computer viruses, worms, and Trojan horses. To help prevent the most current virus, you must update your anti-virus software regularly. You can set up most types of anti-virus software to update automatically. These software programs can also  be set to automatically scan disks when inserted into the disk drive, scan files when downloaded from the Internet, or scan emails when received.

The availability of anti-virus programs brought an end to many common types of computer virus. Some anti-virus software is available free of charge. Some anti-virus sellers maintain websites with free online scanning capability for the entire computer or for critical areas such as local disks, folders or files only.

Independent testing on all the major virus scanners consistently shows that none of them provides 100 percent virus detection.

Some of the most popular anti-virus software are Norton, McAfee Virus Scan, Panda and Quick Heal.

General steps to run and update an anti-virus

You can get your system installed with a good anti-virus software. To run the scan, you generally follow the these steps:

1. Open the Anti-virus program's main window. Initiate virus scan by clicking on the scan options.

2. Once the scanning is complete, you get a detailed list of viruses in your system and the infected files. You will be asked to repair, delete or quarantine the infected file.

   a. *Repair*: This option eliminates the virus and repairs the infected file.

   b. *Delete*: This option removes or erases the virus and the infected file completely from the system.

   c. *Quarantine*: This option can be used when you are not sure of the virus present on the file. In this way, you can separate the infected file from the non-infected files.

The more viruses that are known to the anti-virus database, the easier it becomes to detect them on your system. For this, it is important to keep your anti-virus software updated. To update the anti-virus, you should follow the steps given here:

1. Connect to the internet.

2. Click on the available update options for your chosen anti-virus software, and download the latest version.

3. Restart your computer.

You can help protect your computer from a virus by keeping the following points in mind.

1. Load software from original disks or CDs. Pirated or copied software always comes with a risk of virus.

2. Do not open email attachments if you do not recognise the sender (though you may also receive viruses from people you know). Scan the attachments with anti-virus software before opening or saving them.

3. Computer uploads and changes in the System Configuration should always be performed by the person who is responsible for the computer. Password protection should be used.

4. Download files only from reputable internet sites and be careful when exchanging removable media with friends.

5. Purchase an anti-virus program that runs as you boot or works independently on your computer. Update it frequently.

6. Install a **firewall** on your system. This is a security system that can protect software or hardware or both. It monitors the movement of information both in and out when turned on.

A. How does a worm works in a computer as a destructive code? Try to find out more about it and make a document file on it.

B. What is spyware? Find out more about it.

GLOSSARY

Anti-virus software   Software used to prevent, detect and remove destructive programs.

Boot sector   The area of the computer that is accessed when the computer starts.

Boot sector virus   A virus that infects the boot sector.

Firewall   A security system that protects hardware or software or both.

Logic bomb   A destructive program that lies dormant until the target program logic is activated.

Macro computer virus   A virus that infects macro files.

Multipartite virus   A virus that infects both boot records and program files.

Trojan horses   A harmful program containing malicious codes.

Worms   A destructive software program designed to spread through computer networks.

YOU ARE HERE

10

1. A computer virus may corrupt or delete data on a computer.
2. A virus is inactive until you have executed an infected program or application.
3. Computer viruses cannot infect write-protected discs.
4. Viruses cannot do physical damage to computer hardware.
5. Some common types of computer virus are Boot sector viruses, Macro computer viruses, Multipartite viruses, and Polymorphic viruses.
6. Do not open email attachments if you do not recognise the sender.

EXERCISE

A. Fill in the blanks.

1. Once a virus is active, it loads onto the computer's .... and is saved there.

2. A biological virus destroys the .... of the body, while a computer virus destroys the .... that is stored in it.

3. Computer viruses cannot infect ....

4. .... is a set of commands written by the user to be executed later.

5. The name of the .... virus comes from Greek mythology.

B. True or false?

1. Spyware passes on information to advertisers or third parties.

2. Boot sector virus infects the boot sector only.

3. Both boot records and program files are infected by worms.

4. You cannot update anti-virus software once installed.

5. Multipartite viruses infect the computer with encrypted copies of it.

C. Give one word for the following.

1. It may corrupt or delete data on a computer.   ....

2. The area of the computer that is accessed when the computer starts.   ....

3. It can be installed when a user downloads something from the internet.   ....

4. A harmful program containing malicious codes.   ....

5. It is used to protect computers from viruses.   ....

D. Answer the following questions.

1. Define a computer virus. How is it different from a biological virus?

2. What damage can be caused by viruses?

3. Discuss how a computer virus spreads.

4. List the various types of computer viruses.

5. Why do you need anti-virus software?

LAB WORK

A. Find out which anti-virus software is installed in the computers of your school lab.

B. Note down the steps to scan the files on your system using your anti-virus software.

C. Ask your teacher if there is a different type of anti-virus software installed for the server.

D. List some anti-virus software that is available free of charge.

PROJECT WORK

In groups of four, work together to create a multiple-choice quiz on the topic 'Computer Viruses' with 10–15 questions. You can do this either on paper, or use a PowerPoint Presentation. Each group should come forward with their quiz and run it with the rest of the class.

11 Troubleshooting

Introduction

As wonderful as computers can be, at times they can also be incredibly troublesome. Sometimes, it is worth having a look to see if you can solve simple PC problems yourself before calling a technician. In this chapter, you will learn about a few simple tips on how you can avoid some of the most common problems that you face while working on computers.

Computer Troubleshooting

Troubleshooting is the identification of a problem in a system caused by a failure of some kind. The problem is initially experienced as symptoms of malfunction and troubleshooting is the process of determining the causes of these symptoms. You can also say that troubleshooting is a process of identifying a computer problem so that it can be fixed.

Some people use their instincts while others use advice from experts to get an idea about the different types of troubleshooting. A few common steps can then be followed to find out the problem. You can try these steps whenever you come across any problem in your computer. If these steps do not help you, then you can call an expert, a computer engineer, to troubleshoot.

Why is Computer Maintenance important?

It is important to take proper care of your computer for the following reasons:

- It will increase the speed and the life of your PC.
- It prevents errors.
- It secures your data and information from unwanted damage.
- It saves your precious time.

Areas to Troubleshoot

There are three areas to troubleshoot. These are discussed here.

Hardware

Computer hardware is the physical part of a computer and it is not frequently changed or updated. Most computer hardware is in-built and cannot be seen by users. There are a large number of computer hardware devices, including the hard disk, CD-ROM, RAM, motherboard, monitor, printer and other peripheral devices. In order to identify the problem with your system hardware, you first need to identify the type of hardware.

Some of the basic hardware problems that you may face are:

- Power failure in the computer.
- Device problems like a keyboard, mouse and printer not being recognised.

Software

Computer software can be any program file or application running on the computer. Software problems could be unexplained crashes or strange error messages. Before calling up a software expert, you need to identify the problem.

Some of the basic software problems that you may face are:

- You are unable to install a program.

FACT FILE

The term **debug** is used when the problem is within the software program. The process of finding and reducing the number of bugs, or defects in a computer program is known as **debugging**.

- The program or utility does not load. It has an error when you attempt to load it.
- The system crashes when you are working with a specific software.

Operating system

Probably the most frustrating problem computer users experience are startup problems where your computer fails to boot up properly.

Some of the most common problems involving the operating system of a computer are:

- Windows restarts without warning.
- Windows stops responding.
- Windows files do not boot.
- Windows starts in a safe mode.
- Windows slows down.

Steps for Troubleshooting

In this section you will learn how you should handle any problem that you experience with your computer.

Step 1: Find out the problem

This is a very important step, as it gives you an idea of just how frequently you experience this problem. On the basis of your findings you can also decide if it needs attention. Once you are able to answer these two questions, you can think of how to troubleshoot your computer system. Some of the common problems that you may face are:

- The system is not getting a proper power supply.
- The system restarts on its own after a few minutes.
- Sometimes the system stops responding.
- The system is running slow.
- An error message is displayed.
- Windows does not load.

Step 2: Categorise your problem

Once you have found out whether the problem is related to the hardware or the software, then half of the work is done.

For hardware related problems

- Check the power supply points.
- Check whether devices like the keyboard, mouse, printer and system unit are connected properly.
- Ensure that during the startup process all the peripherals attached are recognised properly.

For software related problems

- Check the operating system files.
- Check the software files that are frequently used.
- Check the device drivers are properly installed.

Step 3: Check the service manual

You have learnt how to find out the type of problem that your computer system may be facing. The service manuals contain instructions for troubleshooting and service information. Almost every computer and peripheral device made today has a set of service documentation in the form of books, service CD-ROMs and websites. Websites are the most popular place for this documentation to be held as more service centres are connected to the internet. For example, if the computer is not able to recognise any device attached, like a printer, then you should search the service documentation for this issue and it will be able to tell you the most common causes for this issue and their solutions.

Step 4: Back to Its original state

When you troubleshoot, make one change at a time in the problem sector. If the change does not solve the problem, restore back to the original state. You should not make too many changes at a time as this may lead to more complications. Whenever changes are made with no results, then it is always advisable to undo the changes.

Step 5: Call an expert

If you feel that you will not be able to solve the problem in your computer, then you should call a technician. This avoids creating more complications rather than solving the problem.

Troubleshooting common problems

The computer locks up

If the computer is frozen and does not respond to any commands follow the steps given below:

1. Press **Ctrl + Alt + Del** (all three keys at the same time).
2. Click on the **Start Task Manager** option in the list.
3. The **Windows Task Manager** window displaying the **Task** list appears.

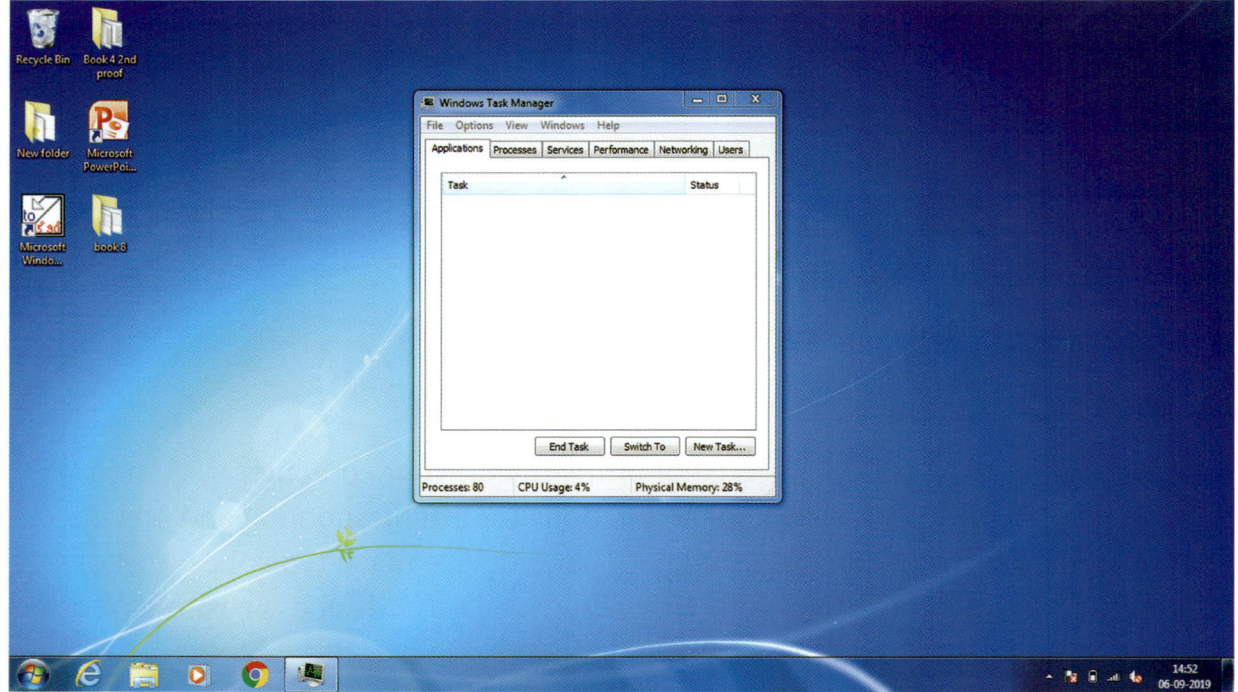

Windows Task Manager

4. Select any program that says 'Not responding' in the **Status** section.
5. Click on the **End Task** button. Repeat until the tasks come to an end.

If this does not work, shut down the computer, wait for several seconds, turn the computer on again and scan the disks, files and folders to check for any virus.

Error messages displayed on the monitor

If an error message is displayed on your monitor screen, you must **reboot** it, that is, restart your computer. A majority of problems that occur while you are using your computer can be fixed by rebooting.

Applications sometimes do not release memory when they are closed. This at times results in the computer acting in an unexpected manner. When you reboot, memory space is cleared of any application that is not in use and most things are reset.

178

The computer is completely dead with no power supply

Under adult supervision, check all the connections, the cables between the CPU, the monitor and all the electrical cables. Check the wall socket. After doing so, keep the following options in mind.

- If you have a light on your monitor but not on your CPU, then there is a problem with your CPU.

- If there is a light on your CPU but not on your monitor, then you have a problem with your monitor and your CPU may be fine.

- If you have another monitor in working condition, the quickest way to test is to put another monitor on the machine and see if you get an image on the screen.

- If you have a light on both the monitors and the CPU, ask an adult to check the pins of the data cable between the monitor and the CPU. A single bent pin can also cause an image problem.

The mouse and keyboard do not work

Check the connection of the computer mouse and the computer keyboard wire with the computer. If the wire is plugged in, yet the device is not detected, you may have to reboot your computer. You can also check the following:

1. Click on the **Start** button.
2. Select **Control Panel** from the list.
3. Click on the **Device Manager** option from the list of tasks given.
4. The **Device Manager** window appears.

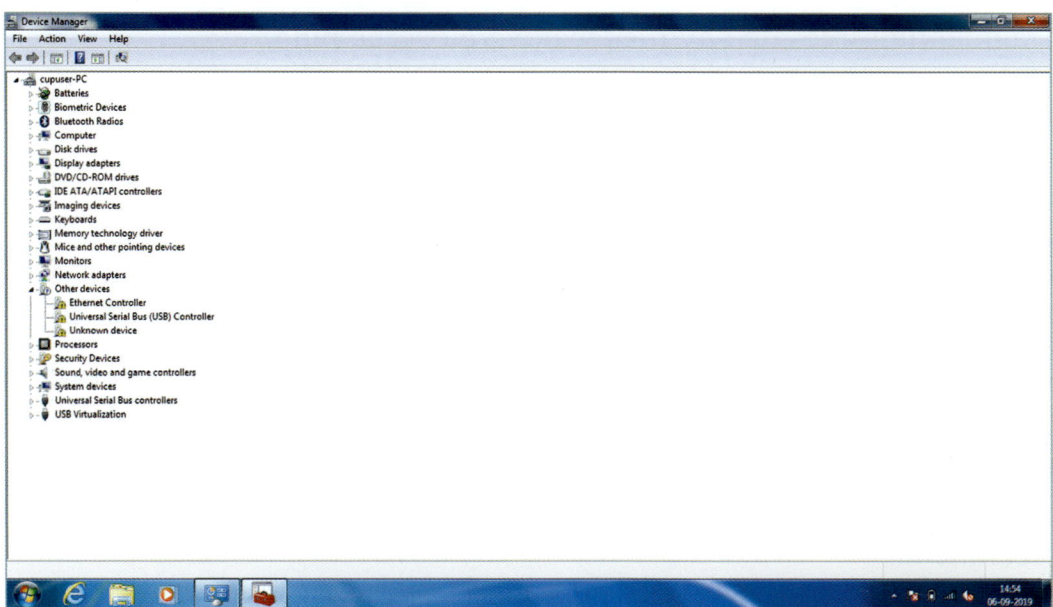

Device Manager window

There can be other reasons for the devices not working. At times dust particles may hamper the functioning of your devices. To prevent this you should always keep your computer covered and clean it regularly.

The computer displays a disk error or non-system disk message

You should check your disk drives for any CD left inserted. If one is found, remove it and reboot the computer.

If you do not have any disk in a drive, and the message is accompanied by a sound, shut down your computer and call a technician.

The computer starts up in safe mode

If any problem occurs with the operating system, the system files get loaded in the safe mode to avoid system crash. Only the minimum necessary programs will load. You may then try solving the problem by running a scan of the disks.

When the scan is completed, reboot your computer to see if the problem has been fixed. Along with scanning your system, you may also try defragmenting the files by following the steps given below:

1. Click on the **Start** button.
2. Type **Disk Defragmenter** in the **Search programs and files** box.
3. Click on **Disk Defragmenter** in the **Search Results** list.
4. Once the defragmentation is over, restart your computer and check.

   Defragmenting frees up any files that were overlapping.

5. You must call a technician if the problem still persists.

The printer does not work

If there is an error when printing files, first find out whether it is due to any problem in the printer or an incorrect command from the computer.

Many printer models have a built-in self-test option which allows you to print a test page by holding down the feed button for a few seconds. The power button will begin to flash and a test page will print. If the printer self-test fails, then the problem is with the printer rather than the printer cable or the computer. If this occurs, you need to contact a technician.

If the printer self-test prints, the next step is to instruct Windows to print a test page. You should follow the steps given below:

1. Click on **Start** ⟹ **Control Panel** ⟹ **Devices and Printers**, and right-click on the **Printer** icon.

2. Select **Printer properties** and press the **Print Test Page** button. If the test page fails to print, make sure the printer cable is firmly fixed in both the computer and the printer.

3. You should also check the ends of the printer cable to make sure that none of the prongs are bent.

4. If the test print fails, or if the print consists of unwanted characters or a few characters printed over many pages, you need to uninstall and then reinstall the drivers for your printer.

A lot of computer problems can be solved by troubleshooting. However, you should always remember that interfering with the system files and computer hardware may sometimes lead to more errors. Therefore, when you feel that the problem is too difficult for you to solve, you should always ask for help from an adult or call a computer technician.

ACTIVITY

A. Make a presentation on the topic 'Steps for Troubleshooting'. Use the internet for collecting more information and images.

B. List different problems that you've come across in your daily life which you have solved without help from an outside source. Your list could be about fixing a cracked pipe, taping a broken wire or fixing a loose door knob or anything else that comes to mind.

What are the five qualities that have helped you to fix things on your own rather than seeking help?

GLOSSARY

Reboot   Restarting a computer.

Troubleshooting   The identification of trouble in a system caused by a failure of some kind.

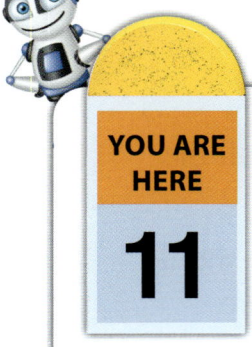

YOU ARE HERE

11

1. It is important to take proper care of your computer.

2. The three areas to troubleshoot are: hardware, software and operating system.

3. The steps for troubleshooting help you to deal with the problem in a more systematic way.

4. If the computer is frozen or any program is not responding, press Ctrl + Alt + Del keys at the same time and start the Task Manager.

5. When the problem is too complicated, you should attempt to solve it only under the supervision of an adult or a computer technician.

EXERCISE

A.   Fill in the blanks.

1. You can speed up your computer by running the .... utility.

2. The restarting of a computer is called ....

3. Many printer models have a built-in .... option.

4. You check the power supply points for .... related problems.

5. Disk defragmenter is available in ....

B. True or false?

1. Troubleshooting is the identification of a problem in a system caused by a failure of some kind. ⬚

2. It is not important to take proper care of your computer. ⬚

3. The three areas to troubleshoot are: hardware, software and operating system. ⬚

4. If your Windows restarts without warning, then there is a problem in the computer hardware. ⬚

5. Proper maintenance will increase the speed and the life of your PC. ⬚

C. Identify the troubleshooting areas for each of the following problems.

1. Windows stops responding.

2. The system crashes when you are working with a specific software.

3. Power failure in the computer.

4. You are unable to install a program.

5. Windows restarts without warning.

6. Windows starts in a safe mode.

D. Answer the following questions.

1. Give a brief explanation of troubleshooting.

2. Why is it important to take proper care of a computer?

3. What are the areas to troubleshoot?

4. Write about two common problems related to software that you might have experienced.

5. Give troubleshooting steps for an error message displayed on the monitor.

LAB WORK

A.   Jay has opened several files and applications on his computer. He noticed that his MS Excel window has suddenly stopped responding. What can he do to prevent data loss?

B.   Amber is facing some trouble with the hardware devices attached to her computer. Some of them are not working right. Can you suggest where she should check to see that devices are connected properly?

C.   Find out if any part of the system or any device is not working in your lab class. Talk to your school technician to find out the problem and how it can be solved.

PROJECT WORK

Work in groups. Discuss one common problem that people face with their computers which can be solved without expert help. Draw pictures of the problem and the steps involved in solving it. Create a flowchart to help explain to the rest of the class.

Tick (✓) the correct option.

1. **Select the incorrect match.**

   a. Table   It stores information in the form of rows (records) and columns (fields). ☐

   b. Queries   These cannot be used for sorting, grouping or filtering data in MS Access. ☐

   c. Forms   Customised screens to provide an easy way to enter and view data in a table or query. ☐

   d. Reports   These present data from a table or query in printed format. ☐

2. **Which of the following views is represented by icon ⬜ ?**

   a. Datasheet View ☐   b. PivotTable View ☐

   c. PivotChart View ☐   d. Design View ☐

3. **Select the icon that represents the OpenOffice application used for creating presentations.**

   a. ⬜ ☐   b. ⬜ ☐

   c. ⬜ ☐   d. ⬜ ☐

4. **Which of the following components in the OpenOffice Impress window displays different tasks like Slide Layouts, Slide Transition, Custom Animation, Master Pages and Table Design that can be used to design slides?**

   a. Slides pane ☐

   b. Workspace ☐

   c. Status bar ☐

   d. Tasks pane ☐

5. **Identify the incorrect statement about OpenOffice Calc.**

   a. A file is referred to as a Workbook with the default name Calc1. ☐

   b. A cell is formed by the intersection of a row and a column. ☐

   c. In a spreadsheet, you can generate a series of number or text values by using AutoFill handle. ☐

   d. A function can be entered either through Function Wizard or by typing the function, beginning with an equal sign, with the values in a cell. ☐

6. **All the files created in the OpenOffice suite are saved as an ODF document. What is the full form of ODF?**

   a. Open Data Format ☐

   b. Open Document Format ☐

   c. Organised Document Format ☐

   d. Open Document Font ☐

7. **Which of the following HTML code is incorrect with respect to tags and their attributes?**

   a. <FRAMESET rows="45%, *"cols="*, 50%" frameborder="yes" border="7" bordercolor="blue"> ☐

   b. <FRAME src="A.HTML" name="F1" frameborder = "Yes", bordercolor="Red" scrolling="No", marginheight="30", marginwidth="30"> ☐

   c. <FRAMESET rows= "50%, 50%">

      <FRAME noresize="noresize" > ☐

   d. <FRAMESET rows= "50%, 50%">

      </FRAMESET> ☐

8. **What error message will you get if the src file 'A' mentioned in the following frame tag does not exist?**

   <FRAME src="A.HTML" name="A">

   a. Files Not Found ☐

   b. No Such File exists ☐

   c. Unable to Find File ☐

   d. None of the above ☐

9. The .... method is used for displaying text in the browser window. It uses an object called document, which refers to the current document on the browser window.

   a. document.display()　　☐　　b. doc.write()　　☐

   c. document.show()　　☐　　d. document.write()　　☐

10. The following rules are to be followed to assign name to variables. Select the correct sentence(s).

    a. It must start with a letter or an underscore character.　　☐

    b. It cannot contain empty space (white space).　　☐

    c. It cannot have more than 255 characters.　　☐

    d. All of the above.　　☐

11. Match the following operators used in Python.

	Column-I		Column-II
a.	Arithmetic operator	i.	*=
b.	Assignment operator	ii.	*
c.	Relational operator	iii.	or
d.	Logical operator	iv.	==

    a. (a)-(i), (b)-(ii), (c)-(iv), (d)-(iii)　　☐　　b. (a)-(ii), (b)-(i), (c)-(iv), (d)-(iii)　　☐

    c. (a)-(ii), (b)-(i), (c)-(iii), (d)-(iv)　　☐　　d. (a)-(ii), (b)-(iii), (c)-(iv), (d)-(i)　　☐

12. Select the Python program which is incorrect.

    a. X=10　　　　　　　　　　　　b. p=10
       X=X+10　　　　　　　　　　　　q=20
       X=X-5　　　　　　　　　　　　p*=q//3
       print (X)　　☐　　　　　　　　print(p,q)　　☐

    c. input ('Enter a number', A)　　　d. All are correct
       Print ('The number is' A)　　☐

13. Which of the following gives the ranged specified by: range (0,-9,-1)

    a. [0,-1,-2,-3,-4,-5,-6,-7,-8]　　☐　　b. [-1,-2,-3,-4,-5,-6,-7,-8]　　☐

    c. [0,-1,-2,-3,-4,-5,-6,-7,-8, -9]　　☐　　d. [0,1, 2, 3, 4, 5, 6, 7, 8]　　☐

14. **The two types of loops used in Python are:**

   a. for and continue

   b. for and while

   c. while and break

   d. continue and break

15. **Intelligence is the ability of a system to reason, learn from experience, solve complex problems, comprehend new ideas, use natural language fluently, adapt new situations, store and retrieve information. It is composed of:**

   a. Reasoning, learning and problem solving

   b. Perception and linguistic intelligence

   c. Perception, reasoning, learning and problem solving

   d. Perception, reasoning, learning, problem solving and linguistic intelligence

16. **Choose the correct order of steps used for problem solving in AI.**

   a. Identification of solutions

   b. Implementing

   c. Defining a problem

   d. Analysing the problem

   e. Choosing a solution

   a. a, b, d, c, e

   b. c, d, a, e, b

   c. b, e, c, d, a

   d. c, a, b, d, e

17. **................ is a customised screen for viewing, entering, modifying and deleting data in a table or a query.**

   a. Field

   b. Form

   c. DBMS

   d. Report

18. **In Python, the range() function is used to create a list containing a sequence of numbers starting from .... and ending with one less than ....**

   a. step, stop

   b. step, start

   c. start, step

   d. start, stop

19. **Which of the following are macro viruses?**

   a. W97M.Melissa, WM.NiceDay and W97M.Groov

   b. W97M.Groov, Anthrax and Tequilla

   c. Jerusalem and Cascade

   d. One_Half, WM.NiceDay and Anthrax

20 **Which program prevents your computer from the following?**

- Virus
- Worms
- Trojan horse

a. Linux ☐

b. Ant-virus ☐

c. Cyber security ☐

d. All of the above ☐

21. **Some of the common problems involving the operating system of a computer are:**

1. Windows stops responding.
2. Power failure in the computer.
3. Windows restarts without warning.
4. Windows starts in a safe mode.

a. 1 and 3 ☐

b. 2, 3 and 4 ☐

c. 1, 2 and 3 ☐

d. 1, 3 and 4 ☐

22. **Which of the following shows the correct order of troubleshooting steps?**

1. Categorise your problem.
2. Check the service manual.
3. Call an expert.
4. Back to its original state.
5. Find out the problem.

a. 5, 4, 3, 2, 1 ☐

b. 5, 3, 4, 2, 1 ☐

c. 5, 1, 2, 4, 3 ☐

d. 3, 4, 5, 2, 1 ☐

23. **Select the word from the given options which can fill both the blanks given in the sentence below.**

Many printer models have a …………… option which allows you to print a test page by holding down the feed button for a few seconds. The power button will begin to flash and a test page will print. If the printer …………… fails, then the problem is with the printer itself rather than the printer cable or the computer.

a. built-in self test ☐

b. power-on self test ☐

c. built-in printer test ☐

d. built-in power test ☐

24. Which of the following sentence(s) is/are correct with reference to HTML5?

1. HTML5 is an independent markup Language and is no longer a part of SGML.
2. It can be used on desktop as well as mobile devices like tablets and smartphones.

a. Only 1   b. Only 2
c. Both 1 and 2   d. Both are incorrect

25. Select the type of script to which the following sample code belongs.

```
<doctype html>
<html>
<head>
<meta charset="UTF-8">
<title>Sample document</title>
</head>
<body>
<h1><u>My first page</u></h1>
</body>
</html>
```

a. HTML   b. HTML5
c. XML   d. JavaScript